Using
Professional Write™

Katherine Murray

CORPORATION

LEADING COMPUTER KNOWLEDGE

Using Professional Write™

Copyright © 1989 by Que® Corporation

Library of Congress Catalog No.: LC 89-62440
ISBN 0-88022-490-8

91 90 89   8 7 6 5 4 3 2 1

Interpretation of the printing code: the rightmost double-digit number is the year of the book's printing; the rightmost single-digit number, the number of the book's printing. For example, a printing code of 89-4 shows that the fourth printing of the book occurred in 1989.

Using Professional Write is based on Version 2.1 and the earlier Versions 2.0 and 1.0.

DEDICATION ▽

To my husband, Bob, who doesn't complain nearly as much as I would if our roles were reversed. Thank you for your encouragement, enthusiasm, and endurance.

-km

Publishing Director

Lloyd J. Short

Production Editor

Gregory Robertson

Editors

Jo Anna Arnott
Mary P. Arthur
Fran Blauw
Kelly D. Dobbs

Technical Editor

Ron Holmes

Editorial Assistant

Stacie Lamborne

Index by

reVisions Plus, Inc.

Book Design and Production

Dan Armstrong   Joe Ramon
David Kline   Dennis Sheehan
Lori Lyons   M. Louise Shinault
Jennifer Matthews Peter Tocco
Cindy Phipps

Composed in Garamond and Excellent No. 1
by Que Corporation

ABOUT THE AUTHOR ▼

Katherine Murray

K atherine Murray is the president of reVisions Plus, Inc., a writing, editing, and desktop publishing company that deals primarily with the development and production of microcomputer-related materials. Author of *Using PFS: First Choice, Using PFS: First Publisher*, the *IBM PC, XT, and DOS Workbook*, and the *IBM PC, XT, and DOS Instructor's Guide*, as well as a contributing author to *Using HyperCard: From Home to HyperTalk* and *1-2-3 QuickStart*, Katherine also has published many family-related articles in national general interest publications.

CONTENTS AT A GLANCE

TABLE OF CONTENTS ▼

I   Professional Write Basics ▼

1   Introducing Professional Write   11

▼ ACKNOWLEDGMENTS

I'd like to thank the following people who helped me assemble, write, and debug *Using Professional Write*:

Greg Robertson, production editor, who doesn't let even the teeniest error escape his hawk-like vision,

Kelly Dobbs, editor, for applying her usual editorial savoir faire to the manuscript,

Fran Blauw, Jo Anna Arnott, and Mary Arthur, who skillfully edited this manuscript into a better book,

Ron Holmes, technical editor, for exterminating the bugs in this manuscript,

Lloyd Short, publishing director, who knows what it's like in the trenches, and expects the most out of everybody anyway.

TRADEMARK
ACKNOWLEDGMENTS

Que Corporation has made every reasonable attempt to supply trademark information about company names, products, and services mentioned in this book. Trademarks indicated below were derived from various sources. Que Corporation cannot attest to the accuracy of this information.

Conventions Used in This Book

*U*sing *Professional Write* uses several conventions of which you should be aware. They are listed here for your reference.

❑ Information that you are to type (usually found in examples with numbered steps) is indicated by italic type. For example, "At the prompt, type *cd \pw*." In some cases, material you type is set on a line by itself.

❑ Names of menus (such as File/Print, Edit, and Format) are shown with the initial letter capitalized. Options on those menus appear in boldface type (for example, **Get a file** and **Insert blank line**).

❑ Messages and prompts that appear on-screen are represented here in a special typeface (Printer number).

❑ Special tips and questions asked often by Professional Write users are highlighted by a special design box.

❑ Sidebars have been used to provide additional material related to each chapter's topic. Sidebars have titles and are contained in boxes.

❑ Icons have been used to indicate new information that is related to Version 2.1 of Professional Write.

Introduction

Once in a while, you pick up a software product that drastically changes the way you perform work-related tasks. Professional Write is one of those products. If you are accustomed to pounding out routine memos, letters, or reports on some sort of roaring electric typewriter (which may or may not have correction capabilities), you will be awed by the amount of time and effort Professional Write can save as you go about your daily tasks. Even for more complicated tasks like mail merging, producing elaborate reports, or importing spreadsheets or graphs, the features of Professional Write make creating, revising, and printing professional-looking documents as easy as possible.

What Is Professional Write?

Professional Write is a full-featured word processing program that is designed to be so easy to use that even a computer neophyte can produce a document at the first sitting. Geared for the fast-paced world of business meetings and power lunches, Professional Write is perfect for the person who is besieged by paperwork and doesn't have a lot of time available for learning software programs.

Even though Professional Write is available at a fraction of the cost of other popular word processing programs like WordPerfect or WordStar, the program contains a variety of extra features built-in to make your work easier.

A 77,000-word dictionary checks your spelling; a 22,000-word thesaurus helps you find synonyms; an address book helps you maintain important data about clients, employees, or contacts and enables you to create and print form letters easily.

If you have been using other popular word processing programs, Professional Write enables you to import and work with those files directly. Suppose that your office previously used WordPerfect, but you found the command system to be too cumbersome for your limited needs. When you switch to Professional Write, you won't need to retype all those files you entered in WordPerfect—Professional Write converts and imports the file with just a few menu selections from you. You can import files you have previously created in the following word processing programs:

- ❏ Microsoft Word
- ❏ MultiMate
- ❏ OfficeWriter
- ❏ PFS: First Choice
- ❏ PFS: Write
- ❏ Wang PC
- ❏ WordPerfect
- ❏ WordStar

In addition to importing these files, you can export the files you create with Professional Write in formats accepted by those programs. Similar to many other popular programs, Professional Write also accepts files in ASCII or DCA format.

Using Professional Write Highlights

In *Using Professional Write*, you will find descriptions and how-to tutorials about the various aspects of the Professional Write program. By using many examples, this book takes you from a beginning overview of the program to procedures for creating professional-looking, sophisticated documents that include imported graphs and spreadsheets and make use of the program's address book feature. Among the features highlighted in this book are the following:

Importing data from other programs. Using Professional Write helps you make the most of text you have already entered by showing you how to import it into Professional Write and add the finishing touches. Professional Write 2.1 now supports more popular word processing programs than versions previously released.

Editing and enhancing techniques. Learn to produce quality copy with just a few keystrokes. Enhance your document by adding effective headers and footers. How do you know when to use which font? Do your memos look like ransom notes? In addition to offering step-by-step instructions on editing and sprucing up your documents, *Using Professional Write* provides tips on planning, editing, and streamlining your document by using various program features.

Using the page preview feature. Page preview, new with Version 2.1 of Professional Write, enables you to display the document on-screen with the fonts you have selected and the formats you have chosen. This preview mode even enables you to make modifications without returning to the work screen. *Using Professional Write* shows you how to use this page preview feature to get the majority of your work done before you see it in print.

Printer support. The land of printers is getting more varied all the time. Just a few years ago, you were limited to a choice of dot-matrix or letter-quality printer. Now you have a choice of dot-matrix, letter-quality, dot-matrix printers that can produce letter quality output, laser printers, and PostScript laser printers. How do you know which printer you need? Professional Write enables you to select two printers and provides support for more than 150 popular printers. *Using Professional Write* helps you work with your printer to produce effective materials in just a fraction of the time and trouble required by other word processing programs.

Working with address books. Professional Write has a mini-database feature that you can use to create address books to store up to 2,000 records of information. This address book can be a great timesaver. For example, suppose that you are working with a series of distributors and you currently have all the names, addresses, and phone numbers of the distributors written on your Rolodex cards. When you need to type a form letter that will be sent to each of these people, you must type each name and address at the top of each letter. With Professional Write, you can have the program plug in the information for you; with no extra typing and no extra time. This book will help you plan and use the address books you create for your Professional Write data.

Macro capability. If you have ever worked with computers before, you have probably heard the term *macro*. A macro, put simply, is a series of keystrokes or menu selections that you assign to one key or key combination so that when you press that key (or key combination), the keystroke series is carried out automatically. *Using Professional Write* teaches you how to create and use macros and offers many sample macros that you can use or modify as needed.

Who Should Read This Book?

Using Professional Write is written for the person who wants to produce effective, professional documents in the shortest amount of time possible. Whether your needs are as simple as producing a standard memo once a week or as complex as creating and printing an elaborate multipage annual report, *Using Professional Write* includes procedures, tips, and examples that will help you get up to speed quickly. Specifically, *Using Professional Write* addresses the following users:

❏ Businesspersons who are evaluating Professional Write as the new standard for their word processing needs

❏ Managers who often need to produce a printed document as fast as possible

❏ Workers who are responsible for creating, editing, and publishing annual and quarterly reports

❏ Owners of small businesses who want an easy-to-use program that is capable of producing professional documents quickly

❏ Support personnel who use word processing infrequently and want on-line help and pull-down menus

❏ Anyone who seeks an easy-to-use, yet powerful word processing program that provides a wealth of features within a reasonable price range

Whether you use Professional Write infrequently or as a part of your daily routine, you will find the examples, figures, and tips in *Using Professional Write* informative and helpful.

Conventions Used in This Book

Using Professional Write uses several conventions to help you learn to produce Professional Write documents as easily as possible. These conventions are listed here for your reference.

❏ Information that you are to type (usually found in examples with numbered steps) is indicated by italic type. For example, you may see a line such as "At the prompt, type *cd \pw*."

❏ Names of menus (such as Help, Options, and Fonts) are shown with the initial letters capitalized. Options on those menus appear in boldface type (for example, **Change a font** or **List available fonts**).

❏ Messages and prompts that appear on-screen are represented here in a special typeface, such as `Printer number`.

❏ Sidebars have been added to provide additional material related to each chapter's topic.

❏ Special tips and questions often asked by Professional Write users are highlighted by a special design box.

 Special icons are used to highlight information that is new with Version 2.1 of Professional Write.

What Is in This Book?

Using Professional Write is divided into parts and chapters as indicated in the following paragraphs. The content of each part and chapter is briefly described.

Part I

Part I, "Professional Write Basics," teaches you the basics of the program and helps you install the program on your system. Additionally, Part I includes a Quick Start chapter that gives you a hands-on tour of the program.

Chapter 1, "Introducing Professional Write," explains the basic elements and highlights of the program. Sample documents show you what you can do with the program, and overviews of each of the main features of Professional Write give you a closer look at the tools you will be using as you create your own documents.

Chapter 2, "Getting Started with Professional Write," lets you know what hardware and software you need to run the program and shows you how to make backup copies and install the program on your system. For hard disk users, this chapter includes important information on organizing files and directories. This chapter also teaches you to configure Professional Write for your particular system. Additionally, you learn how to start and exit Professional Write.

Chapter 3, "A Professional Write Quick Start," takes you on a whirlwind tour of the basic elements in the program, enabling you to gain hands-on experience by entering and editing text, setting margins and tabs, adding headers, changing fonts, running the spelling checker, and printing the document. References are provided so that you can find a more complete discussion of each activity in the appropriate chapters of this book.

Part II

Part II, "Creating Professional Write Documents," takes you step-by-step through the procedures for creating, formatting, editing, enhancing, previewing, and printing Professional Write documents.

Chapter 4, "Creating, Formatting, and Saving Documents," explains typing and importing text into the Professional Write document; teaches you to set tabs, margins, and indents; shows you how to specify boldface or underline features; and explains how to save the file in various formats.

Chapter 5, "Editing Documents," shows you how to perform various editing operations, such as highlighting, moving, copying, deleting, or reformatting text. This chapter explains all these aspects of editing Professional Write documents.

Chapter 6, "Enhancing Documents," takes you a step further toward producing an effective document. Now that you have gotten the text into the document and have edited to your heart's content, what are you going to do to spruce it up? Does you report require headers and footers? Do you want to use the draw feature to highlight important items? Do you need to add page numbers or a cover page? This chapter shows you how to make your document more visually appealing by using additional features of the program.

Chapter 7, "Understanding and Working with Fonts," provides you with information you need for setting up, working with, and modifying fonts. A troubleshooting section is included to help you solve any problems you might encounter while working with fonts in your Professional Write documents.

Chapter 8, "Previewing and Printing Documents," introduces you to an important new feature in Professional Write 2.1: previewing. The new preview feature enables you to see on-screen how your document looks—with all the correct font assignments and headers and footers—before you print. Printing procedures also are discussed, as are tips for deciding which type of printout you need. The chapter also explains the various print options. Laser printer advocates can find important information on using built-in, cartridge, and soft fonts with Professional Write.

Part III

Part III, ''Professional Write Special Features,'' focuses on the features you will use as you become proficient with Professional Write. Specifically, this part includes chapters on the address book feature, creating and using macros, designing and using templates, and using data from other programs in Professional Write documents.

Chapter 9, ''Special Features: The Dictionary, Thesaurus, and Calculator,'' offers important information on each of these timesaving Professional Write features.

Chapter 10, ''Creating and Working with Address Books,'' shows you how you can organize and enter database information so that all your information is easily accessible. Want Professional Write to insert addresses on your form letters? Are you tired of typing mailing labels by hand? This chapter gives you ideas for planning your own address books and shows you how to produce form letters and mailing labels by using the data in the address books you create.

Chapter 11, ''Using Professional Write Macros,'' teaches you how to create and use macros that cut down on the time and keystrokes required to produce documents. You can automate often-repeated routines so that Professional Write can do them for you. This chapter also provides many sample macros that you can use as-is or modify to suit your own word processing needs.

Appendixes and Glossary

This book concludes with four appendixes and a glossary. Appendix A highlights the new features introduced with Version 2.1 of Professional Write. Appendix B provides a listing of speed keys. Appendix C lists editing and cursor-movement keys. Appendix D shows you how you can use PFS: First Publisher to spruce up your Professional Write documents. Finally, the Glossary provides definitions of various terms used throughout the book.

Now that you know the general game plan, it's time to get down to business.

Part I

▼

Professional Write Basics

Includes

Introducing Professional Write

Getting Started with Professional Write

A Professional Write Quick Start

1

Introducing
Professional Write

Correction fluid. Erasable bond. Carbon paper. Eraser pencils. Think of all the things you will miss about producing documents on your typewriter.

Whether you have been using a computer for years or you have only recently been introduced to the word processing arena, you will find that the benefits of word processing—and of Professional Write, specifically—far outweigh any sentimental attachment you have to the tools of the typewriter era.

In this chapter, you will learn about the Professional Write word processing program and find out how word processing can speed up both routine and complicated tasks, helping you do more in less time. This chapter highlights the basic elements of the program and shows you a few sample documents you can produce as your experience with Professional Write grows.

Before introducing the basics of the program, however, this chapter shows you how electronic word processing has changed the way businesses do business.

The Benefits of Word Processing

Before the advent of personal computers, general office work required a massive amount of time to perform a limited number of tasks. If you were a number cruncher, you typed numbers on your adding machine and wrote totals on your accountant's pad. If you were a wordsmith, you composed, typed, and revised your documents by using a typewriter. Today, it seems almost impossible to imagine that producing a report could take the following steps:

1. Gather notes for the report.

2. Type (or write long-hand) the first draft of the report.

3. Edit and revise the report.

4. Type the second draft.

5. Edit the report again or turn over to supervisor for approval.

6. Make any necessary changes.

7. Type the final version of the report.

This report would be a basic, humdrum version of a typed report. No headers and footers. No cover page. No rules, boxes, or bold headlines. No graphs. How effective can such a report be?

To produce a report in this way, you need to type the entire report *three* times. And, unless you are a superlative typist, each time you retype the report, you increase the chance for misspellings and punctuation errors.

Although the actual task of typing the report is the same whether you use a Smith-Corona typewriter or Professional Write on a PC, word processing enables you to get away with typing the report only once. No matter how many errors you need to correct, no matter how drastically you revise the document, you don't need to type the entire report more than once. And, with word processing, you may be able to bypass even the typing phase—if the document is already in a file that can be imported into Professional Write. The program makes it easy to import text from other files—meaning that you can copy reports or sections of reports from other word processing files you have created—which cuts down the text entry time even further.

In addition to cutting down on data-entry time and effort, word processing enables you to do the following:

❏ Edit text easily without retyping the entire document

❏ Mark and move blocks of text

❏ Insert text

❏ Add to or revise text easily

❏ Reformat text

❏ Check spelling (not available with all word processing programs)

❏ Find synonyms for overused words (not available with all word processing programs)

❏ Change font style and size (not available with all word processing programs)

If you are new to word processing, it may seem as if all the new commands and options involved with a new software program are more trouble than they are worth. Particularly if this is your first experience with computers, you may think that pounding out documents on the Smith-Corona is less confusing than learning how to use today's technology to (eventually) save time on your memos and reports.

If you are the least bit wary of word processing, or if you have only a limited amount of time to spend learning a new program, you will be pleased with your investment in Professional Write. Created for the businessperson who has unlimited demands and limited time, Professional Write enables even new users to get up to speed quickly, producing memos, letters, reports, and a myriad of documents in the smallest amount of time possible.

The next section highlights the features of Professional Write.

The Benefits of Professional Write

Professional Write helps you create documents—memos, letters, reports, whatever—as fast and as easily as possible. Although Professional Write is easy to use, the program offers a number of features that will appeal to you and your workload whether you are a new or experienced word processing user.

Perks for New Users

If you are new to word processing or to computers in general, Professional Write makes the transition to computerized word processing easy. You don't have to worry about forgetting an important option: Professional Write displays all the options on-screen for you, each tucked away neatly in the appropriate pull-down menu (see fig. 1.1). You open the pull-down menus by pressing the function key that is displayed as part of the menu name (for example, F2—File/Print).

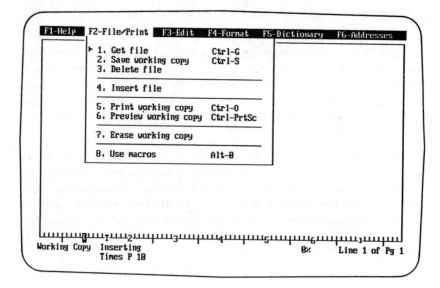

Fig. 1.1. *The File/Print pull-down menu.*

Professional Write also has a context-sensitive help system that helps you quickly find the answers you need. *Context-sensitive* help means that the help system is capable of providing help that is based on the current cursor position. For example, if you are unsure how to use the **Save working copy** option, you can highlight that option and press F1. Professional Write then displays whatever help is available for that subject (see fig. 1.2).

The program also gives you the option of displaying the Help Menu, which lists all help subjects available. This menu can be particularly helpful when you are wanting to perform a certain operation, like indenting a paragraph, for example—but you don't know which option to use. By highlighting the

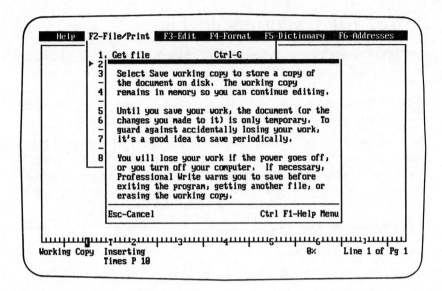

Fig. 1.2. A context-sensitive help screen.

Formatting and page layout option in the Help Menu and then selecting **Indenting a section of text** and pressing Enter, you cause Professional Write to display the help you need for that topic.

If you have trouble remembering that *i* comes before *e* except after *c*, Professional Write's spelling checker will appeal to you. With a built-in dictionary of 77,000 words, Professional Write is able to detect spelling errors in your documents and suggest the correct spelling. You also can create your own custom dictionary so that you, in effect, teach Professional Write to recognize words that are particular to your line of business. Additionally, a thesaurus provides you with on-screen synonymns, enabling you to make your documents more interesting and effective.

If your work mandates that you prepare, write, and mail massive volumes of mail—often form letters that are identical except for the names and addresses—you will find that Professional Write's address book feature gives you an electronic alternative to the desktop Rolodex file. Not only do you have the names and addresses at your disposal, you can have Professional Write put the names and addresses in the form letters for you automatically, cutting hours of routine typing tasks off your To Do list.

Power for Experienced Users

Although the developers of Professional Write focused on creating a product that is easy for a person to sit down and use on the spur of the moment, they did not overlook the need for power in the program. Professional Write offers several powerful features for those users who want to get the most speed and professional quality from their word processing programs.

The macro capability of the program enables you to record often-used keystrokes or menu selections and play them back by pressing one key combination. A *macro* is actually a miniprogram that carries out a series of steps. For example, suppose that you routinely update a certain record file at the end of every day. Doing this requires the following steps:

1. Close the file you are working on.

2. Open the record file.

3. Move the cursor to the end of the file.

4. Update the file by entering the names of the projects you worked on during the day.

With Professional Write, you can assign the first three steps to a macro so that all you need to do is press one key combination and then update the file as needed. (Macros are explained fully in Chapter 11.)

As printers become more powerful and desktop publishing features begin creeping into word processing programs, more and more users are wanting the ability to control and change how the type looks. Just a few years ago, word processing advocates didn't worry much about typefaces and sizes—there just wasn't enough variety to provide many options, unless you owned a full-blown typesetting system.

Today, laser printers make it possible to print documents in a variety of typefaces, styles, and sizes. Professional Write is equipped to deal with this variety by enabling you to specify fonts that are supported by your printer.

Professional Write also enables you to specify more than one printer, which comes in handy if you print drafts of the document on a fast dot-matrix printer and print final copies on a slower letter-quality or laser printer. (More about printer setup is discussed in Chapter 2.)

The preview feature, new with Version 2.1, enables you to get a look at the way the document is shaping up before you print. On the document work screen, you cannot see the different fonts you assign to headlines, body text, and so forth, but on the preview screen, you can see, edit, and, if desired, delete the fonts. You get an accurate screen representation of the document as it will appear when it is printed (see fig. 1.3).

What Are Fonts?

When you begin to explore fonts, typefaces, sizes, and styles, it is best to start with a few basic definitions.

As you may know, a *typeface* is a family of type. For example, Times Roman is a typeface. Within the Times Roman typeface family, you can have any variety of sizes and styles—such as Times Roman 12-point bold type, Times Roman 36-point italic type, and Times Roman 6-point type. All these different sizes and styles are considered the same typeface because they are Times Roman, even though they are different sizes and styles.

The *style* of the type is usually bold, italic, underline, or normal (no style). Type size is measured in *points*, with 72 points equaling one inch. The size of type can range from a minute 6 points to a whopping 72 points (and, depending on the fonts and capabilities of your printer, the size may range further than this).

A *font*, then, is one size and style of a particular typeface. For example, each of the following is a font:

Times Roman 10-point
Avant Garde 8-point bold
New Century Schoolbook 36-point bold
Garamond 12-point italic
Times Roman 12-point bold

The fonts you can use with your printer depend on the type of printer you have and the fonts available for it. For more information on working with fonts, see Chapter 9.

Those are just a few of the features you will be exploring throughout this book. Whether you are a new or experienced user, Professional Write has features that can help you improve the speed—and quality—of your word processing tasks.

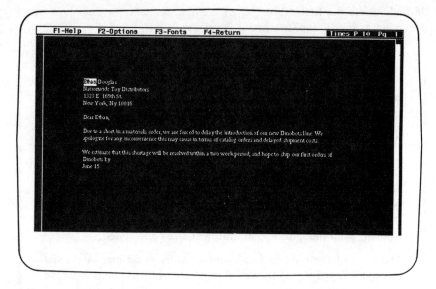

Fig. 1.3. *The preview screen.*

New Features of Professional Write 2.1

Professional Write 2.1 became available in the spring of 1989. With this new release, Software Publishing Corporation enhanced (or added) features in the following areas:

❏ File maintenance and compatibility

❏ Formatting

❏ Graph importing

❏ On-screen display (preview)

❏ Printing

File Maintenance and Compatibility Enhancements

With Professional Write 2.1, you can choose any number of ways to sort the files in a specified directory. This feature can be particularly helpful if you are looking for a particular file and you can't recall its name. (The 40-

character file description and the keyword search capabilities also help you locate files quickly. These features are discussed more fully in Chapter 2.)

Although Professional Write 2.0 was able to read and write files in formats compatible with many popular word processing programs, Professional Write 2.1 further increases the number of formats available. Now you can work with files (and save files to be used with) PFS: First Choice Version 3.0, WordPerfect 5, Microsoft Word Version 4.0, and OfficeWriter Version 6.

Formatting Enhancements

Professional Write 2.1 now enables you to change margins and tabs without marking text blocks, as you had to do in previous versions of the program. Additionally, you can set margins without setting tabs, and you can change margins either by typing the new margins on the ruler (as in previous versions) or by entering a number at the appropriate on-screen prompt. (This procedure is explained in Chapter 4.)

Importing Graphs

Now you can spruce up your reports by importing graphs from PFS: First Graphics. Professional Write 2.0 supported graphs created in Harvard Graphics, Professional Plan, and PFS: First Choice, and all these products are still supported in addition to PFS: First Graphics.

On-Screen Display (Preview)

Because the word processing screen does not show you the effects of the fonts you specify, the new version of Professional Write has a preview feature that shows you how your document will look when it is printed. This new feature can save you considerable time and trouble, particularly if you are unsure whether you have chosen effective fonts for your particular document. Preview also helps you determine whether you need to make any formatting changes before you print.

Printing Enhancements

Professional Write supports a number of new printers and enables you to specify more than one printer setup for your system. Additionally, when you are working with a printer that supports fonts, you will find it important that Professional Write now displays in the information line whether the font at the cursor position is a portrait or landscape font and what size has been chosen for that font. (More about portrait and landscape fonts in Chapter 9.)

What Can You Do with Professional Write?

If you are new to Professional Write, or to computers in general, you may be wondering what type of documents you can produce with Professional Write. This section provides three examples of documents produced by BrightStar Toys, Inc.

A Sample Memo

This first example, a simple memo from one department to another, was entered and printed in less than five minutes (see fig. 1.4).

To: Mike Rodgers
From: Leslie Young
Re: Overages
Date: 08/15/89

In reviewing our expenditures for July, it has come to my attention that each of the following accounts has exceeded the maximum materials allowance.

I have spoken with Mark Williams, the account representative for each of these accounts, and have requested a detailed expense report to account for the overages.

Account	Materials Cost
Shutterbug, Inc.	$1,350.57
Mongo's Music	$1,260.00

Fig. 1.4. *A sample memo.*

A Sample Letter

The sample letter took a little longer to compose than the memo because of the length and format of the text. Also, because this letter is to be sent to a customer, the spelling checker was run to ensure that there were no spelling mistakes. Figure 1.5 shows the sample letter.

Ethan Douglas
Nationwide Toy Distributors
1323 E. 165th St.
New York, NY 10016

Dear Ethan,

Due to a short in a materials order, we are forced to delay the introduction of our new Dinobots line. We apologize for any inconvenience this may cause in terms of catalog orders and delayed shipment costs.

We estimate that this shortage will be resolved within a two week period, and hope to ship our first orders of Dinobots by June 15.

Perhaps I may make a few suggestions about other toys we have available from BrightStar Toys, Inc.:

In addition to our new Dinobots line, we have Prehistoric Pals, fuzzy little bedtime friends that can be scrunched to the size of an orange.

Another new item along this line is the Bubblesaurus; a spongy Nerf-like dinosaur that has suction cups on his feet and doubles as a liquid soap decanter and sponge.

Our Christmas line promises to be an exciting and profitable array of new toys from America's favorite toymaker, as well. Monkey See Monkey Do, the new charade game for children ages 4 to 8, encourages new thinking skills and gives children entertaining objects to act out. Coast-to-Coast Dolls is a new collection of miniature dolls of the highest quality available, in a range of ethnic and regional representatives. From Ashley in Alabama to Winnie in Wisconsin, girls everywhere will love the beautiful costumes and accessories that are included with each doll. For the preschool set, Yellow House Yonker Blocks are the answer this Christmas season. These large bright yellow blocks, made of a high synthetic fiber that is both washable and durable, help children with both fine and gross motor development and provide countless hours of bright, safe, and clean fun.

This spring, watch for the introduction of our new Home Science line. Twelve project packs are currently planned for introduction in the spring, with an additional twelve packs planned for the fall show in Las Vegas. Each packet includes everything children need to perform six science experiments related to a particular topic; for example, kitchen science, water science, temperature science, etc. The Home Science line has been rated favorably in all test markets around the country and is currently up for adoption in several leading school systems.

Once again, I'd like to apologize for the delay of our newest product line. I hope that BrightStar Toys will be able to meet your needs again in the future.

Sincerely,

Robert Murray
Account Manager

Fig. 1.5. *A sample letter.*

A Sample Report

The sample report took still longer than the letter and the memo because of the more complicated tasks involved. However, the total time involved in typing, editing, and designing the first page of the report took an experienced Professional Write user only 15 minutes. In this document, the text within the box was formatted so that it is indented, and the drawing feature was used to add a design element to the boxed information. Figure 1.6 shows the first page of the sample report as it appears on-screen.

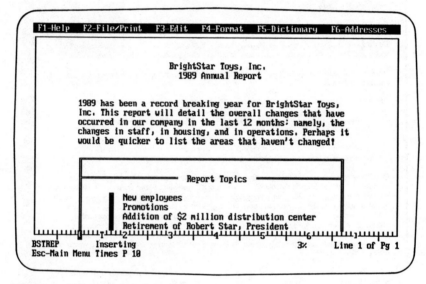

Fig. 1.6. *A sample report.*

An Overview of Professional Write

This section provides you with an introduction to the basic elements in the Professional Write program. References are provided so that you can turn to the appropriate chapters in order to find additional information about the topics introduced here.

The Main Menu

When you first start Professional Write, the Main Menu is displayed. On this menu, you see only three options: **Create/Edit**, **Setup**, and **Exit** (see fig. 1.7).

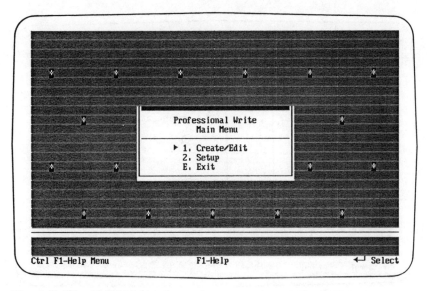

Professional Write
Main Menu

► 1. Create/Edit
  2. Setup
  E. Exit

Ctrl F1-Help Menu   F1-Help   ← Select

Fig. 1.7. The Main Menu.

You use the first option, **Create/Edit**, for most of your tasks in Professional Write. Every document you work with—whether you are writing it for the first time or revising it—is accessed through this menu option. **Setup** is used, as you might expect, to set up your computer equipment and communicate to Professional Write what type of hardware you are using. The last option on the Main Menu, **Exit**, takes you out of Professional Write and deposits you at the DOS prompt.

Working with the Directory

When you select the **Create/Edit** option from the Main Menu, Professional Write displays a blank screen with the title Working Copy in the bottom left corner. If you want to retrieve an existing file, you do so by selecting **Get file** from the File/Print menu. A box is then displayed, asking for the name of the file you want to retrieve. You can enter the name of the file, if you know it, or you can press Enter to have Professional Write display a listing of all the files in that directory. The listing displays the name of the file, the size, and the description you assigned the file when you last saved it. Figure 1.8 shows a sample listing.

You can work with the directory screen in several different ways: you can sort, search, or select files by using function keys assigned to those purposes. For more information on managing Professional Write files, see Chapter 2.

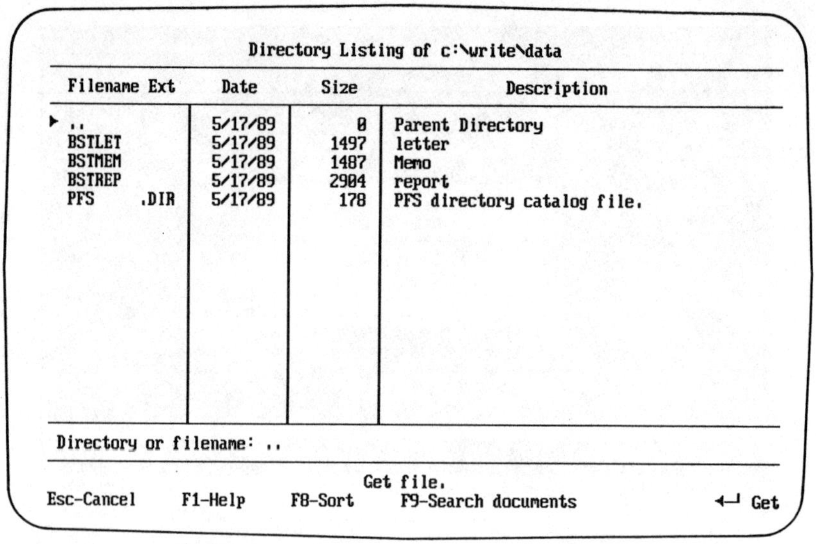

```
                Directory Listing of c:\write\data

   Filename Ext    Date      Size           Description

 ▶ ..            5/17/89        0   Parent Directory
   BSTLET        5/17/89     1497   letter
   BSTMEM        5/17/89     1487   Memo
   BSTREP        5/17/89     2904   report
   PFS     .DIR  5/17/89      178   PFS directory catalog file.




   Directory or filename: ..

                          Get file.
   Esc-Cancel    F1-Help    F8-Sort    F9-Search documents        ⏎ Get
```

Fig. 1.8. The file directory screen.

Professional Write Pull-Down Menus

After you open a file by using the **Create/Edit** option, the Create/Edit screen is displayed. On this screen, you do all your word processing tasks. The predominant feature of this screen is the line of pull-down menus across the top of the screen (see fig. 1.9).

Using Help (F1)

As already mentioned in this chapter, Professional Write has an elaborate help system that is designed to help new users get up to speed quickly. Professional Write actually has two different ways of providing assistance:

❏ Context-sensitive help

❏ Help Menu

The term *context-sensitive help* means that this aspect of Professional Write's help system "knows" what you need help with and supplies help information about that topic. Suppose, for example, that you are planning to draw a line around a paragraph in a report, but you are unsure how to use the **Draw lines** option on the Edit menu. To use context-sensitive help, you position the highlight on that option and press F1. Professional Write then

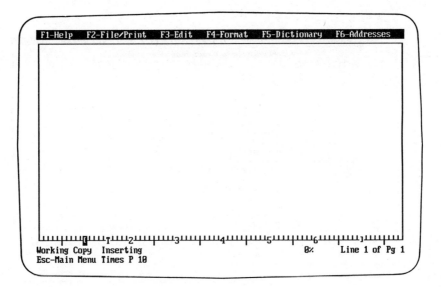

F1-Help   F2-File/Print   F3-Edit   F4-Format   F5-Dictionary   F6-Addresses

Working Copy Inserting   0%   Line 1 of Pg 1
Esc-Main Menu Times P 10

Fig. 1.9. The Create/Edit screen.

displays a screen of information that tells you about drawing lines. The program "sees" which option you select before you press F1 and displays any available help information on that topic.

You also can find help on drawing lines by using the Help Menu (see fig. 1.10). To display the Help Menu, you simply press Ctrl-F1. When the Help Menu is displayed, use the down-arrow (↓) key to move the highlight to the **Drawing lines** option and press Enter. Professional Write then displays the appropriate help screen.

The File/Print (F2) Menu

The File/Print menu provides you with the options you need to work with files in various ways (see fig. 1.11). For example, you use the options on this menu to save and retrieve files, print and preview files, delete files, and activate macro capability. Table 1.1 gives you an overview of the features available on the File/Print menu.

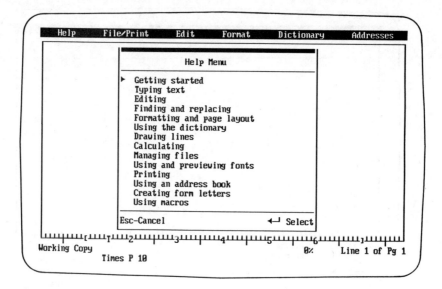

Fig. 1.10. *The Help Menu.*

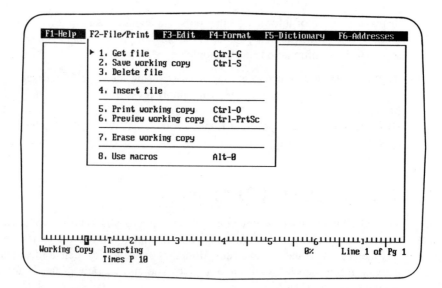

Fig. 1.11. *The File/Print menu.*

Table 1.1
File/Print Menu Options

Option	Speed Key	Description
Get file	Ctrl-G	Enables you to retrieve a file
Save working copy	Ctrl-S	Saves a copy of the document that is on-screen
Delete file		Deletes the current file
Insert file		Inserts a stored file into the working copy
Print working copy	Ctrl-O	Prints the document displayed on-screen
Preview working copy	Ctrl-PrtSc	Displays current document in preview mode
Erase working copy		Erases the copy of the document currently displayed on-screen
Use macros	Alt-0	Enables macro capability

The Edit (F3) Menu

The Edit menu gives you the tools you need to work with the text in your document (see fig. 1.12). Whether you need to add text, delete text, mark text blocks, change the style of the text (that is, make the text bold or underlined), use the find and replace feature, or calculate an equation, you will find the options on the Edit menu shown in table 1.2.

Table 1.2
Edit Menu Options

Option	Speed Key	Description
Insert blank line	Ctrl-I	Inserts a blank line at the cursor position
Delete word	Ctrl-W	Deletes the word at the cursor position
Delete line	Ctrl-L	Deletes the line at the cursor position

Table 1.2—*continued*

Option	Speed Key	Description
Mark text	Ctrl-T	Marks the beginning of a text block
Mark rectangle	Ctrl-R	Marks the beginning of a rectangular text block
Paste	Ctrl-P	Places items from the clipboard into the document
Boldface word	Ctrl-B	Puts word at the cursor position in boldface type
Underline word	Ctrl-U	Underlines word at the cursor position
Draw lines		Turns on the line draw feature
Find & Replace	Ctrl-F	Activates the find and replace feature
Calculate	Ctrl-M	Enables you to perform a calculation and paste the result in the document

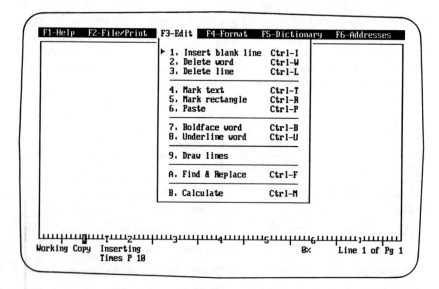

Fig. 1.12. The Edit menu.

The Format (F4) Menu

The Format menu enables you to control the format of the text in your document (see fig. 1.13). You also use options on this menu to add headers and footers to your document. Table 1.3 describes the options on this menu.

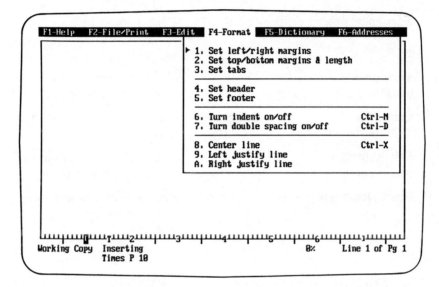

```
 F1-Help   F2-File/Print   F3-Edit   F4-Format   F5-Dictionary   F6-Addresses

                              ▶ 1. Set left/right margins
                                2. Set top/bottom margins & length
                                3. Set tabs

                                4. Set header
                                5. Set footer

                                6. Turn indent on/off              Ctrl-N
                                7. Turn double spacing on/off       Ctrl-D

                                8. Center line                      Ctrl-X
                                9. Left justify line
                                A. Right justify line


 Working Copy   Inserting                          0%      Line 1 of Pg 1
                Times P 10
```

Fig. 1.13. *The Format menu.*

Table 1.3
Format Menu Options

Option	Speed Key	Description
Set left/right margins		Set and/or change margins for current document
Set top/bottom margins & length		Set and/or change top and bottom margins
Set tabs		Set tabs for the current document
Set header		Set a header for the current document

Table 1.3—*continued*

Option	Speed Key	Description
Set footer		Enter a footer for the current document
Turn indent on/off	Ctrl-N	Control whether document is to be indented
Turn double spacing on/off	Ctrl-D	Controls whether text is double- or single-spaced
Center line	Ctrl-X	Centers any text on line at cursor position
Left justify line		Left-justifies any text on line at the cursor position
Right justify line		Right-justifies any text on line at the cursor position

The Dictionary (F5) Menu

The Dictionary menu contains the items you need in order to use the dictionary feature of Professional Write (see fig. 1.14). Table 1.4 highlights the options on this menu.

Table 1.4
Dictionary Menu Options

Option	Speed Key	Description
Proof word	Ctrl-A	Checks spelling of word at the cursor position
Proof to end of document	Ctrl-V	Checks spelling from the cursor position to the end of the document
Find synonyms		Displays synonyms for word at cursor position or can suggest synonyms for entered word

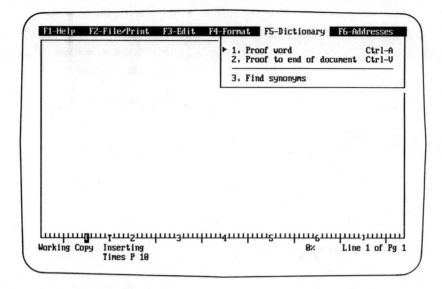

Fig. 1.14. *The Dictionary menu.*

The Addresses (F6) Menu

As you might expect, you use the Addresses menu when you are working
with Professional Write's address book feature (see fig. 1.15). Table 1.5
highlights the options on the Addresses menu.

Table 1.5
Addresses Menu Options

Option	Speed Key	Description
Select address book		Enables you to choose an address book file you have already created
Add an address		Adds an address to an existing address book
Find an address		Enables you to search for a particular address
Specify copy format		Enables you to specify the copy format the program uses to copy address book information to the working copy

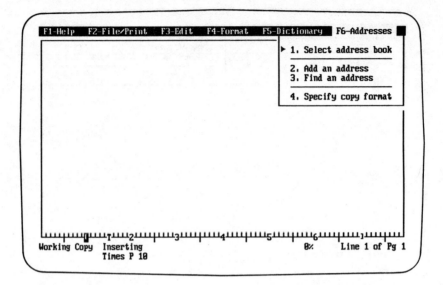

Fig. 1.15. The Addresses menu.

Understanding the Create/Edit Screen

As mentioned previously in this chapter, the Create/Edit screen is the screen on which you do all of your word processing in Professional Write. Now that you have gotten familiar with the pull-down menus of the program, you need to take a look at the screen itself. (If you are new to computers, some of the terms used here may sound foreign. For clarification, turn to the glossary at the end of this book.)

The Create/Edit screen is shown in figure 1.16. Across the top of the screen, you see the menu bar. (Each menu was described in the preceding section.) Below the menu bar is an open area, called the *work area*, in which you create and edit documents. In the upper left section of the work area you can see the cursor, which is a small flashing rectangle that marks the place on the screen where the next character will appear when you begin typing. At the bottom edge of the work area is the ruler. The ruler line resembles an ordinary ruler, except that the symbol [indicates the setting of the left margin,] indicates the right margin, and T shows where the current tab settings are placed.

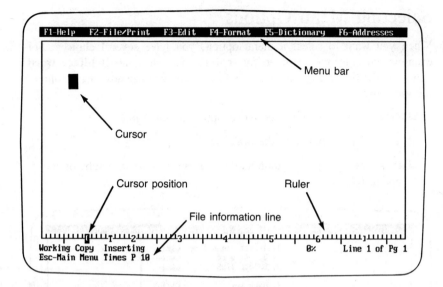

Fig. 1.16. *Parts of the Create/Edit screen.*

Under the ruler line is a file information line that displays the name of the file (or Working Copy, if the file is a new file). This line also tells whether insert mode is on or off, what percentage of the file memory allotment has been used, and at what position the cursor is currently placed (Line 1 of Pg 1).

Methods of Using Professional Write

With Professional Write, you can select menu options several different ways. First, to open a menu, you simply press the function key that appears to the left of the menu name. The following list shows the menu names and the functions keys used to open the menus:

F1   Help
F2   File/Print
F3   Edit
F4   Format
F5   Dictionary
F6   Addresses

Selecting Menu Options

When you want to select a menu option, you have several choices. For example, consider the menu in figure 1.17. To select the **Boldface word** option on the Edit menu shown in the figure, you can use any of the following methods:

❏ Press ↓ until the **Boldface word** option is highlighted.

❏ Type 7 (the number of the option).

❏ Press the speed key combination that appears to the right of the option (Ctrl-B).

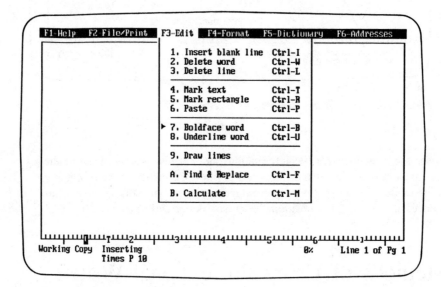

Fig. 1.17. *Selecting menu options.*

Speed Keys

Speed keys are key combinations that enable you to bypass the menu selections and carry out an operation more quickly. For example, instead of opening the Edit menu, using the down-arrow (↓) key to highlight the **Boldface word** option, and pressing Enter in order to boldface one word, you can just press Ctrl-B from within the document. Professional Write then boldfaces the word at the cursor position.

Additional Professional Write Features

Above and beyond the call of word processing features, Professional Write offers several additional features that help you ensure the accuracy of your work and help reduce the amount of time you spend working with words. This section gives you an introduction to the following Professional Write features:

❏ Dictionary

❏ Thesaurus

❏ Font Support

❏ Preview Feature

❏ Macros

❏ Address Books

Dictionary

Professional Write comes with a 77,000-word dictionary, ready to spotlight spelling errors at the press of a speed key. The program gives you the option of spell checking the word at the cursor position (Ctrl-A) or checking from the cursor position to the end of the document (Ctrl-V).

In addition to the built-in dictionary, Professional Write provides you with room for a 5,000-word dictionary that you can create for words that are specific to your business. For example, if you deal in computers and the words RAM, ROM, and BIOS are often embedded in your document, the Professional Write dictionary is going to stop each time it comes across those words and tell you that something's wrong. Rather than repeat each time that you do, in fact, mean to have those words spelled that way, you can personalize a dictionary so that Professional Write knows that those are acceptable words.

Thesaurus

Professional Write also is equipped with a 22,000-word thesaurus. If you have ever been stuck in a word rut, where you just seem to keep saying the same thing over and over, you will appreciate the luxury of having the program ''think'' of alternative words for overworked phrases. To access the thesaurus, you use the command **Find synonyms** from the Format menu.

Font Support

Professional Write enables you to take full advantage of the capabilities of your printer. Not all word processors have evolved to that point. When you set up your printer (in the next chapter), you take care of specifying whether your printer supports fonts in any form—soft fonts, built-in fonts, cartridge fonts, and so on.

Using different fonts to highlight information, make headings stand out, and set off text produces a more polished, professional-looking document. For more information on understanding, setting up, and using fonts with Professional Write, see Chapter 9.

Preview Feature

Professional Write's preview feature gives you a chance to look over the document before you print it. Preview shows fonts as they will appear in print and shows a better representation of the document's format and line and page breaks. Figure 1.18 shows a document as it appears on-screen; figure 1.19 shows the same document in preview mode.

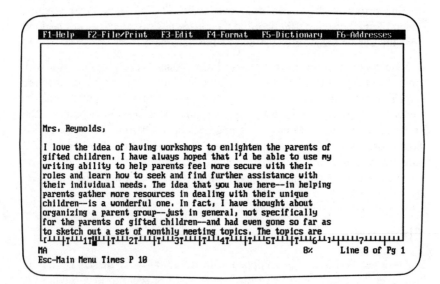

Fig. 1.18. The document on the Create/Edit screen.

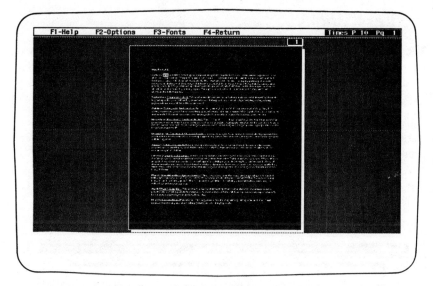

Fig. 1.19. *The document in preview mode.*

When the display is in preview mode, a new set of menus is presented on the menu bar. You can change views, modify the fonts used, or edit the document as needed. When you return to the Create/Edit screen, all changes you made are reflected in the working copy of the document.

Macros

Macros are like mini-programs that execute a string of commands or actions at the push of one key combination. In fact, you can think of a macro as a line of dominos—when you push the first domino, it falls and pushes the second, and so on, until all the dominos have fallen. With macros, the first command or action leads to the second, then the third, and so on, until all the actions you specified are carried out.

With Professional Write, you can create macros to take care of all kinds of routine tasks, such as

❑ Adding a salutation to correspondence

❑ Adding the date at the beginning of letters

❑ Setting a ruler line for a bulleted list

❑ Drawing a box

❑ Adding product information

Address Books

The address book feature enables you to keep an electronic file of names and addresses you use often. This feature is invaluable if you frequently send out any mailing that requires printed labels, envelopes, or form letters.

If you have ever worked with any kind of database or filing program, you will recognize some of the features of the address book. You can store names, addresses, phone numbers, and a variety of other information about people or companies that are important to your business. Each address book can store up to 2,000 records. Figure 1.20 shows a typical address book entry. Information on setting up and using your own address books is included in Chapter 10.

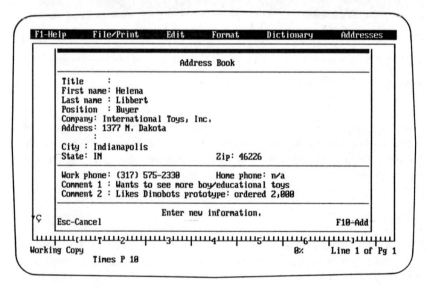

Fig. 1.20. *An address book entry.*

Chapter Summary

In this chapter, you have gotten a bird's-eye view of the various aspects of Professional Write. From an introduction to word processing, this chapter has progressed through the basic Professional Write tools to the more specialized features of the program. In the next chapter, you make backup copies of the program, install the program, set up Professional Write to work with your hardware, learn to manage Professional Write files, and get the program up and running.

2

Getting Started with Professional Write

N ow that you have been introduced to the basics of the Professional Write program, you need to make backup copies of the Professional Write disks, set up subdirectories for the program (if you are using a hard disk system), and install the program on your computer. This chapter explains all the basic procedures for getting Professional Write up and running, and provides basic introductions to various hardware and software elements, which will be especially helpful for users who are new to word processing or computers in general.

What Comes with Professional Write?

The number and the size of disks included in your Professional Write package depends on the capabilities of the system for which you are purchasing the program. Professional Write is available on both 5 1/4-inch and 3 1/2-inch disks. When you open the package containing 5 1/4-inch disks, you should see

❑ Start Up disk (Disk 1)

❑ Program disk (Disk 2)

❏ Printer disk (Disk 3)

❏ Preview disk (Disk 4)

❏ Dictionary disk (Disk 5)

❏ Conversion disk (Disk 6)

❏ *Professional Write User's Manual*

❏ *Professional Write Printer Manual*

If you are using the 3 1/2-inch version of Professional Write, the following items should be included in the package:

❏ Start Up and Program disk (Disk 1)

❏ Printer and Preview disk (Disk 2)

❏ Dictionary and Conversion disk (Disk 3)

❏ *Professional Write User's Manual*

❏ *Professional Write Printer Manual*

If you are missing any of the items listed here, contact the dealer who sold you the program.

What Do You Need to Run Professional Write?

The following list shows the hardware and software you need to run Professional Write:

❏ An IBM PC, PC XT, or PC AT; an IBM Personal System/2 (PS/2) Model 30, 50, or 60; or any 100% IBM-compatible desktop, portable, or laptop computer (including COMPAQ, EPSON, Tandy, Toshiba, NEC, and others)

   Note: Software Publishing Corporation recommends using a computer based on the 80286 microprocessor if you plan to use the preview feature now available with Professional Write Version 2.1.

❏ Two double-sided disk drives or one disk drive and a hard disk

❏ A minimum of 512K of random-access memory (RAM)

❏ A monitor (monochrome or color)

❑ One of the following video adapters: Enhanced Graphics Adapter Card, Hercules Graphics Card, or IBM Color/Graphics Adapter Card.

❑ A printer supported by Professional Write

❑ The Professional Write program

❑ DOS (Version 2.0 or higher)

The next section provides examples of several types of hardware setups that can run Professional Write. If you already have your hardware, you may want to skip to the section ''Making Backup Copies of Professional Write'' elsewhere in this chapter.

Sample Hardware Setups

Several examples of hardware setups capable of running Professional Write are described in the following paragraphs. The first example, listed in table 2.1, shows the minimum hardware setup—one that requires a minimal investment. This system is an IBM PC compatible with two disk drives, 512K of memory, a CGA monochrome monitor, and an EPSON LX80 dot-matrix printer.

Table 2.1
Minimum Hardware and Software Setup for Professional Write

Component	Minimum Setup Has
System Unit	8088 microprocessor
Disk drives	Two 5 1/4-inch floppy drives
Memory	512K
Monitor	Monochrome
Display adapter	CGA
Printer	EPSON LX80 dot-matrix
Operating system	MS-DOS or PC DOS (Version 2.0 or later)

A second configuration, shown in table 2.2, involves an IBM PC XT/286, one hard disk drive, one floppy disk drive, 640K of memory, and a Toshiba P1351 letter-quality printer. (Remember that these configurations are simply examples of types of systems that could be used; they are not meant to recommend one specific brand over another.)

Table 2.2
Enhanced Hardware and Software Setup for Professional Write

Component	Enhanced Setup Has
System unit	80286 microprocessor
Disk drives	One 5 1/2-inch disk drive One 20M hard disk
Memory	640K
Monitor	Monochrome or color
Display adapter	EGA
Printer	Toshiba P1351 letter-quality
Operating system	MS-DOS or PC DOS (Version 2.0 or higher)
Mouse	LOGITECH mouse
Additional software	PFS: First Graphics

A third sample configuration, shown in table 2.3, is a top-of-the-line system that shows the capabilities of a PS/2 Model 60. This system has a 44M hard disk, one 3 1/2-inch disk drive, and a Hewlett-Packard LaserJet Series II printer.

Table 2.3
Top-of-the-Line Hardware and Software Setup for Professional Write

Component	Top-of-the-Line Setup Has
System unit	80386 microprocessor
Disk drives	One 3 1/2-inch disk drive 44M hard disk
Memory	1M memory[1]
Monitor	VGA color monitor
Display adapter	VGA
Printer	Hewlett-Packard LaserJet Series II
Operating System	MS-DOS or PC DOS (Version 2.0 or higher)

Component	Top-of-the-Line Setup Has
Additional software	PFS: First Graphics (for creating graphs to be displayed in reports and presentations)
	PFS: First Choice (for spreadsheet, database, report, and communications capabilities)

[1] Professional Write can automatically use expanded memory available on most EMS boards.

The next section describes the basic components included in a computer system. If you are a new user, the section may introduce you to topics you have not seen before (if any terms are unfamiliar, consult the Glossary at the end of this book). If you are an experienced computer user, you may want to skip to the section "Making Backup Copies of Professional Write."

The Computer System

The purchase of computer equipment is a serious decision that requires a great deal of thought and fact-gathering. Whether you are the owner of a small business or a purchaser responsible for buying systems for 100 employees, you need to examine your present computer needs and make predictions about future needs before you invest in a system to solve your problems now, give you room for future growth, and stay within your budget.

Professional Write can also be run on a network, which brings another dimension into your decision. In general, if you are considering a major purchase, you may want to talk to a consultant while you are considering the various systems available.

Choosing a Computer: What Do You Need?

As you explore the possibilities of the many systems you can choose, the following questions will help you analyze the type of features you need in a computer system. If you already own a system, these questions will help you identify areas in which you may want to enhance the system you already have.

1. Is processing speed a major consideration? If so, you may want to look at systems with 80386 microprocessors. The 80286 offers significantly increased speed over the 8088 microprocessor, but currently the 80386 is the top of the line.

2. How much storage capacity do you need? Will you be creating and maintaining documents that are significant in terms of length or number? Will you use your word processing program to create and store correspondence with hundreds —or thousands—of clients? Will Professional Write be used by only one person who creates two or three letters a month? Is the program the standard adopted by your entire public relations department? Consider how much storage space you may need before you invest in a hard disk or limit yourself by buying a floppy disk drive system. Remember to evaluate the future needs of your business, and don't buy a computer without room to expand.

3. Will you (or your employees) be spending a considerable amount of time at the computer? The answer to this question affects the type of monitor and graphics adapter you buy. Currently the VGA monitor and adapter give the best display available, but EGA monitors also provide clear characters, a variety of colors, and good graphics formation. Although you can use a VGA monitor and graphics card with Professional Write, the program will display output in EGA mode; the program, as yet, does not support VGA mode. The CGA monitor and card generally offer poor resolution, black-and-white graphics, and a slower screen update than EGA or VGA. You should also be sure to purchase a monitor and adapter that can support Professional Write's preview mode (any of those listed previously will be able to do this).

4. What sort of print quality do you need? The quality of the output you need to produce depends, of course, on how you use the output after you print it. If you print memos only for your own use, you may not need a printer with more capabilities than a dot-matrix printer has to offer. If, however, you are responsible for producing press releases sent to prospective buyers and review agents, you should print on a laser printer in order to get the best quality possible.

Memory

The computer's available memory, called RAM (random-access memory), is a major concern for most users. RAM is the work area into which the computer loads Professional Write and the data files you work with during the work session.

Professional Write requires 512K of RAM, 384K of which must be available to the Professional Write program. In that 512K, the computer loads the operating system (MS-DOS or PC DOS) and the COMMAND.COM program, which translates the DOS commands you type (such as DIR and RENAME) into commands understood by the operating system. The 512K also holds Professional Write and the data files that you need to create or modify.

Depending on the system you have, you may have from 512K to 1M (megabyte) of RAM. If you are unsure of the amount of RAM available in your system, you can use the DOS CHKDSK command to display the amount of RAM available and the amount of RAM currently in use. When you type CHKDSK at the DOS prompt and press Enter, a screen similar to the one shown in figure 2.1 is displayed. (The files listed on your screen will differ from the ones shown here.)

```
[C:\PW] chkdsk

Volume RVP        created 04-22-1989 7:02a
Volume Serial Number is 0758-07EC

  65255424 bytes total disk space
     75776 bytes in 4 hidden files
    184320 bytes in 74 directories
  39499776 bytes in 1795 user files
    120832 bytes in bad sectors
  25374720 bytes available on disk

      2048 bytes in each allocation unit
     31863 total allocation units on disk
     12390 available allocation units on disk

    655360 total bytes memory
    401232 bytes free

[C:\PW]
```

Fig. 2.1. *Using CHKDSK to determine the amount of RAM in use.*

Professional Write 2.1 supports EMS, or the Expanded Memory Specification. If your system is equipped with expanded memory, this capability enables you to use more memory for your data files than DOS normally provides.

What's the Difference between RAM and Disk Storage Space?

New users are often confused about the difference between RAM and hard disk or floppy disk storage space. If RAM stores the programs and the data, what does the hard disk store? If a hard disk offers 20M for program and data file storage, why is 512K of RAM so important?

An analogy best answers these questions. Imagine that you are at the library, doing research for a report on the effects of black-and-white print advertising. You have found a file of 100 manila folders from which you need to gather the necessary statistics. You also have five sheets of instructions given to you by your boss on how to reference various research facts. You sit down at a library table, open several of the folders, and lay out only the instruction sheets you need for this part of the research—after all, a library table can only hold so much.

When you finish gathering data from the first set of manila folders, you put those back and get the second set. Similarly, when you complete the first few pages of instructions, you put those back and get the remaining pages.

You can think of the library table as the RAM in your computer. RAM stores only the instructions and the data you need during that portion of your work session. RAM is the work area used as you work with files in Professional Write, or, for that matter, in any other program.

The 100 manila folders are stored in *disk storage*—whether that is on a hard disk or floppy disks. In Professional Write, when you request to see another file, it is retrieved from storage and loaded into RAM. Sometimes, depending on how limited the available RAM space is, the computer may discard a file that is now unneeded in order to make room for the incoming file. By keeping only those files needed for the current work session in RAM, you can work much faster than if you had to retrieve data from disk storage while using these files.

What is Expanded Memory?

A computer equipped with an expanded memory board gives you more room for your Professional Write data files. Expanded memory is additional memory beyond the DOS limitation. Your computer accesses this memory by using *bank switching* or *memory paging*.

Although the amount of expanded memory in your system can be as high as 32M, your computer accesses only 64K at one time. The concept becomes clearer if you imagine a 64K window that opens onto a 32M block of memory. When your computer needs to access data that is stored in another part of the 32M block, the 64K window is moved to the appropriate position. (The system also stores a directory that it consults in order to find the various data blocks.)

For Professional Write users, having access to expanded memory means being able to open files more quickly, work with larger documents, and use a variety of features without worrying about memory limitations.

The Monitor

Consider how difficult word processing would be without a monitor. Sure, it would be possible—but how accurate can your typing be if you can't see what you're doing? If you are like many typists, you wind up backspacing and deleting at least once every few hundred characters.

Now consider how draining it would be to work eight hours a day in front of a monitor that displays poorly formed characters, bad contrast, and has slow display times. Are you patient enough to not mind typing several words ahead of the monitor display? Some low-end adapters and systems can be excruciatingly slow, especially if you are a fast typist. All these facets play into the decision you make when you purchase a monitor that you will be living with for the major portion of your computer work time. Because the monitor is your link to the workings of your computer, this purchase is one you should make cautiously.

You have several options for the type of monitor you may use with Professional Write. You can use a monochrome or a color monitor, along with a CGA, EGA, VGA, or Hercules Graphics Card. The display quality of each of these types will be discussed later in the chapter.

On all monitors, the display is composed of hundreds of small dots of light, called *pixels*. Each character is a pattern of pixels displayed on-screen. The higher the number of pixels used to display a character, the better the quality of the display. Monitors that can display a high number of pixels are known as *high-resolution* monitors; monitors capable of displaying a lower number of pixels are called *low-resolution* monitors.

A CGA (Color Graphics Adapter) monitor offers the lowest resolution of the various adapters: this card displays a character in a grid of 8 by 8 pixels. By comparison, an EGA (Enhanced Graphics Adapter) monitor displays an 8-by-14-pixel grid for one character, and the Hercules Graphics Card provides a display grid of 9 by 14. The VGA (Video Graphics Adapter) is capable of displaying characters in an 8-by-16 grid on a color monitor, and in a 9-by-16 grid on a monochrome monitor. As yet, Professional Write does not support VGA mode. When you use Professional Write on a VGA monitor and with a VGA adapter, the program displays output in EGA mode.

> The higher the resolution of your monitor, the clearer the characters appear.

The selection of the monitor and graphics card for Professional Write depends only on your preference and your computer needs. Be sure that the monitor and card you buy will support Professional Write's preview mode, however.

The Printer

The choice of printer is another decision that depends on the way in which you use the computer and the type of output you produce. Will you be printing only memos and an occasional letter? Are you responsible for producing press releases that are sent to important clients? Do you produce annual reports that carry year-end information to stockholders?

If your work is circulated only among office personnel, a dot-matrix printer may be all you need. If, on the other hand, you send documents to clients, customers, or reviewers, you need to make sure that the documents are the highest quality possible, which may mean investing in a laser printer.

Like monitors, printers vary greatly in terms of capabilities and cost. A low-end, dot-matrix printer can be obtained for under $200. A top-of-the-line laser printer runs upwards of $4,000. The following paragraphs give you a brief explanation of the different printer types and their capabilities.

When data is sent to a dot-matrix printer, the printer puts the characters on the page by pushing pins onto the ribbon, which in turn prints the characters on the paper. The *printhead* is the hardware mechanism in the printer that controls the placement of the pins. Nine-pin and 24-pin dot-matrix printers are available from many manufacturers.

Each printed character is composed of a pattern of dots; in the printed document, you can see the individual dots easily, especially on low-end dot-matrix printers. Like the screen resolution of monitors, printers have a print resolution that varies depending on the capabilities of the printer. A 9-pin dot-matrix printer, for example, prints at 72 dpi (dots per inch), and a 24-pin dot-matrix printer prints at 120 dpi. The more dots per inch, the better the resolution of the printed characters and graphics.

The following list shows the dot-matrix printers compatible with Professional Write. For more information regarding individual models, consult the *Professional Write Printer Manual*.

ALPS	Kyocera
Brother	NEC
C. Itoh	OKIDATA
Canon	Panasonic
DEC	Qume
Diablo	Star
EPSON	Tandy
Fujitsu	Texas Instruments
Hewlett-Packard	Toshiba
IBM	Xerox

Some dot-matrix printers—and all laser printers—support the use of fonts. Professional Write supports the use of fonts on the following printers:

EPSON LQ-800/1000, LQ-500, LQ-850/1050, LQ-950,
    FX-850/1054, LQ-2500, LQ-2550
IBM ProPrinter X24/XL24, X24E/XL24E
IBM QuickWriter
Kyocera
OKIDATA 390, 393, 393C
Panasonic KX-P4450
Texas Instruments 875/877

Later in this chapter, you will learn how to install your dot-matrix printer for Professional Write. Also, if your dot-matrix printer supports fonts, you can choose the font you want to use for your document text.

The advent of laser printers opened new doors in the printer market. Although some dot-matrix printers are capable of printing up to 120 dpi, laser printers can produce 300-dpi resolution. This added print resolution makes a significant difference in the appearance of characters. The clarity and formation of the characters is so good, in fact, that the average reader does not notice any difference between output produced on a 300-dpi laser printer and output produced on a typesetting system.

Most laser printers also support a variety of fonts. The Hewlett-Packard family of laser printers relies on font cartridges or soft fonts to provide the necessary instructions for printing certain fonts. PostScript laser printers, however, like the QMS or the Apple LaserWriter, can print up to 35 fonts from their built-in font libraries. Chapter 7, "Understanding and Working with Fonts," provides more information about the various font options available.

At present, the following laser printers can be used with Professional Write:

Apple LaserWriter
AST TurboLaser /PS
Hewlett-Packard DeskJet[1]
Hewlett-Packard LaserJet/Plus
Hewlett-Packard LaserJet II
IBM Personal Pageprinter
NEC LC-890
PostScript printers
QMS PS 800+

[1] Although the Hewlett-Packard DeskJet is actually an ink jet printer and *not* a true laser printer, the output produced comes close in quality to that of a laser printer, and for that reason it is listed here.

For more information regarding various laser printer specifications, see Chapter 8, "Previewing and Printing Documents."

Software

Now that you've learned about the various hardware setups you can use to produce documents with Professional Write, you need to explore the software you use with the system. In this section, you are introduced to the operating system your computer uses to interact with you. Additionally, you learn about other programs that you may want to use with Professional Write.

Operating System

The operating system your computer uses is the link between your computer hardware and you. Professional Write works with MS-DOS or PC DOS. (As you may know, DOS stands for Disk Operating System. The original version, MS-DOS, was developed by Microsoft Corporation. PC DOS, from IBM, is more widely used.) You use operating system commands to perform tasks such as changing drives, naming files, creating directories, copying files, and erasing files, among many other operations.

To operate Professional Write, you must have DOS (PC DOS or MS-DOS) Version 2.0 or higher. If you have an older version of DOS (the release number will be lower than 2.0), contact your local computer dealer for information on obtaining a more current version of DOS.

Other Application Programs

If you haven't already done so, you may eventually invest in other programs that complement the capabilities of Professional Write. PFS: First Publisher, for example, is a natural addition to Professional Write. A low-cost solution for desktop publishing for the IBM, First Publisher can spruce up your company reports, enliven your press releases, and customize your company masthead.

Professional Write also can be used with other word processors, spreadsheets, and databases. Spreadsheets can be brought into your company report. You can pull dBASE III information into an existing address book. You can use PFS: First Graphics to illustrate important points in your year-end summary. For more information on using Professional Write with additional software products, see Appendix D, "Using Professional Write Documents with First Publisher."

Now that you have learned everything you need to know about the hardware and the kinds of software you will use, you are ready to make backup copies of your Professional Write disks and install the program on your computer. The next two sections explain these tasks.

Making Backup Copies of Professional Write

Before you install and configure the Professional Write program, you need to make backup copies of the original program disks and store the originals in a safe place. If the backups are damaged, you can use the originals to make another set. Whether you have a two-disk drive system or a system with a hard disk, having copies of the original disks is a safety measure no one should omit.

Remember to format your backup disks before copying the Professional Write program to them. You can use the DOS command FORMAT to do this. Simply place the disk to be formatted in drive A, close the drive door, type at the prompt

FORMAT A:

and press Enter. *Caution:* Before you use this command, however, make sure that no important files are stored on the disk in drive A. After you enter the FORMAT command and press Enter, all files on the disk are erased, and the disk is formatted.

A special note to hard disk users: Be extremely careful when using the FORMAT command. Be sure to add the drive designation (in this case drive A) or DOS will assume that you mean the current directory on the active drive (which is probably drive C). If you fail to enter the drive designation, you may wind up with a reformatted hard disk, which means that all data and program files in the current directory have been erased.

If you use 5 1/4-inch disks, you need to make backup copies of six Professional Write disks. If you use 3 1/2-inch disks, you need to make copies of only three disks. With either size disk, the procedures listed in the following sections are similar.

Before backing up the Professional Write program disks, be sure to label the backup disks. Use names that indicate that the disks are backups of the program—not usable data disks. To avoid damaging the disks, write on the labels before pressing them on your disks.

Backing Up on a Hard Disk System

After you have turned on the computer and answered the necessary DOS date and time prompts (if applicable), make sure that the C› prompt is displayed on-screen. Then follow these steps:

1. Insert the Start Up disk in drive A and close the drive door.

2. Type *diskcopy a: b:* and press Enter. (Even though you have only one disk drive, DOS knows to alternate the read and write procedures as though two disk drives are being used.)

3. When DOS prompts you to insert the blank backup disk, remove the disk in the drive and insert the first formatted and labeled backup disk.

4. Press Enter. DOS then writes information to the backup disk.

Repeat these steps until you have made backup copies of all the Professional Write program disks.

> After you make the backup copies of the program disks, it's a good idea to protect the copies by putting a write-protect tab over the enable notch (on 5 1/4-inch disks) or by sliding the built-in write-protect tab (on 3 1/2-inch disks). After you write-protect a disk, no one can write information to the disk, perhaps accidentally overwriting information already stored there.

Backing Up on a Two-Disk Drive System

On a system without a hard disk, it is very important to have a set of program disks that you can use for day-to-day Professional Write operations. Because your copy of the Professional Write program is not on a hard disk, if something happens to the originals and you haven't made backup copies, you cannot get into and use any Professional Write data saved on other disks.

To make backup copies of Professional Write disks on a two-drive system, follow these steps:

1. Insert your DOS disk into drive A.

2. Turn on the computer (or reboot by pressing Ctrl-Alt-Del).

3. Answer the date and time prompts as necessary.

4. At the A› prompt, type *diskcopy a: b:* and press Enter.

5. Remove the DOS disk from drive A and insert the Start Up disk (Disk 1). If you are using 3 1/2-inch disks, insert the Start Up and Program disk.

6. Insert the formatted and labeled backup disk into drive B.

7. When prompted, press Enter. DOS copies the contents of the disk in drive A to the disk in drive B.

Repeat steps 4 through 7 until you have copied all the Professional Write program disks.

> After you make backup copies, remember to store the original Professional Write disks in a safe place.

Installing Professional Write

Now that you have made backup copies of the original Professional Write program disks, you are ready to install the program on your system. If you have a two-drive system, you don't really "install" the program; you simply load the program into RAM from the backup copies each time you start Professional Write. For that reason, if you use a two-drive system, skip to the section "Starting Professional Write" so that you can begin to use the program.

The next sections explain how to set up your hard disk to store the Professional Write program and data files.

Making Professional Write Subdirectories

The way in which you plan the subdirectories of your hard disk now greatly affects how easily you can find and manipulate files later. Anyone who has ever lost hours in a frantic search for a lost file knows how important it is to organize the hard disk into logical subdirectories.

You can think of the directories on the hard disk as a tree structure (see fig. 2.2). At the base of the tree is the root directory; below that are several subdirectories.

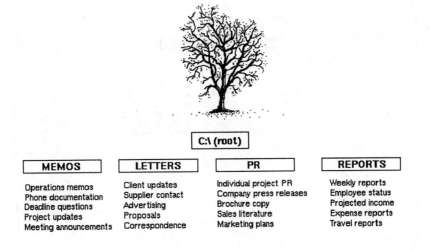

MEMOS	LETTERS	PR	REPORTS
Operations memos	Client updates	Individual project PR	Weekly reports
Phone documentation	Supplier contact	Company press releases	Employee status
Deadline questions	Advertising	Brochure copy	Projected income
Project updates	Proposals	Sales literature	Expense reports
Meeting announcements	Correspondence	Marketing plans	Travel reports

Fig. 2.2. A tree diagram of subdirectories on the hard disk.

The client relations division of the Houston Rose Advertising Agency needs four separate directories for Professional Write files:

MEMOS   For internal memos

LETTERS   For client correspondence

PR   For press releases regarding client projects

REPORTS   For weekly, quarterly, and annual reports that are submitted from the client relations division.

As you can see in figure 2.2, various files related to these four topics can be stored in the subdirectories.

Figure 2.3 shows how the directory in figure 2.2 would look if the DOS command DIR were used to display the files and subdirectories in the WRITE directory.

To make a directory to store your Professional Write program files, follow these steps:

1. If your computer is already on, type *cd* to get to the root directory. If you haven't turned on your computer, do so now and answer the DOS date and time prompts.

2. To make a directory for your Professional Write files, type *md\write* and press Enter. (The *md* stands for "Make Directory," and the backslash tells the operating system that the WRITE subdirectory is one level below the root directory.)

```
[C:\PW] dir

Volume in drive C is RVP
Volume Serial Number is 0758-07EC
Directory of  C:\PW

.            <DIR>      06-25-89   3:03p
..           <DIR>      06-25-89   3:03p
MEMOS        <DIR>      06-25-89   3:03p
LETTERS      <DIR>      06-25-89   3:03p
REPORTS      <DIR>      06-25-89   3:03p
PR           <DIR>      06-25-89   3:03p
       6 File(s)   25372672 bytes free

[C:\PW]
```

Fig. 2.3. Using DIR to display files.

3. If you want to change to the new directory, type *cd\write*. This command tells the operating system to "change directories" to the WRITE directory.

> If you don't use the backslash when you make a directory (for example, MD DATA), a subdirectory with the specified name is created under the current directory by default.

If you want to create subdirectories beneath the WRITE directory, you can model your commands after the following examples:

    md\write\hradocs
    md\write\sales
    md\write\hraaccts

Installing the Program

The actual installation of the Professional Write program is really nothing more than another copy operation. To install Professional Write on your hard disk system, follow these steps:

1. Type *cd\write* and press Enter to make the WRITE subdirectory the current directory.

Understanding Paths

To a new computer user, the concept of paths may seem confusing. If you think of a path as a line of directions you give to the computer when you tell it to look for a file, the concept becomes clearer. For example, the path

c:\write\client\letters\sl8-30.doc

tells Professional Write to look for a letter named SL8-30.DOC in the LETTERS subdirectory of the CLIENT subdirectory of the WRITE directory on drive C.

To remove the computer terms and take the ''directions'' analogy one step further, suppose that you are telling a friend how to get to the local market to get some sunscreen. The path

San Diego:\Surf City market\aisle 4\top shelf\sunscreen

tells your friend to start in San Diego, go to Surf City market, and find the sunscreen on the top shelf of the fourth aisle.

---

2. Insert the Start Up disk (Disk 1) in drive A. If you are using 3 1/2-inch disks, insert the Start Up and Program disk (Disk 1).

3. Type *copy a:*.* c:* and press Enter. Repeat this step for each disk until you have copied all Professional Write files into the WRITE subdirectory.

Starting Professional Write

After Professional Write has been copied to the WRITE directory, you can start the program from the hard disk. To start Professional Write, follow these steps:

1. Make sure that you are in the WRITE directory by typing *cd\write* and pressing Enter.

2. Type *pw* and press Enter. The Professional Write Main Menu is displayed on-screen (see fig. 2.4).

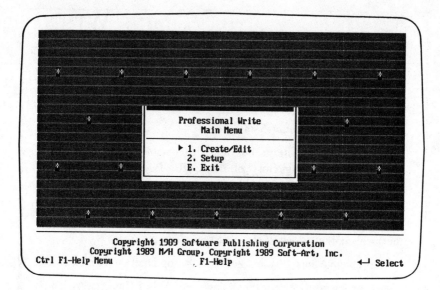

Copyright 1989 Software Publishing Corporation
Copyright 1989 M/H Group, Copyright 1989 Soft-Art, Inc.

Fig. 2.4. The Professional Write Main menu.

If you use a two-drive system, follow these steps:

1. Make sure that drive A is the current drive. (The A› prompt should be displayed on-screen.)

2. Insert the Start Up disk (Disk 1) for 5 1/4-inch systems (or the Start Up and Program disk for 3 1/2-inch systems) into drive A.

3. Type *pw* and press Enter. The Main Menu appears.

4. You are now ready to work with Professional Write. If you choose, you can store files you create on a separate data disk. (This is a must if you are working on a two-drive system without a hard disk.) Insert a blank, formatted data disk into drive B and you're ready to go.

> If you are using a two-drive system, at various points during the work session, Professional Write may prompt you to remove the disk in drive A and insert a different program disk.

Configuring Professional Write

Although the term *configuring* may sound like computer jargon, it actually means little more than telling the program what type of printer and monitor you're using. Now you are ready to configure Professional Write. Select **Setup** from the Main Menu by pressing ↓ once to highlight the option and then pressing Enter (see fig. 2.5). The Setup menu pops up over the Main Menu (see fig. 2.6).

Using the Setup Menu

Using the Setup menu, you tell Professional Write about the hardware you use as you work with the program, the drive and directories you work with most frequently, the screen colors and update speed you prefer, and whether you want the text mode set to insert or replace mode (discussed later in this chapter).

This section explains the various options available on the Setup menu and shows you how to enter the correct information for your particular setup. Table 2.4 lists the options available on the Setup menu and provides a brief description of each option.

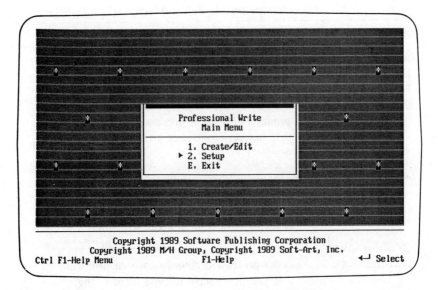

```
                    Professional Write
                       Main Menu

                    1. Create/Edit
                  ▶ 2. Setup
                    E. Exit




          Copyright 1989 Software Publishing Corporation
        Copyright 1989 M/H Group, Copyright 1989 Soft-Art, Inc.
Ctrl F1-Help Menu                F1-Help                  ↵ Select
```

Fig. 2.5. *Selecting the Setup option.*

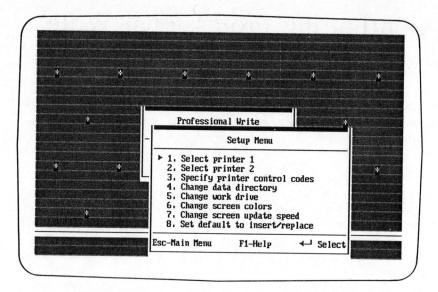

Fig. 2.6. The Setup Menu.

Table 2.4
The Options on the Setup Menu

Option	Description
Select printer 1	Sets up the printer you will use most often with Professional Write. For example, if you print most documents for in-house use, you may want to set up your dot-matrix printer as printer 1. (Note: If you are using a printer that supports fonts, set up that printer as printer 1.)
Select printer 2	Chooses a second printer. This is especially helpful when you infrequently use a second printer and you don't want to reconfigure the program each time you use that printer.
Specify printer control codes	Customizes the printer routine so that control codes are issued automatically at print time and you don't have to type them in the working copy.

Option	Description
Change data directory	Sets the default directory Professional Write uses to retrieve and store files.
Change work drive	Changes the drive Professional Write uses to retrieve and store files.
Change screen colors	Chooses one of three color schemes for the screen display.
Change screen update speed	Chooses a faster update speed for the screen. (With some monitors and graphics cards, a faster update is not possible.)
Set default to insert/replace	Sets insert or replace mode. (The default setting is Insert.)

The following sections explain how to use each option available on the Setup Menu.

Setting Up Your Printers

Professional Write provides you with a great deal of flexibility when it comes to setting up a printer to work with the program. Compatible with over 100 popular printers, Professional Write also enables you to set up two different printers to work with the program and to specify the font you want to use as body text.

Set up the printer you use most often as printer 1, and the printer you use less frequently as printer 2. If your department produces high-quality reports on a laser printer, for example, you may want to specify the laser as printer 1, if you produce most of your documents on that printer. If you print occasional memos on a dot-matrix printer, you can set up that printer as printer 2. Then, when you want to print your document, you simply tell Professional Write which printer to use, and the program sends the correct printer routine to the printer, without any further intervention from you. Remember, however, that in order to use fonts, you must set up as printer 1 the printer that has font capabilities. If you set up a font printer as printer 2, you will not be able to select fonts for your document, and a default font will be used.

Setting Up Printer 1

When you choose **Select printer 1** from the Setup menu, the Printer 1 Selection screen appears (see fig. 2.7). At the bottom of the screen, you can see the printer and printer port currently selected. On the left side of this screen, a two-column listing of printers supported by Professional Write is displayed. On the right side of the screen, the printer ports available to the printer are displayed.

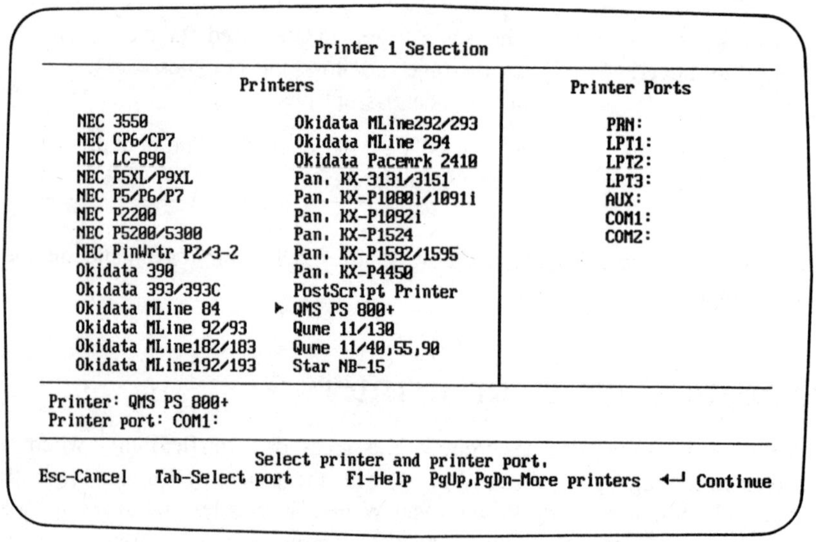

```
                           Printer 1 Selection

                 Printers                          Printer Ports

        NEC 3550       Okidata MLine292/293            PRN:
        NEC CP6/CP7    Okidata MLine 294               LPT1:
        NEC LC-890     Okidata Pacemrk 2410            LPT2:
        NEC P5XL/P9XL  Pan, KX-3131/3151               LPT3:
        NEC P5/P6/P7   Pan, KX-P10801/10911            AUX:
        NEC P2200      Pan, KX-P1092i                  COM1:
        NEC P5200/5300 Pan, KX-P1524                   COM2:
        NEC PinWrtr P2/3-2  Pan, KX-P1592/1595
        Okidata 390    Pan, KX-P4450
        Okidata 393/393C   PostScript Printer
        Okidata MLine 84  ▶ QMS PS 800+
        Okidata MLine 92/93  Qume 11/130
        Okidata MLine182/183  Qume 11/40,55,90
        Okidata MLine192/193  Star NB-15

        Printer: QMS PS 800+
        Printer port: COM1:

                        Select printer and printer port,
      Esc-Cancel   Tab-Select port      F1-Help  PgUp,PgDn-More printers  ◄┘ Continue
```

Fig. 2.7. The Printer 1 Selection screen.

Choosing the Printer

To choose the printer that you will be using with Professional Write, use the arrow keys to move the highlight arrow to the model of printer you use. If you do not see your printer on the menu, you can do one of three things: select another model made by the same printer manufacturer, choose **Unlisted printer**, or select a model that your printer can emulate (your printer's manual should be able to supply this information). To display a second screen of printers, press PgDn.

Choosing the Port

After you have moved the highlight arrow to the printer model you need, press Tab to get to the Printer Ports side of the screen. If you are unsure which port is which, you may want to have a person with technical savvy determine which port you are using. Choose the correct printer port by using the same method you used to select the printer.

> Depending on the port you select, an additional screen may be displayed, asking you to provide information about the port you have selected. Your printer manual should be able to help you solve questions about baud rates, parity bits, and other items relevant to your particular printer.

When you have specified the printer and the port, press Enter. If you have chosen a printer type (other than the HP family) that supports fonts, the Select Regular Font screen pops up over the Printer 1 Selection screen. If you have chosen a Hewlett-Packard printer, another Setup menu is displayed. On this menu, you select any font cartridges or soft fonts that you plan to use with your printer. This menu also provides you with an option that enables you to tell Professional Write where to find soft font files. For more information about working with soft fonts for Hewlett-Packard printers, see Chapter 7.

Choosing Fonts

On the Select Regular Font screen, you select the font for the text in your documents (see fig. 2.8). This screen is set up in tabular form, showing you the font name, orientation, point, pitch, and style settings available for each font. The following list explains each of these items:

Font
: This varies with the type of printer you use and your printer's capabilities. If you are using a PostScript laser printer, your screen may show a wide variety of fonts, such as Times Roman, Zapf Chancery, Courier, and others. If you are using a dot-matrix printer with only limited font capability, you may see several sizes and variations of the Courier typeface.

Orientation
: The orientation of a font is the way the font is placed on the page. Two orientations are available: *portrait*, which is the regular printout style, and *landscape*, which prints the text across the length of the page. Landscape style is good for items such as slides, handouts, and items that will be folded.

```
                        Printer 1 Selection

                       Select Regular Font

    NE  Font               Orientation   Point   Pitch   Styles
    NE
    NE  Courier            Landscape     14      8.5     N,B,I,BI
    NE  Times              Portrait      8       Prop.   N,B,I,BI
    NE ▶ Times             Portrait      10      Prop.   N,B,I,BI
    NE  Times              Portrait      12      Prop.   N,B,I,BI
    NE  Times              Portrait      14      Prop.   N,B,I,BI
    NE  Times              Portrait      18      Prop.   N,B,I,BI
    Ok  Times              Landscape     8       Prop.   N,B,I,BI
    Ok  Times              Landscape     10      Prop.   N,B,I,BI
    Ok
    Ok  Selection: Times
    Ok
    Ok  Esc-Cancel              PgUp,PgDn-More              ↵ Select

    Printer: QMS PS 800+
    Printer port: COM1:
```

Fig. 2.8. Selecting the font for your document.

Point	The height of a font is measured in points. A point is actually 1/72 of an inch; 72 points make an inch.
Pitch	The number of characters the font prints in one inch. A 10-pitch Courier font, for example, prints 10 characters in one inch.
Styles	Lists the text styles that are available with the displayed font. For example, suppose that one Courier font shows N,B,I,BI in the Styles column. This means that the font can be printed in normal, bold, italic, and bold italic type.

Depending on the number of fonts supported by your printer, you may be able to display a second screen of fonts by pressing PgDn. If you want to cancel the font selection, press Esc. Use the ↑ or ↓ keys to highlight the font you want to use. After you choose the font, press Enter. You are returned to the Setup menu.

If you are using a Hewlett-Packard laser printer, you select the font for your documents by choosing the Select Regular Font option displayed on the HP Setup menu.

Setting Up Printer 2

The procedure for setting up the second printer is almost the same as the procedure for setting up the first. With this selection, however, you don't have the option of selecting a font for the text in your documents.

> You cannot select fonts for printer 2.

Although Professional Write enables you to specify the same printer port for printer 1 and printer 2, installing the printers for different ports is more efficient. For example, suppose that after you print a draft of a document on printer 2, you want to produce the final version on printer 1. If you have both printers set up for the same port, in order to change printers, you must unhook the cable for printer 2, and attach the cable for printer 1. If you set the printers up for different ports, at print time you can enter the printer number to show Professional Write which printer (and port) to use. (This procedure is discussed in Chapter 8, "Previewing and Printing Documents.")

> You can change the printer settings at any time by selecting the appropriate option from the Setup Menu and choosing the correct settings.

Working with Printer Control Codes

Depending on the type of work you do and the capabilities of your printer, you may need to send printer control codes to your printer. Printer control codes may vary from manufacturer to manufacturer, so check your printer manual to find the correct control codes for your printer.

To access the Printer Control Codes screen, select **Specify printer control codes** from the Setup Menu. The menu shown in figure 2.9 is then displayed.

After the appropriate setting, type the printer control code that performs the function you want. If you don't need to specify a code after an item, leave the item blank.

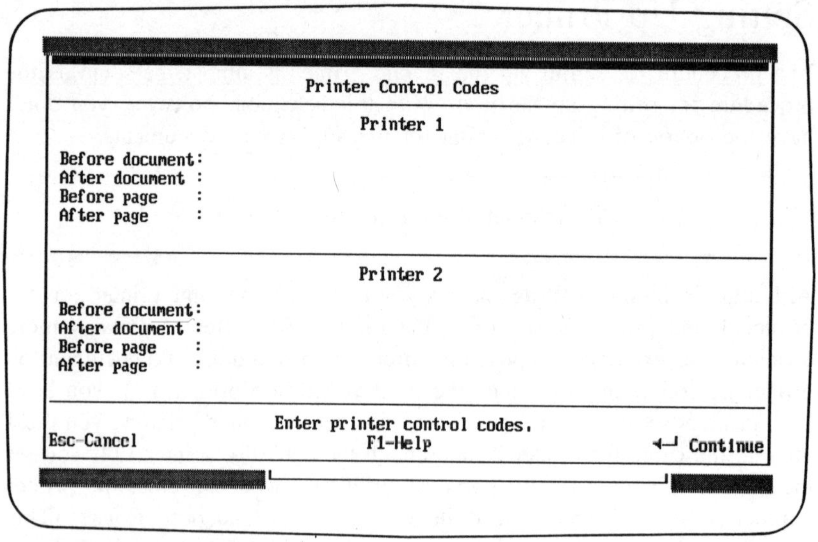

```
                    Printer Control Codes
                         Printer 1

Before document:
After document :
Before page    :
After page     :


                         Printer 2

Before document:
After document :
Before page    :
After page     :


                 Enter printer control codes.
Esc-Cancel              F1-Help              ↵ Continue
```

Fig. 2.9. *The Printer Control Codes screen.*

Specifying Work Defaults

As you become proficient with Professional Write, you may want to customize the directory and drive paths you use. As you may recall, Professional Write uses a path to locate the place from which you want to retrieve and store files. This section explains how you can change the default directory and drive so that Professional Write automatically looks in those places for the files you specify.

Setting a Default Data Directory

Earlier in this chapter, you learned to set up directories to store your Professional Write files. Professional Write comes preset with a default data directory of c:\, which means that all files will be stored in the root directory, unless you specify otherwise. If you set up your directories as suggested earlier, you will now want to change the default data directory so that the files you create and edit will be stored in the appropriate directory.

To change the default data directory, select the **Change data directory** from the Setup Menu. A window pops up over the Setup Menu, displaying the current default directory and prompting you to enter the name of the directory that you want to make the default directory (see fig. 2.10).

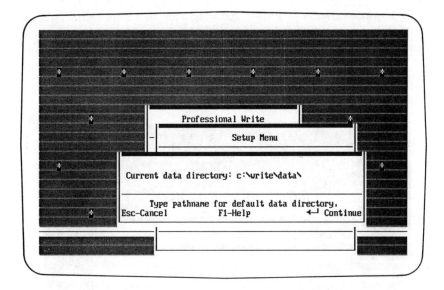

Fig. 2.10. *The Change Data Directory screen.*

Enter the path of the new directory (for example, c:\write\letters) and press Enter. You are then returned to the Setup Menu. Now, each time you select the options for saving or retrieving files, Professional Write automatically looks in the new default data directory that you have specified.

> If you are using a two-drive system, you can change the default data directory to drive B, if you prefer. This will enable you to place a data disk in drive B and have Professional Write automatically go to that drive instead of a default data directory.

Setting the Default Work Drive

You can also change the default work drive so that Professional Write goes automatically to the right place to locate the files you need. In most cases, if you are using a hard disk, you will want to leave the default data directory set to drive C. If you are using a two-drive system, you may want to set the directory to drive B.

If you use a RAM disk (an alternate section of memory that your computer recognizes as a separate drive), you may want to set that drive up as your work drive. (Often, RAM disks are called drive D.) Additionally, if you are using Expanded Memory (EMS), you may want to set the EMS up as a RAM disk. For more information about RAM disks, consult your computer dealer. To change the default work drive, select **Change work drive** from the Setup Menu. The screen shown in figure 2.11 appears over the Setup Menu.

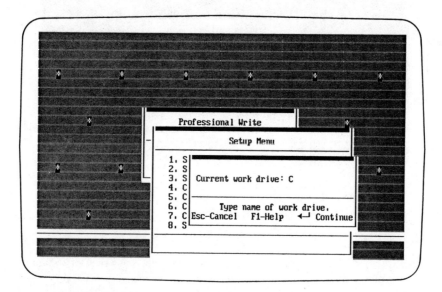

Fig. 2.11. *The Change Work Drive screen.*

Enter the name of the drive that you want to make the default drive and press Enter. Now Professional Write will look on that drive when saving or retrieving files.

Controlling the Screen Defaults

The new options on the Setup menu control the screen display. If you are using a color monitor, you can choose from three color schemes for the program (you cannot mix and match colors, however; you must choose one of Professional Write's preset color schemes). If you are using a mono-chrome monitor, you need to select the **Monochrome** option. Additionally, you can control the speed with which Professional Write updates the screen display by using one of the options on the Setup menu. This section explains both of these screen settings.

Choosing Screen Colors

If you are using a color monitor with Professional Write, you will notice as soon as you start the program that blue seems to be the dominating color: blue background, blue pull-down menus, blue screens. Depending on your preferences, you may want to choose a different color scheme.

To change the display colors on Professional Write, select the **Change screen colors** option from the Setup Menu. A small pop-up window is then displayed over the Setup Menu (see fig. 2.12).

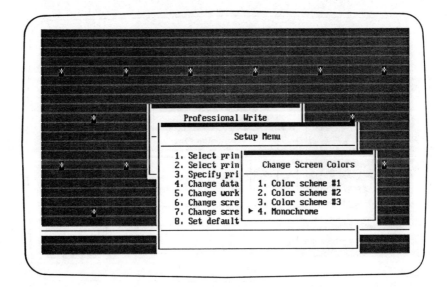

Fig. 2.12. *The Change Screen Colors box.*

Use the arrow keys to move the highlight to the option you want and press Enter. The change in color takes effect immediately. If you don't like the colors displayed, repeat the steps and choose a different color setting. Experiment until you find the color combination you want.

Setting Screen Update Speed

The screen update speed is one of the simplest options to change. Not many people are interested in having a slower screen update, but, unfortunately, some color monitors are unable to work with the faster update without sacrificing some display quality. The screen update speed simply controls how quickly the screen is redrawn when you make major modifications, choose menu options, or start the program.

Note: If you are using a monochrome monitor, Professional Write automatically sets the screen update speed to fast mode.

To try a faster update speed, choose the **Change screen update speed** from the Setup menu. When the Screen Update window appears, press Y in answer to the Fast screen update? prompt. Depending on the monitor you use, you may see a message telling you that the update speed cannot be modified (see fig. 2.13).

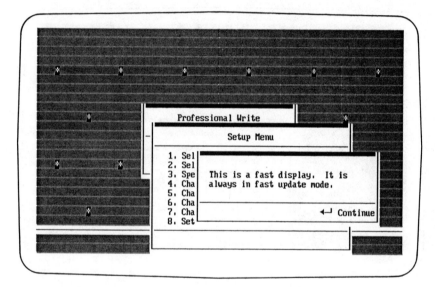

Fig. 2.13. A screen update message.

If you notice a problem with the way the program operates after you return to the Setup menu, reselect the options and change the Fast screen update? setting to N. Not all systems can support fast screen update.

Setting Editing Defaults

As you become more proficient with Professional Write, you will read more about the insert and replace modes. Here, a few definitions are warranted.

The Professional Write cursor works in two modes: insert mode and replace mode. When the cursor is in *insert* mode, any characters you type are inserted at the cursor position; characters following the cursor position are moved to the right to accommodate the inserted letters. For example, if the cursor is positioned after the word *Professional* in the line

New Professional features

and you type the word *Write*, the line becomes

New Professional Write Features

However, if the *replace* cursor is active, the characters you type are inserted at the cursor position, but any existing characters are overwritten, or replaced, by the new characters. So, with the replace cursor active, the line in the preceding example becomes

New Professional Writeres

As you can see, the letters that were not replaced by the word *Write* (*es*) remain at the end of the word. You can remove those letters by pressing the space bar twice.

Some people prefer using the insert cursor as they write and edit; others prefer using the replace cursor. Professional Write automatically defaults to the insert cursor when you begin working in a document. If you want to change the program setup so that the program makes the replace cursor active at start-up, simply select the **Set default to insert/replace** option from the Setup Menu.

A pop-up window is displayed so that you can change the status of the cursor (see fig. 2.14).

After the prompt, type *r* (for replace). From that point on, whenever you load or open a new document, the replace cursor is the active cursor. To turn off the replace cursor, you can press Ins at any time while you are working with a document; then the insert cursor will be active for the rest of the work session (unless you press Ins again).

> If you are a user new to Professional Write, you may want to leave the defaults as they are for now. Later, after you have gained some experience with the program, you will have a better idea of which defaults you want to modify.

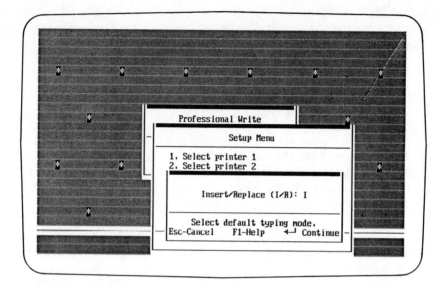

Fig. 2.14. *Setting the Insert/Replace cursor mode.*

Chapter Summary

In this chapter, you were introduced to the hardware and software you need in order to run Professional Write 2.1. Additionally, you learned essential procedures like backing up your Professional Write disks, creating subdirectories, installing the program on your computer, and setting up the program to work with your printer and monitor. Finally, this chapter showed you how you can modify some of Professional Write's defaults in order to make working with the program as comfortable as possible.

In the next chapter, you will explore all the fundamental features of the program in a Professional Write Quick Start.

3

A Professional Write
Quick Start

Learning to use a new computer program is the same as learning any new skill. Becoming proficient at anything requires practice and patience, whether you are learning to speak Swedish or paddle a canoe.

When you set out to explore a new program, you need to learn how to do the following important things:

- ❏ Use the menu system

- ❏ Find the menus that contain the options you will use most often

- ❏ Select options

- ❏ Open and save files

- ❏ Enter data in the files

In other words, you need to learn about as many of the basics as possible in a short, introductory time frame. This chapter takes you through the basic procedures you will use as you become proficient with Professional Write. In addition to the topics listed previously, you will find information on working with text blocks, basic editing techniques, and changing the format of documents.

First...Some Basics

This section first introduces you to the procedure for starting—also known as *booting*—the program. After you have started the program, you can then explore each of the menus available in Professional Write.

Starting Professional Write

If you are using a hard disk system and you have already installed Professional Write on the hard disk, you can boot the program by following these steps:

1. Change to the directory in which you have stored the Professional Write program files by typing *cd c:\write* (where *write* is the name of the directory) and pressing Enter.

2. Type *pw* and press Enter.

After a moment, the Professional Write Main menu appears on-screen (see fig. 3.1).

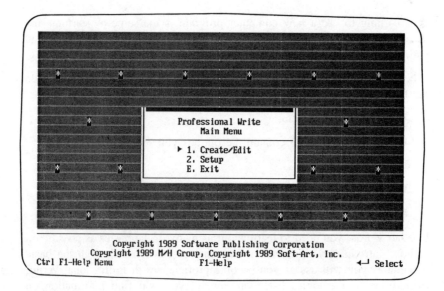

```
                        Professional Write
                           Main Menu
                      ▶ 1. Create/Edit
                        2. Setup
                        E. Exit


                Copyright 1989 Software Publishing Corporation
             Copyright 1989 M/H Group, Copyright 1989 Soft-Art, Inc.
     Ctrl F1-Help Menu                      F1-Help              ↵ Select
```

Fig. 3.1. *The Professional Write Main menu.*

Note: If you have not installed Professional Write on your hard disk system, follow the installation procedures detailed in Chapter 2 before trying the preceding steps.

If you are using a two-drive system, start Professional Write by following these steps:

1. Make sure that your DOS disk is in drive A and turn on the computer.

2. Enter the time and date, if necessary, and remove the DOS disk from the drive when you see the DOS prompt (which should appear as A›).

3. Insert the Start Up disk into drive A. (If you are using 3 1/2-inch disks, this disk is called the Start Up and Program disk.)

4. Type *pw* and press Enter.

If you are using 5 1/2-inch disks, Professional Write then tells you to remove the Start Up disk and insert the Program disk. If you are using 3 1/2-inch disks, this step is eliminated because all necessary files are stored on the Start Up and Program disk. The Professional Write Main menu is then displayed on-screen.

Selecting Menu Options

If you are new to computers, the suggestion that you ''select the **Create/Edit** option'' may leave you in a fog. Exactly how do you select an option?

As you can see from the Main menu shown in figure 3.1, on all Professional Write menus, one menu option is highlighted; that is, one option is displayed in a different color and a sideways triangle appears to the left of the highlighted option. The option that is automatically highlighted is called the *default* option. To select the default option, you simply press Enter.

If you want to select an option other than the one automatically highlighted by the program, you can use one of two methods: you can type the number (or in the case of the **Exit** option on the Main menu, type the letter *e*), or you can press the up-arrow (↑) key or the down-arrow (↓) key to move the highlight triangle to the option you want and select the option by pressing Enter. Professional Write then carries out your request.

Opening a Document

The way in which you open a document depends on whether the document is a new document or one you have created previously. In both cases, you need to begin the session by selecting the **Create/Edit** option from the Main menu. The Create/Edit screen shown in figure 3.2 appears.

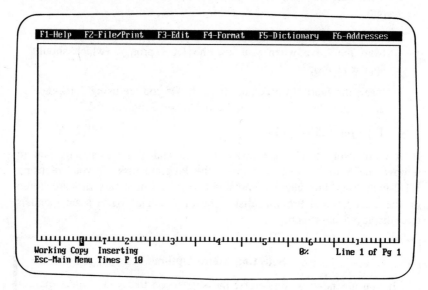

Fig. 3.2. The Create/Edit screen.

After the Create/Edit screen is displayed, you can enter or import text (if you are creating a new document) or open the file you want to work with (if the file already exists). For the examples in this Quick Start, you will be entering text in a new document, so this is the screen with which you will start. For the sake of completeness, however, the following procedure tells you how to open a file that you have created previously.

To open an existing file, follow these steps:

1. Press F2 to open the File/Print menu.

2. Select the **Get file** option by pressing Enter. (This option is already highlighted as the default selection.)

3. A window is displayed that shows you the directory in which your data files are stored. (You set this data path by using the Setup Menu, which is discussed in Chapter 2.) If you know the name of

the file, you can enter it after the path and press Enter (see fig. 3.3). If you do not know the name of the file, you can press Enter to display a listing of the files in that directory (see fig. 3.4).

4. Select the file you want by using the arrow keys to highlight the file name and pressing Enter. The file is then displayed on-screen (see fig. 3.5).

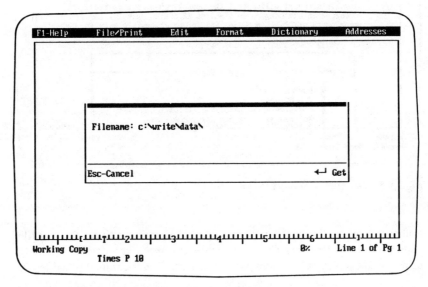

Fig. 3.3. *The default directory path is displayed.*

Directory Listing of c:\write\data

Filename Ext	Date	Size	Description
▶ ..	5/17/89	0	Parent Directory
ADDRESS .SPC	5/17/89	896	BrightStar Customer List
BSTLET	5/17/89	1497	letter
BSTMEM	5/17/89	1487	Memo
BSTREP	5/17/89	2904	report
P	6/22/89	211	sample paragraph
PFS .DIR	6/22/89	294	PFS directory catalog file.
POEM	6/28/89	1312	

Directory or filename: ..

Get file.

Esc-Cancel   F1-Help   F8-Sort   F9-Search documents   ↵ Get

Fig. 3.4. *Professional Write lists all the files in the directory.*

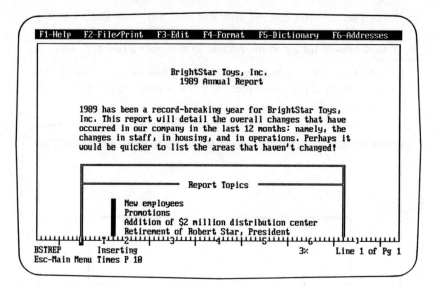

F1-Help   F2-File/Print   F3-Edit   F4-Format   F5-Dictionary   F6-Addresses

BrightStar Toys, Inc.
1989 Annual Report

1989 has been a record-breaking year for BrightStar Toys,
Inc. This report will detail the overall changes that have
occurred in our company in the last 12 months; namely, the
changes in staff, in housing, and in operations. Perhaps it
would be quicker to list the areas that haven't changed!

Report Topics

New employees
Promotions
Addition of $2 million distribution center
Retirement of Robert Star, President

BSTREP   Inserting   3%   Line 1 of Pg 1
Esc-Main Menu Times P 10

Fig. 3.5. The file is displayed on-screen.

Rather than going through this menu sequence, you can activate the **Get file** option by simply pressing Ctrl-G, which is the speed key combination. By using the speed key, you can bypass steps 1 and 2 and go directly to step 3.

Entering Text

Entering text is the easy part. If you have ever typed on a typewriter, key-ing text into your document will come naturally. You don't need to worry about pressing Enter at the end of every line; Professional Write has a word-wrap feature that automatically continues flowing the text onto the screen for you.

In this exercise, you will type a paragraph into the document. In addition to typing the text, you can import the text from files created with other popular word processors.

Typing Text

Type the following paragraph (including mistakes):

> Due to a short in a meterials order, we are forced to delay the intro-
> duction of our new Dinobots line. We apologize for any inconve-
> nience this may in terms of catalog orders and delayed shipment
> costs.

Making Corrections while Typing

If you are like most people, your typing is not 100 percent accurate 100
percent of the time. For that reason, you need to know how to correct typos
that you make as you type a document.

There are two errors in the sample paragraph:

1. *Materials* is misspelled as *meterials*.

2. The word *cause* was left out of the last sentence.

After you finish typing the paragraph, the cursor is positioned after the
period at the end of the last sentence. To move the cursor up to the first
misspelling (*meterials*), press ↑ three times. Then, press ← to move the cursor to the error. The cursor should now be positioned on the first *e* in
meterials. To remove the error, press Del. The letter is deleted. Before you
proceed to make corrections, make sure that insert mode is in effect. As
you may recall from Chapter 1, when insert mode is active, any characters
you type are inserted at the cursor position and existing characters are
moved to the right accordingly. If the replace cursor is active, any existing
characters to the right of the cursor position are overwritten by the characters you type. When insert mode is active, the cursor is a flashing rectangle;
when replace mode is active, the cursor is a small flashing underscore.

Next, type *a* to correct the misspelling. The word *materials* should now be
correct.

Next, you need to add the word *cause* to the last sentence. To get to the
space between *may* and *in*, press ↓ twice. Then, press → until the cursor is
placed on the first letter of the word *in*. Type *cause* and press the space bar
once. The last sentence should now be correct (see fig. 3.6).

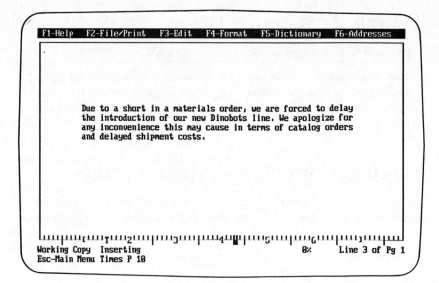

Fig. 3.6. *The corrected paragraph.*

> ***Reminder:*** When the *replace* cursor is active, any characters you type overwrite the text at the cursor position, while the *insert* cursor inserts the typed text and moves any existing text to the right.

Chapter 4, "Creating, Formatting, and Saving Documents," introduces you to the various cursor-movement keys you use to move the cursor around within Professional Write documents. For a quick reference, you can also turn to Appendix C, "Editing and Cursor-Movement Keys," to find a listing of editing and cursor-movement keys.

For the next few exercises, you need a larger selection of text to work with, so we need to add some more text. Use the arrow keys to position the cursor in the space after the period at the end of the paragraph. Press Enter twice. Then type the following:

> We estimate that this shortage will be resolved within a two-week period and hope to be able to begin shipping our first orders of Dinobots by June 15.

At the end of the paragraph, press Enter twice. Then type the following paragraph:

Because of the delay of our shipping date, we have arranged to offer wholesalers a price break of 10% on all Dinobot orders of 100 or more. Orders of 1000 or more will be given a 15% price break. We hope that this monetary savings will help compensate you for the inconvenience this delay may have caused you.

Editing the Document

Your document should now have three paragraphs of text. What if you decide that you would like to have paragraph 2 placed after paragraph 3?

Professional Write enables you to work with blocks of text. A text block is any highlighted area of text (from one character to an entire document) on which you can perform many operations, such as copying, moving, cutting, pasting, and so on. In this Quick Start section, you will learn to highlight a block of text and perform several of these important operations.

Highlighting Text Blocks

Before you can perform any operation on text, you must select it as a text block. Suppose that you do want to copy paragraph 2 and place it after paragraph 3. The first step in this procedure involves highlighting the block.

In this instance, we will use **Mark text**, because there are no special formats to preserve. To highlight the second paragraph, follow these steps:

1. Move the cursor to the beginning of the second paragraph.

2. Press F3 to open the Edit menu.

3. Use the ↓ key to move the highlight to the **Mark text** option and select it by pressing Enter or typing *4*. (You may use the speed key Ctrl-T, if you prefer.) At the bottom of the Create/Edit screen, instructions appear telling you to use the arrow keys to move to the end of the block you want to mark and then to press F10. As you press the arrow keys, the highlighted area expands. Move to the end of the paragraph. Your screen should be similar to the one shown in figure 3.7.

4. Press F10.

Text Blocks versus Rectangular Blocks

On the Edit menu, you see two options for marking text: **Mark text** and **Mark rectangle**. If both options mark a block of text so that you can cut, copy, erase, and move the block, why have two options?

Put simply, the only difference between the two options is that **Mark rectangle** does not wrap the text when the text is placed back into the document. For example, suppose that you want to move a highlighted column of words and you want to preserve the format of the column. If you select **Mark text**, when the block is moved, the format will be lost. If you select **Mark rectangle**, Professional Write preserves the format.

After you select **Mark text**, the Text Block Operations menu is displayed. After you select **Mark rectangle**, the Rectangular Block Operations menu appears. Both menus contain similar options, although the Text Block Operations menu does provide a few more options related to formatting. For more detailed information on using these options, see Chapter 5, "Editing Documents."

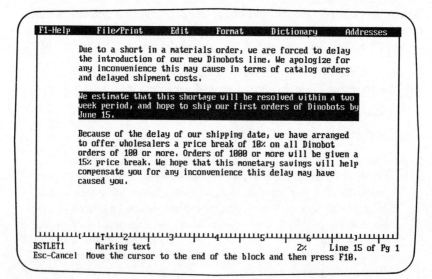

Fig. 3.7. The highlighted text block.

> You can use the speed key Ctrl-T to begin marking a text block.

The block of text is now marked so that you can perform any of the following operations:

- ❏ Cut (remove) the block from the document
- ❏ Copy the block to the clipboard or to another place in the document
- ❏ Change the type style of the block
- ❏ Change the font or the type size of the block
- ❏ Change the margins, tabs, or indents
- ❏ Change the spacing
- ❏ Save the block as another document
- ❏ Print the block
- ❏ Calculate any values in the block

Note: Some of the options are different if you highlight a block of text by using the **Mark rectangle** option. For more information on the options available with rectangular block operations, see Chapter 5, ''Editing Documents.''

In the next section, you will copy the paragraph to the end of the document.

Copying Text

Now that you have identified the block of text you will be working with, you can copy the block to another position in the document.

To copy a text block, follow these steps:

1. Make sure that the text block (paragraph 2) is highlighted. (If you have not done this already, refer to the preceding section). After the text block is selected, the Text Block Operation menu is displayed.

2. Select the **Copy** option in one of three ways: by typing *2*, by pressing Ctrl-C (the speed key combination), or by pressing ↓ once to highlight the option and then pressing Enter.

After you press Enter, Professional Write copies the text block to the clipboard. You can think of Professional Write's clipboard as an unseen place in memory where the program places blocks of text that you copy, cut, or erase. You use the Edit menu's **Paste** option (discussed in the next section) to place a block of text from the clipboard into the document.

Moving Text

Suppose that you now want to move the second paragraph to the end of the document. There isn't a ''move'' option with Professional Write; instead, you use the **Cut** and **Paste** options to remove the block from one position in the document and place it in another position.

To move a text block, follow these steps:

1. Select the text block as described in the section ''Highlighting Text Blocks.''

2. From the Text Block Operations menu, choose the **Cut** command in one of three ways: by pressing Enter (because the option is already selected as the default), by typing *1*, or by pressing Del (see fig. 3.8). Professional Write then cuts the highlighted block from the document and places the block on the clipboard.

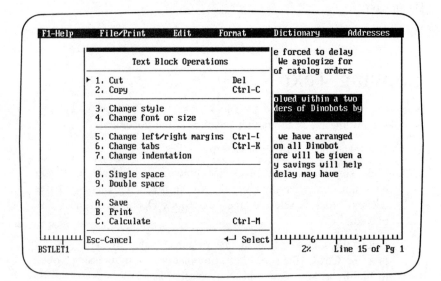

*Fig. 3.8. Selecting the **Cut** option.*

3. Move the cursor to the point in the document where you want the block to be inserted—in this case, to the end of the document.

4. Select the **Paste** option in one of three ways: by pressing F3 to open the Edit menu and typing 6, by opening the Edit menu and using the arrow keys to highlight the option and pressing Enter, or by pressing Ctrl-P (the speed key combination). Professional Write then pastes the text block to the cursor position (see fig. 3.9).

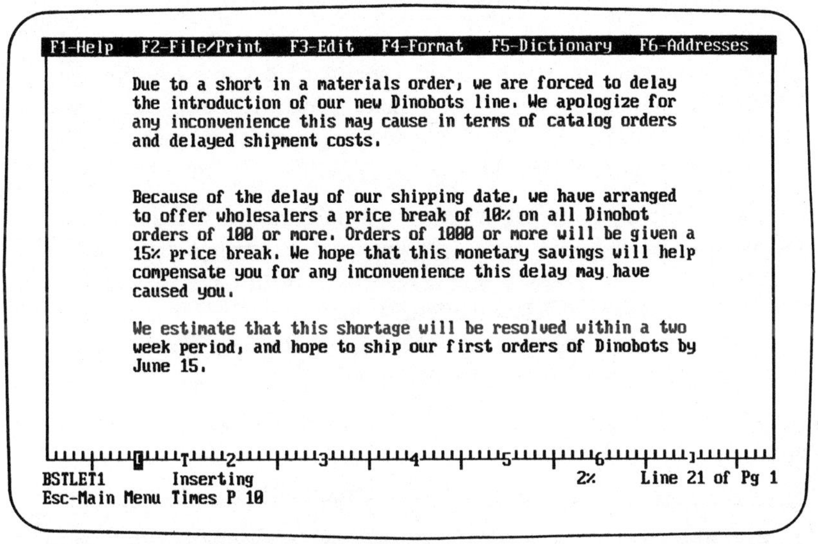

```
 F1-Help   F2-File/Print   F3-Edit   F4-Format   F5-Dictionary   F6-Addresses

         Due to a short in a materials order, we are forced to delay
         the introduction of our new Dinobots line. We apologize for
         any inconvenience this may cause in terms of catalog orders
         and delayed shipment costs.

         Because of the delay of our shipping date, we have arranged
         to offer wholesalers a price break of 10% on all Dinobot
         orders of 100 or more. Orders of 1000 or more will be given a
         15% price break. We hope that this monetary savings will help
         compensate you for any inconvenience this delay may have
         caused you.

         We estimate that this shortage will be resolved within a two
         week period, and hope to ship our first orders of Dinobots by
         June 15.




 BSTLET1        Inserting                          2%      Line 21 of Pg 1
 Esc-Main Menu  Times P 10
```

Fig. 3.9. The moved text block.

When you are using a rectangular block operation, you can use the **Erase** option to remove the text but preserve the space; in other words, when you erase text in a rectangular block, spaces are inserted in the place the text occupied, thus preserving the format of the block. Chapter 5 explains the **Erase** option more thoroughly.

Changing Fonts

After you have marked a block (a text block or a rectangular block), you have the option of changing the font, style, or size of the characters— provided, of course, that your printer supports different fonts. (For more information about installing your particular printer, see Chapter 2, "Getting Started with Professional Write.")

To change the font of a section of text, follow these steps:

1. Highlight the text block to be used (paragraph 2).

2. The Text Block Operations menu appears; select the **Change font or size** option by typing *4* or by using the ↓ key to move the high- light to the option and pressing Enter. *Note:* You also can change the fonts, sizes, or styles if you are using a rectangular block. This procedure is explained in Chapter 5.

3. The Select Font or Size window is then displayed. On this screen, you select the font to which you want to change the selected block. Use the ↓ key to move the highlight to the font you want and press Enter to select the font. If the one you are looking for is not shown, it may be on another screen of fonts. Press PgDn to display additional font screens.

Figure 3.10 shows the Select Font or Size window for a system with a PostScript laser printer.

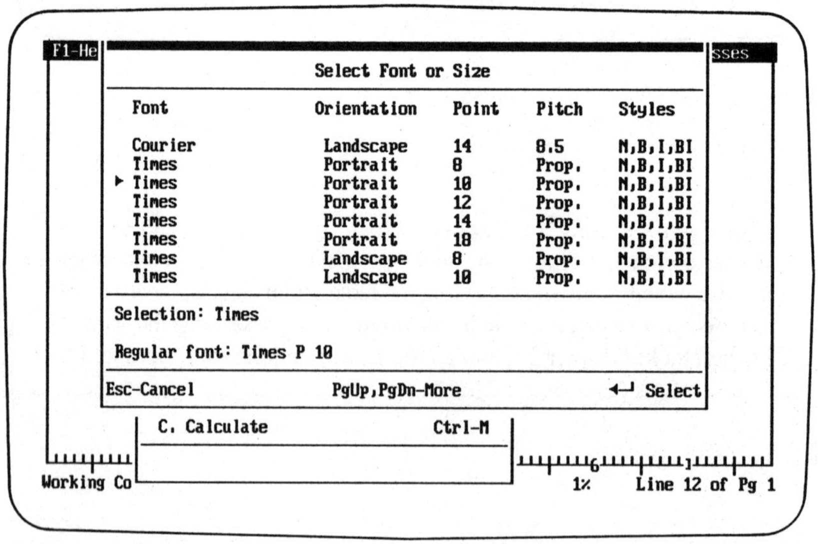

```
 F1-He                                                                sses
                        Select Font or Size

         Font              Orientation   Point   Pitch   Styles

         Courier           Landscape     14      8.5     N,B,I,BI
         Times             Portrait      8       Prop.   N,B,I,BI
       ▸ Times             Portrait      10      Prop.   N,B,I,BI
         Times             Portrait      12      Prop.   N,B,I,BI
         Times             Portrait      14      Prop.   N,B,I,BI
         Times             Portrait      18      Prop.   N,B,I,BI
         Times             Landscape     8       Prop.   N,B,I,BI
         Times             Landscape     10      Prop.   N,B,I,BI

         Selection: Times

         Regular font: Times P 10

         Esc-Cancel            PgUp,PgDn-More           ←┘ Select

               C. Calculate              Ctrl-M

  Working Co                                          1%    Line 12 of Pg 1
```

Fig. 3.10. The Select Font or Size window.

You can change fonts, sizes, or styles only if your printer supports different fonts. Consult your printer manual or Professional Write's *Printer Manual* (enclosed with the software) for more details on the capabilities of your particular printer.

After you select the font and press Enter, you are returned to the working copy. As figure 3.11 shows, even though a larger font size was selected in figure 3.10, the font size shown on-screen does not change. The affected text is shown in a different color on-screen, however, which reminds you that the text will appear as a different font at print time (or in a document preview). Further, you are reminded as to the actual size chosen for the font by the indicator Times P 10 in the file information line at the bottom of the screen.

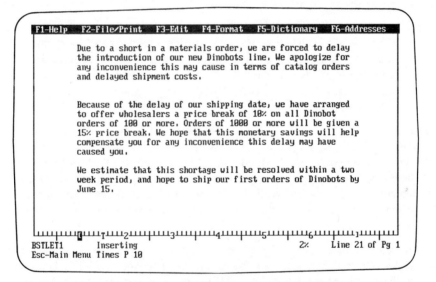

Fig. 3.11. The text does not appear on-screen in a different font.

You also can change fonts from preview mode. Consult Chapter 8 for instructions on using preview.

Deleting Text

Chances are, if you are deleting something, you have already put some effort into it and now you have decided that you don't like what you have done. Perhaps some important information in the document changed, so part of the document needs to be deleted. No matter what your reason for deleting text, you will need to delete items at some time or another.

Professional Write offers the **Delete word** and the **Delete line** options for deleting, as you probably suspect, words and lines. However, Professional Write does not offer an option for deleting entire blocks of text. If you want to delete something larger than a line, you will need to highlight a block and use the **Cut** option to remove the block from the working copy. (Remember, however, that when you cut text from the document, it is placed on the clipboard, overwriting any information that had been stored previously on the clipboard.)

> If you want to delete a section of text from a rectangular block and want to maintain the block's format, use the **Erase** command, available in the Rectangular Block Operations menu.

To delete a word, simply position the cursor anywhere on the word you want to delete, open the Edit menu by pressing F3, and select the **Delete word** option by typing *2* or by pressing ↓ to move the highlight to the option and pressing Enter. Alternatively, you can use the Ctrl-W speed key combination to bypass the menu selections and carry out the command immediately. Be careful with the **Delete word** and **Delete line** options, however. Once the text is gone, it's gone; if you need to get back text you have accidentally deleted, you must retype it.

To delete a line, place the cursor anywhere in the line you want to delete—for this exercise, place the cursor in the second blank line between the first and second paragraphs. Then select **Delete line** from the Edit menu. Figure 3.12 shows the placement of the cursor when **Delete line** is selected. In figure 3.13, the line has been deleted and subsequent lines have been moved up in the document.

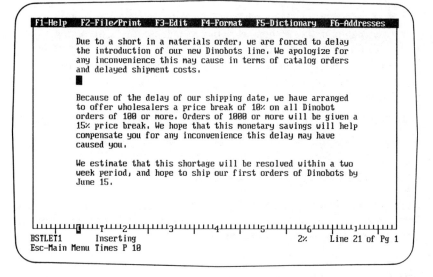

Fig. 3.12. *Deleting a line.*

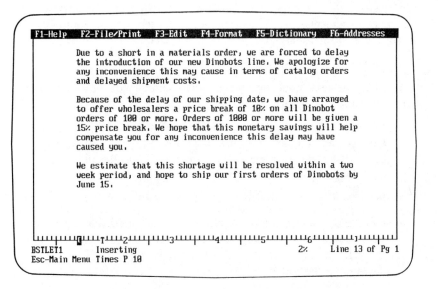

Fig. 3.13. *The document after the line has been deleted.*

If you are unsure about whether you want to delete a section of text, highlight the section as a block and use the **Cut** option to move the block to the clipboard. (Remember, however, that when you place an item on the clipboard, it replaces the item placed there previously.) This way, if you want to recover the text, you can use **Paste** to return the text to the document.

Reformatting Text

Now that you know how to work with the text itself, you need to learn about changing the format of the text. This section shows you how to change the tabs, margins, and indents.

Changing Tabs

Professional Write has one tab set to the indent level you would use if you were beginning a new paragraph. You may find that you need other tabs as you create documents specific to your needs. (A more complete discussion of tabs, indents, and margins is included in Chapter 4.)

To add a tab, follow these steps:

1. Mark the text block that the new tab setting will affect (in this case, mark paragraph 2).

2. When the Text Block Operations menu is displayed, select the **Change tabs** option. (You may also use the speed key combination Ctrl-K, if you prefer.) The cursor moves to the ruler line at the bottom of the screen.

3. Press → to position the cursor on the 2 on the ruler line.

4. Next, add a tab by typing *t* for typewriter tab. (You can also create a decimal tab by typing *d*, or clear an existing tab by pressing the space bar.) Figure 3.14 shows how the ruler line looks after the tab has been added.

5. Press Enter.

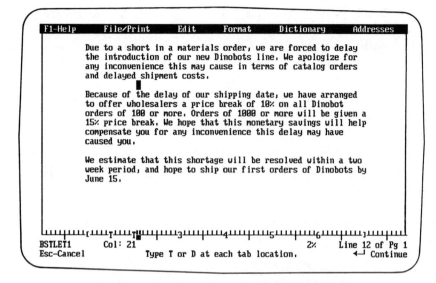

Fig. 3.14. *The ruler line after the tab has been added.*

New tab settings do not affect text you have already typed.

Changing Margins

Occasionally, you will want to vary the margin settings in your document. Maybe you want to include a section of text that is centered within the normal text margin. Or you may want to move the right margin to the center of the page to leave room for a piece of clip art you plan to paste on the document.

To change the margins, follow these steps:

1. Mark the text block that the new margin settings will affect (in this case, mark paragraph 2).

2. When the Text Block Operations menu is displayed, select the **Change right/left margins** option. (You can also use the speed key combination Ctrl-[, if you prefer.) The cursor moves to the ruler line at the bottom of the screen.

3. You can then type margin characters ([for the left margin and] for the right margin) on the ruler line, or you can press F8 to type numeric settings. For this exercise, use → to move the cursor to the 2 and type [; then use → again to move the cursor to the 6 and type] (see fig. 3.15).

4. Press Enter and Professional Write automatically reforms the high-lighted block (see fig. 3.16).

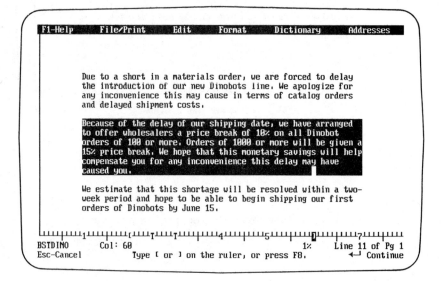

Fig. 3.15. The new margin settings for the block.

Changing Indents

You can also change the indentation of a section of your document. To change the indents, follow these steps:

1. Mark the text block that the new margin settings will affect (in this case, mark paragraph 3).

2. When the Text Block Operations menu is displayed, select the **Change indentation** option. The cursor moves to the ruler line at the bottom of the screen.

3. Position the cursor on the halfway mark between 1 and 2.

4. Press Enter. Professional Write automatically reforms the paragraph.

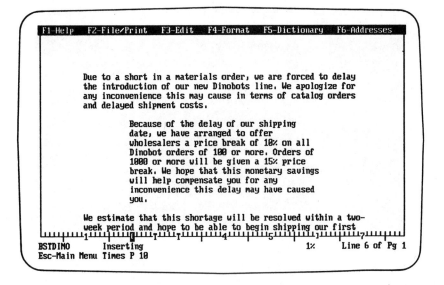

Fig. 3.16. *The reformatted block.*

Previewing the Document

Up to this point, you have worked with text, changed formats, and modified the fonts you use in the document. Most of these changes are shown on-screen, but is what you see *really* what you are going to get when you print the document? Because Professional Write supports the use of different fonts—and not all fonts are the same size and pitch—the program needs to have a way to show you how your document will look when it is printed. In Professional Write, this feature is known as the preview feature.

To preview your document, first open the File/Print menu by pressing F2 and select **Preview working copy**. (You can press the speed key combination, Ctrl-PrtSc, if you prefer.) The document is shown as it will appear on paper. Another menu bar is presented at the top of the screen, showing options you can use to customize the view of your document (see fig. 3.17). When you are ready to return to the working copy, press Esc.

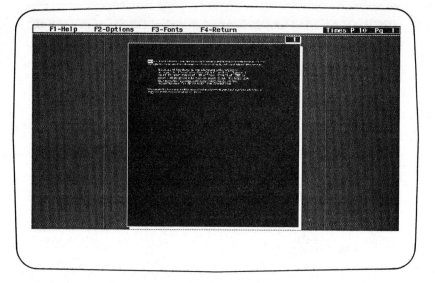

Fig. 3.17. *Previewing the document.*

Saving the Document

Periodically, you must remember to save your document. Even if you are not finished with your work, remember to save the document on a regular basis to protect against power loss or any other calamity that may result in the loss of your data.

To save your document, follow these steps:

1. Open the File/Print menu by pressing F2.

2. Select the **Save working copy** option.

3. Next, enter a file name and a brief description of the file. The description is optional, but can come in handy if you later have trouble remembering the contents of a specific file (see fig. 3.18).

4. Press Enter, and Professional Write saves the file.

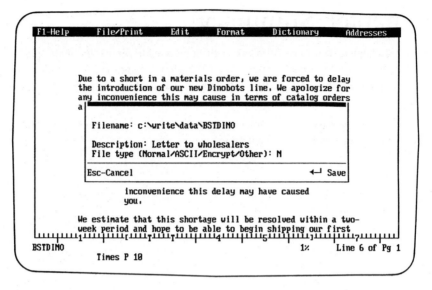

Fig. 3.18. *Naming the document.*

Printing the Document

The final step in this Quick Start involves getting a printed copy of the document you have created. Before you print, make sure that your printer is installed and connected correctly. (If you need to review installation procedures, see Chapter 2, "Getting Started with Professional Write.")

To print the document, follow these steps:

1. Open the File/Print menu by pressing F2.

2. Select the **Print working copy** option. (You can also bypass the menu selections by using the speed key combination Ctrl-O, if you prefer.)

3. When the Print Options window appears, press Enter. (In Chapter 7, "Previewing and Printing Documents," you will learn to work with each of the options on this menu. For now, do not change the default settings.) Professional Write then prints the sample document you have created in this chapter.

Chapter Summary

In this chapter, you have been taken through a whirlwind tour of the basic elements of Professional Write. You have gained hands-on experience by entering and editing text, setting margins and tabs, changing fonts, and previewing and printing the document.

The next chapter begins with more detailed instruction on creating and formatting Professional Write documents.

Part II

▼

Creating Professional Write Documents

Includes

Creating, Formatting, and Saving Documents

Editing Documents

Enhancing Documents

Understanding and Working with Fonts

Previewing and Printing Documents

4

Creating, Formatting, and Saving Documents

In this chapter, you begin the process of creating Professional Write documents. This chapter follows the Houston Rose Advertising Agency, our sample company, through the creation of several different document types.

Before you begin creating documents, it's a good idea to get some picture of where you're headed. Will your documents be used only in the office, or will they be circulated to customers? Do you want the letter to be single- or double-spaced? 12-point or 10-point type?

You can use this checklist to help you determine what type of document you want to create:

❑ Do you want the document to be single- or double-spaced?

❑ Will you be typing or importing the text?

❑ Do you want to use boldface or underlined text to highlight passages in the document?

❑ Will you need to modify the margin settings for some sections?

❑ Will you be saving the document in Professional Write format or in a format supported by other word processors?

Sample Documents

Houston Rose Advertising is a small but creative group of copywriters, artists, and account representatives. This agency produces advertisements for print, video, and audio media. In some cases, Houston Rose needs documents in the form of rough drafts for storyboards; in other cases, a final, professional-looking report is needed to convey an elaborate advertising campaign to a new client.

Figure 4.1 shows a simple memo from one account rep to another. As you can see, no special formats or features have been used; the memo—which took less than 10 minutes to create and print—conveys the necessary information as concisely as possible.

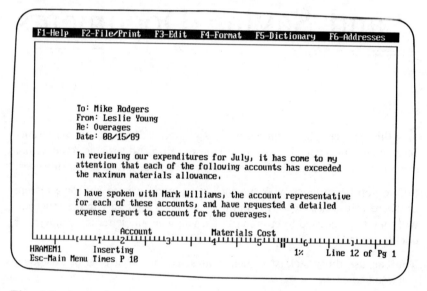

Fig. 4.1. *A sample memo.*

Figure 4.2 shows a more elaborate document that outlines the approach one account representative is proposing to a client. In reality, this document consists of two pages: the first page (unseen here) is a letter conveying the approach suggested by the copywriter; the second page is an outline showing the marketing strategy proposed by Houston Rose.

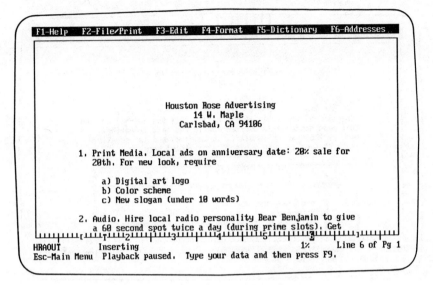

F1-Help   F2-File/Print   F3-Edit   F4-Format   F5-Dictionary   F6-Addresses

```
                       Houston Rose Advertising
                            14 W. Maple
                         Carlsbad, CA 94106

          1. Print Media. Local ads on anniversary date: 20% sale for
             20th. For new look, require

                a) Digital art logo
                b) Color scheme
                c) New slogan (under 10 words)

          2. Audio. Hire local radio personality Bear Benjamin to give
             a 60 second spot twice a day (during prime slots). Get
```

HRAOUT   Inserting   1%   Line 6 of Pg 1
Esc-Main Menu Playback paused. Type your data and then press F9.

Fig. 4.2. *An outline produced with Professional Write.*

Figure 4.3 shows yet another document that makes use of a wide range of Professional Write's capabilities. In this document (a report), the manager of Houston Rose is communicating to stockholders the financial information for the year. To achieve the most professional look possible, the report has headers, footers, and bulleted lists. Graphs have been imported to illustrate complex financial calculations. Most of these "enhancement" features are discussed in Chapter 6.

Opening the Document

The first step in creating a Professional Write document is to start the program. (Refer to "Starting Professional Write" in Chapter 2, if you haven't already done so.)

When the Professional Write Main Menu is displayed on the screen, press Enter to select the **Create/Edit** option.

At the bottom of the screen, you see the words Working Copy. After you name and save the file, the file's name is displayed in this space. For now, you will simply create a memo and assign it a name when you save the file.

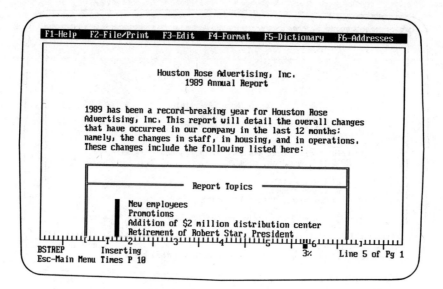

Fig. 4.3. *Creating a more complicated document.*

Reviewing the Create/Edit Screen

The Create/Edit screen is the screen on which you do all of your word processing in Professional Write. This screen has several important elements that you will use throughout your work with Professional Write. Across the top of the screen, you see the menu bar. Below the menu bar is an open area, called the *work area*, in which you create and edit documents. In the upper left section of the work area you can see the cursor, which is a small flashing rectangle that marks the place on the screen where the next character will appear when you begin typing. At the bottom edge of the work area is the ruler. The ruler line resembles an ordinary ruler, except that the symbol [indicates the setting of the left margin,] indicates the right margin, and T shows where the current tab settings are placed.

Under the ruler line is a file information line that displays the name of the file (or Working Copy, if the file is a new file). This line also tells whether insert mode is on or off, what percentage of the file memory allotment has been used, and at what position the cursor is currently placed (Line 1 of Pg 1). If you are using a printer that supports fonts, additional information is displayed, telling you which font is being used, what the orientation of the font is (portrait or landscape), and what point size has been chosen for the text. For more information about these individual elements, see Chapter 1.

Entering Text

Now that you have opened a document, you need to get some text in there. You have two options for entering text into your document: you can type the document in Professional Write, or you can import a file you have created in another word processing program. This section describes both of those procedures.

Typing Text

Typing can be tedious—especially if your job requires you to do it often and in great amounts. Before you begin your labors, review the keys you use to navigate your way around Professional Write's Create/Edit screen (see table 4.1).

You can use the arrow keys even before you have text in the document. Other cursor-movement keys, like Home or End, for example, will not work until you have entered text.

If you make mistakes while you are typing, you can use the Backspace key to "back up" over the text you have typed. This erases the characters so that you can type the words correctly.

To enter text into the document, simply begin typing. The same conventional typewriter rules you may be accustomed to apply to your computer keyboard: Press the Shift key for capitals, the space bar for spaces, and so forth. However, you don't need to enter a carriage return (by pressing Enter) at the end of each line as you would on a typewriter; Professional Write uses a feature called *wordwrap* to determine when the words are getting close to the right margin and acts accordingly so that the text is flowed

Table 4.1
Cursor-Movement Keys

Key	Moves cursor
↑	Up one line
↓	Down one line
→	Right one character
Ctrl-→	Right one word
←	Left one character
Ctrl-←	Left one word
Home	Beginning of current line
Ctrl-Home	Beginning of document
End	End of current line
Ctrl-End	End of document
PgUp	Up one screen
Ctrl-PgUp	To preceding page
PgDn	Down one screen
Ctrl-PgDn	To following page
Tab	To next tab on ruler
Shift-Tab	To previous tab on ruler
Ctrl-J	To another page

automatically to the next line without any intervention from you. Any word that exceeds the right margin is placed on the next line—Professional Write will not hyphenate or break words.

> With Professional Write, you can create macros to help you enter phrases or formats that you use frequently. To find out more about macros, see Chapter 6.

Regular text

As you type the sample paragraph in this section, keep the following typing rules in mind:

❑ Press Enter twice at the end of each paragraph.

❑ Press Tab at the beginning of each paragraph if you want to use paragraph indentations.

❑ Use the Backspace key to erase the most recently typed character(s) if you make a mistake.

❑ If you want to start over, open the File/Print menu by pressing F2 and selecting the **Erase working copy** option.

❑ If you want to enter tabs that will affect the text you type, set the tabs *before* you enter the text. Tabs affect only text that is typed after the tabs are set.

❑ Remember that the way the words are wrapped on-screen may not be the way they will appear as printed. You can use the preview feature to see how Professional Write wraps the text for your particular printer.

Now type the following paragraphs:

In reviewing our expenditures for July, it has come to my attention that each of the following accounts have exceeded the maximum materials allowance.

I have spoken with Mark Williams, the account representative for each of these accounts, and have requested a detailed expense report to account for the overages.

If you pressed Enter twice at the end of both paragraphs, your screen should now look like the one shown in figure 4.4.

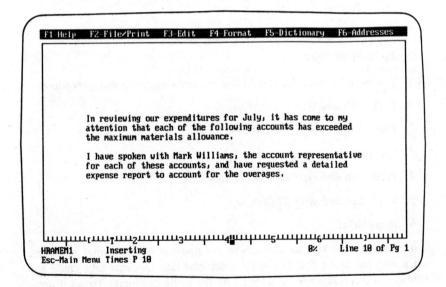

Fig. 4.4. Beginning the sample memo.

Columnar Text

Next, you need to add two columns that list the accounts and the money spent in materials. The only real trick to including columnar material in your reports is to set your tabs first. (Remember, if you set tabs after you enter the text, the text will be unaffected by the tab settings.)

First, set the tabs by following these step:

1. Open the Format menu by pressing F4.

2. Select the **Set tabs** option.

3. When the Set Tabs box is displayed, select **Insert new tabs**.

4. Press → to move the cursor to the T; press the space bar. (This removes the tab preset by Professional Write.)

5. Use → to move the cursor to the 2 and type *t*.

6. Use → to move the cursor to the 4 and type *t*.

7. Press Enter.

Now the tabs are set, and you are ready to enter the headings for the text columns. To do so, follow these steps:

1. Press Tab and type *Account*

2. Press Tab again and type *Materials Cost*

3. Press Enter twice.

Next, you need to enter the text in the columns by using this procedure:

1. Press Tab and type *Shutterbug, Inc.*

2. Press Tab and type *$1,350.57*

3. Press Enter.

4. Press Tab and type *Mongo's Music*

5. Press Tab and type *$1,260.00*

6. Press Enter.

Note: Because the text in the second column involves decimal numbers, you may want to set that tab to be a decimal tab. Decimal tabs cause the numbers in the column to be aligned by the decimal points. To set a decimal tab, simply position the cursor on the ruler line where you want the decimal points to be aligned and type *d*.

You can continue to enter columnar text in this fashion, if you want. Your screen should now look like the one shown in figure 4.5.

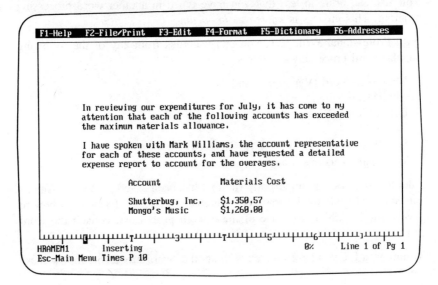

```
 F1-Help   F2-File/Print   F3-Edit   F4-Format   F5-Dictionary   F6-Addresses




         In reviewing our expenditures for July, it has come to my
         attention that each of the following accounts has exceeded
         the maximum materials allowance.

         I have spoken with Mark Williams, the account representative
         for each of these accounts, and have requested a detailed
         expense report to account for the overages.

               Account               Materials Cost

               Shutterbug, Inc.      $1,350.57
               Mongo's Music         $1,260.00

  ⌊⌊⌊⌊⌊⌊ᴵᴵ⌊⌊⌊⌊⌊ᵀ⌊⌊⌊⌊⌊ᴵᴵᴵ⌊3⌊⌊⌊⌊⌊ᴵᵀ⌊⌊⌊⌊⌊ᴵᴵ5⌊⌊⌊⌊⌊ᴵᴵ6⌊⌊⌊⌊⌊ᴵᴵᴵ⌊⌊⌊⌊⌊ᴵᴵᴵ
  HRAMEM1          Inserting                        0%      Line 1 of Pg 1
  Esc-Main Menu Times P 10
```

Fig. 4.5. Entering columnar text.

Remember that if you use columnar text in a document, when you move, copy, cut, and paste the text, you must mark the block by selecting **Mark rectangle** from the Edit menu. By using this option, you preserve the format of the columnar text.

Later in this book, you will learn how to print your Professional Write documents. At this point, however, it is important to introduce a concept that can cause problems when you start to print columnar material.

If you are using a proportional font as the regular font for your document text, your columns may be out of whack when you print the document. Be sure that when you use a proportional font and columnar material, you *do not* select **Font format** on the Print Options menu. (Font format causes Professional Write to "recognize" that you are using a proportional font and reformat the text within the margins you specified. If you have columns of information, Font format will reform the columns.)

Importing Text

You also can bring in text that you have typed in another word processing program. This process is known as *importing*.

With Professional Write 2.1, you can use files from any of the following popular word processing programs:

Microsoft Word (Versions 3 and 4)
MultiMate
OfficeWriter (Version 6)
Wang PC
WordPerfect (Versions 3, 4.1, 4.2, 5.0)
WordStar (Versions 3 and 4)

Additionally, you can import any file that has been saved in ASCII (American Standard Code for Information Interchange) format. To find out how to save a file in ASCII from one of these word processors, consult the word processor's documentation.

To import a file you have created with another word processor, follow these steps:

1. At the Professional Write Main Menu, select the **Create/Edit** option.

2. When the Create/Edit screen is displayed, open the Files/Print menu by pressing F2 and selecting the **Get file** option. (You can bypass the menu selections by pressing Ctrl-G, if you prefer.)

3. When the directory box is displayed, type the path and file name of the file you want to import. (If you are unsure of the file's name, you can press Enter after typing the path and select the file from the list of files displayed.)

4. Press Enter. Professional Write displays a Get File menu, asking you to choose the word processor you used to create the file (see fig. 4.6).

5. Highlight the appropriate program and press Enter. Professional Write displays a message, telling you that the file is being converted (see fig. 4.7).

6. Professional Write displays the file in the working copy.

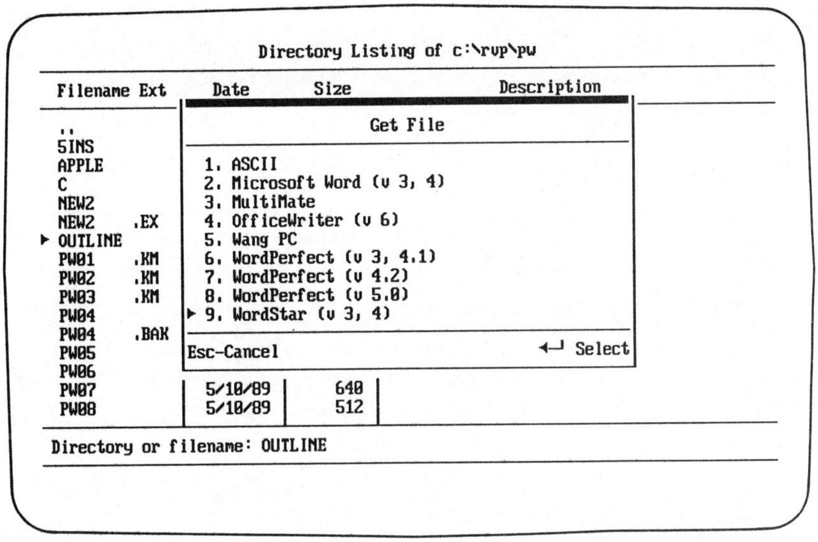

```
                    Directory Listing of c:\rup\pw

 Filename Ext     Date      Size        Description
                        ┌──────────────── Get File ────────────────┐
  ..                    │                                          │
 5INS                   │  1. ASCII                                │
 APPLE                  │  2. Microsoft Word (v 3, 4)              │
 C                      │  3. MultiMate                            │
 NEW2                   │  4. OfficeWriter (v 6)                   │
 NEW2    .EX            │  5. Wang PC                              │
▶ OUTLINE               │  6. WordPerfect (v 3, 4.1)               │
 PW01    .KM            │  7. WordPerfect (v 4.2)                  │
 PW02    .KM            │  8. WordPerfect (v 5.0)                  │
 PW03    .KM            │▶ 9. WordStar (v 3, 4)                    │
 PW04                   │                                          │
 PW04    .BAK           │ Esc-Cancel                   ⏎ Select    │
 PW05                   └──────────────────────────────────────────┘
 PW06
 PW07          5/10/89      640
 PW08          5/10/89      512

 Directory or filename: OUTLINE
```

Fig. 4.6. *Choosing the word processor format from the Get File menu.*

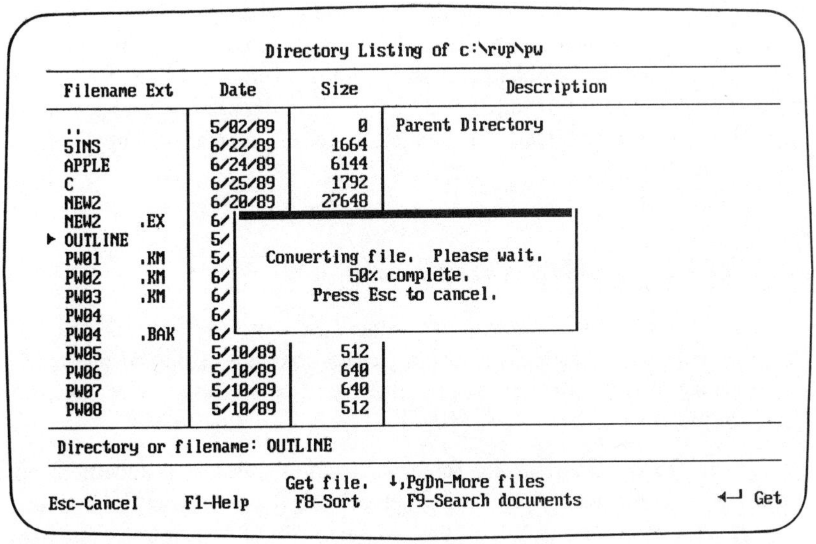

```
                    Directory Listing of c:\rup\pw

 Filename Ext     Date      Size        Description
  ..           5/02/89        0     Parent Directory
 5INS          6/22/89     1664
 APPLE         6/24/89     6144
 C             6/25/89     1792
 NEW2          6/20/89    27648
 NEW2    .EX   6/   ┌──────────────────────────────────┐
▶ OUTLINE      5/   │                                  │
 PW01    .KM   5/   │  Converting file.  Please wait.  │
 PW02    .KM   6/   │         50% complete.            │
 PW03    .KM   6/   │     Press Esc to cancel.         │
 PW04          6/   │                                  │
 PW04    .BAK  6/   └──────────────────────────────────┘
 PW05          5/10/89      512
 PW06          5/10/89      640
 PW07          5/10/89      640
 PW08          5/10/89      512

 Directory or filename: OUTLINE

                       Get file.   ↓,PgDn-More files
 Esc-Cancel   F1-Help   F8-Sort    F9-Search documents      ⏎ Get
```

Fig. 4.7. *Professional Write provides information about the conversion of the file.*

> If you plan to insert a file from another word processor as a *portion* of an existing Professional Write document, first import the file into one Professional Write document, and then insert the new Professional Write document into your existing document. If you try to import the text directly into an existing document by using the **Insert file** option on the Files/Print menu, Professional Write looks for the file in its own format, and if it is not found, imports the file after converting it to ASCII. This can result in a garbled file.

Now that you know how to get text into Professional Write, you need to learn how to work with it. In the next section, you learn to change the format of the text by working with margins, tabs, and indents.

Formatting Text

Depending on the purpose of your document (and on your personal preference), you may have several formatting considerations that you need to address with Professional Write. Perhaps your company always centers the heading in a memo. Maybe your filing system dictates that all account names and numbers must be printed against the right margin in the top corner of the page. Perhaps your editors insist that you double-space all new ad copy so that they can insert massive amounts of red scribbling between each line. In this section, you learn to change the default format of your Professional Write document.

Changing Line Spacing

As you have undoubtedly noticed, the default line spacing for Professional Write documents is single-spaced. That is, the lines are displayed one after another with no blank lines between (unless you press Enter twice, as you do at the end of a paragraph).

You can change the line spacing for a particular section of a document or for the entire document. If you know beforehand that you want to double-space the document, it's probably best to select the **Turn double spacing on/off** option from the Format menu before you type the text. However, it's easy enough to change the line spacing any time you are working with the document.

To change the spacing before you type, open the Format menu by pressing F4 and select the **Turn double spacing on/off** option. (If you prefer, you can press the speed key combination, Ctrl-D.) When the double-space feature is active, the word Double is displayed in the status line at the bottom of the screen.

When you want to turn off the double-space feature and return to single-spaced text, simply select the option again or repeat the speed key combination (Ctrl-D). The Double indicator disappears.

> To double-space a short section of text quickly, you can position the cursor at the beginning of each line and press Ctrl-D.

If you want to double-space a section of text, follow these steps:

1. Highlight the area you want to double-space. (If you need to review highlighting procedures, see Chapter 3.)

2. Select the **Double space** option from the Text Block Operations menu.

The text within the highlighting is then double-spaced (see fig. 4.8).

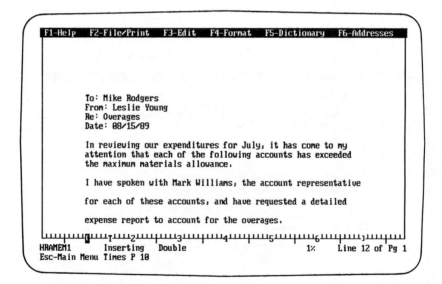

Fig. 4.8. *A portion of the text has been double-spaced.*

Changing Margins

You may want to modify the default settings that Professional Write assigns to your documents. Again, you can make these changes either before you type or after you have already entered text into the document.

Suppose, for example, that you need to move the left margin to leave room for the design printed on the Houston Rose letterhead. To change the left margin before you type, first open the Format menu by pressing F4. Then, select the **Set left/right margin** option. Next, select the **Insert new margins** option from the box that is displayed. A line is displayed at the bottom of the screen, instructing you to position the cursor at the point on the ruler line where you want the left margin to be aligned and type [(see fig. 4.9). If you prefer, you can press F8 to display a window in which you can enter a numeric left margin (see fig. 4.10).

After you either type the indicator or enter the numeric margin setting, press Enter. Professional Write then automatically aligns to that margin any text you type.

You also can set a temporary indent by entering a numeric value after the Indent option in the Print Options menu. (The Print Options menu is discussed fully in Chapter 8.)

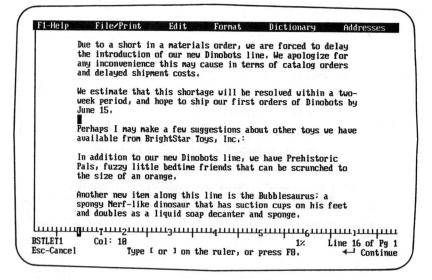

Fig. 4.9. Entering a new left margin.

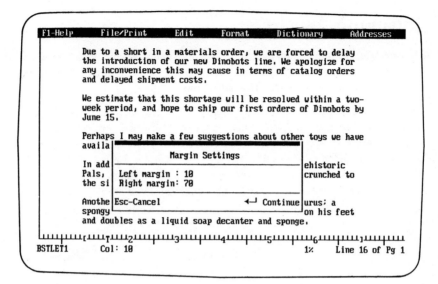

Fig. 4.10. *Setting a numeric left margin.*

You also can change the margin for a selected block of text. To do this, simply highlight the block to be used, press F10, and select **Change tabs** from the Text Block Operations menu (or press Ctrl-K). Then set the tabs in the manner previously described. If you want to clear an existing tab, position the cursor on the tab in the ruler line and press the space bar.

Navigating on the Ruler Line

The ← and → keys are not the only keys available to you as you move the cursor along the ruler line. Use the following keys to help you position the cursor quickly:

This key	Performs this action
Ctrl-→	Moves cursor right in increments of 5
Ctrl-←	Moves cursor left in increments of 5
Home	Moves cursor to the left margin
End	Moves cursor to the right margin

Setting Tabs

Because tabs are a convenience item, not too many people take tabs seriously. They don't affect text already typed. They don't do much except tell the cursor to move five spaces instead of one.

What many people do not know, however, is that with the advent of proportional fonts came uneven spaces. That is, when you use a proportional font, not all letters take up the same amount of space. For example, the capital letter W takes up more room than the letter I. In some fonts—called *monospace fonts*—all letters take up the same amount of room. Consider what happens if you are entering two columns of text and you are using a proportional font. In the first column, you might type the following:

Apples
Bananas
Wilberries

In the second column, you might type

20
30
40

But if you type spaces after each of the fruits so that the second column appears to line up, the second column will be out of alignment when the document is printed because the letters in the words in the first column take up different amounts of space. If you use a tab to set the position of the second column, the numbers in the column will line up.

To make this a little clearer, consider figure 4.11. This screen shows you how the document will look when it is printed (it is displayed in preview mode). In the top part of the page, you see the document as it prints when spaces are inserted between the first column and the second. In the bottom part of the page, a tab was used to align the second column.

To add tabs to your Professional Write document, follow these steps:

1. Position the cursor where you want the tab settings to take effect.

2. Open the Format menu by pressing F4.

3. Select the **Set tabs** option. A window is displayed, asking whether you want to insert new tabs or change existing tabs.

4. Select the **Insert new tabs** option.

5. Use → to move the cursor to the position on the ruler line where you want the tabs to be inserted.

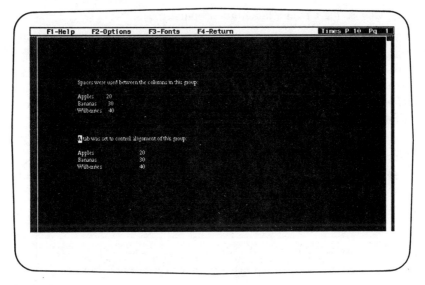

Fig. 4.11. *An example with and without tabs.*

6. Type *t* to set a text tab or *d* to set a decimal tab.

Repeat steps 5 and 6 as necessary to set additional tabs. A tab remains in effect from the point it was inserted to the end of the document, unless you change the settings on the ruler again.

> To remove unwanted tabs, position the cursor on the tab and press the space bar.

Indenting Text

Occasionally, you may want to move the left margin over so that it gives you a temporary indent. You can use this feature, for example, when you are including step-by-step information in a document, or when you want to make a certain passage stand out.

To change the indentation of text, follow these steps:

1. Mark the block to be indented. (Refer to Chapter 3 if you need to review highlighting blocks.) The Text Block Operations menu is displayed.

2. Choose the **Change indentation** option.

3. Use → to move the cursor to the place on the ruler line where you want the indentation to be placed.

4. Press Enter.

Professional Write then automatically indents the section of text that you highlighted (see fig. 4.12).

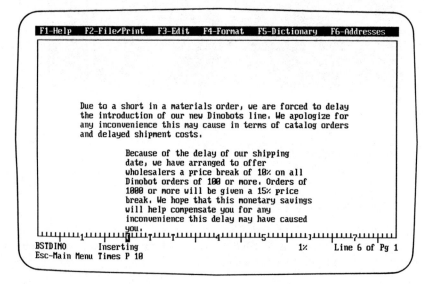

```
 F1-Help   F2-File/Print   F3-Edit   F4-Format   F5-Dictionary   F6-Addresses



        Due to a short in a materials order, we are forced to delay
        the introduction of our new Dinobots line. We apologize for
        any inconvenience this may cause in terms of catalog orders
        and delayed shipment costs.

                Because of the delay of our shipping
                date, we have arranged to offer
                wholesalers a price break of 10% on all
                Dinobot orders of 100 or more. Orders of
                1000 or more will be given a 15% price
                break. We hope that this monetary savings
                will help compensate you for any
                inconvenience this delay may have caused
                you.

 BSTDINO        Inserting                          1%      Line 6 of Pg 1
 Esc-Main Menu Times P 10
```

Fig. 4.12. *The indented text.*

Saving Documents

Saving is a pretty straightforward process. When you save a file, you pre-serve it either on a floppy disk or on the hard disk. Professional Write gives you several options for saving a file. In addition to the "normal" save pro-cedure, you can save the file in several different formats, you can encrypt the file, or you can save a portion of a file as a separate document. This section explains each of those options.

Creating Bulleted Lists and Numbered Steps

If you work in a field that requires the creation of instructional materials or lists of information, you will like Professional Write's automatic hanging indent feature.

A hanging indent causes the number—or bullet—of an item to "hang out." For example, the following line is an example of a hanging indent:

> * *Before starting the program, be sure to place the system disk in drive A.*

The asterisk serves as a bullet, and the text of the second line is aligned with the first line. The asterisk gives the appearance of hanging out in the margin.

Professional Write creates hanging indents automatically when you enter any of the following characters as bullets: +, o, −, or *.

Additionally, when Professional Write recognizes an acceptable enumerator (indicating that an outline follows), the program creates a hanging indent as well. The enumerators recognized by the program are

A.	(A)	a)	a>
1.	1:	1-	1.1.
X.	iii.		

Saving Files . . . Regularly

All save procedures require the use of the Files/Print menu and the **Save working copy** option. The other options that you choose after making these selections vary depending on what you are trying to do.

If you have been working on a document and want to preserve it on disk, follow these steps:

1. Open the Files/Print menu by pressing F2.

2. Select the **Save working copy** option.

3. When the Filename box is displayed, type the name under which you want to save the file and press Tab.

4. After the Description prompt, enter a description of up to 40 characters, and press Tab (see fig. 4.13).

5. After the `File type` prompt, type *n* and press Enter. Professional Write then saves the file.

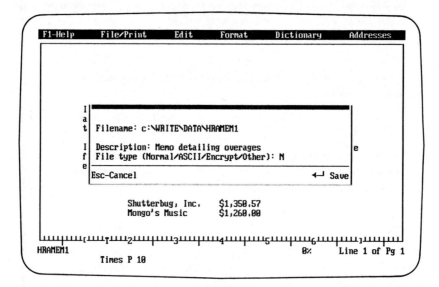

Fig. 4.13. *Entering a file description.*

The procedure for saving files in other formats is identical except for the last step. After the `File type` prompt, type *o* and press Enter. Professional Write warns you that some word processing programs require that you end the file name in an extension recognized by those programs. When you press Enter, Professional Write displays a list of file formats you can use to save the file (see fig. 4.14). Select one of the formats by highlighting it and pressing Enter. Professional Write then saves the file.

When you encrypt a file, you save it in a coded format that allows only authorized persons to have access. To encrypt a file, type *e* after the `File type` prompt and press Enter. Professional Write then prompts you for the password that will be required before the file can be opened (see fig. 4.15). Be sure to enter a password that you can remember easily—forgetting your password could mean that you have no way to access what may be an important file.

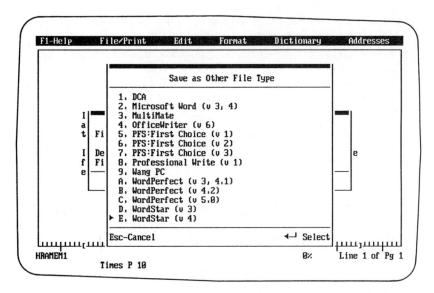

Fig. 4.14. *Formats available for saving the file.*

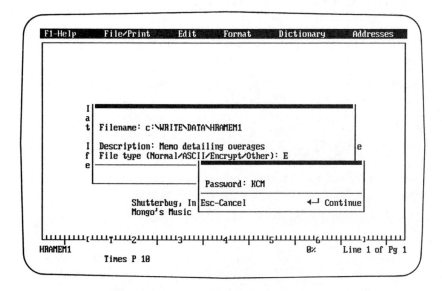

Fig. 4.15. *Entering a password for an encrypted file.*

The last option for the File type prompt is saving the file as an ASCII file. ASCII is a universal code that can be read and written by most software programs. Suppose, for example, that you need to save text that will be used in a format not supported by Professional Write. If you save the file in ASCII format, you should be able to import the file into the other program. Most programs can import data saved in ASCII format. To save the file in ASCII format, type *a* after the File type prompt. Remember, however, that any headers and footers, page numbers, or font styles will be lost with the conversion.

Chapter 4 Quick Start: Creating the Document

This Quick Start section offers some quick step-by-step instructions that help you review the procedures covered in this chapter.

Opening the Document

The first step in creating a Professional Write document is to start the program. (Refer to ''Starting Professional Write'' in Chapter 2, if you haven't already done so.)

When the Professional Write Main Menu is displayed on the screen, press Enter to select the **Create/Edit** option.

Importing Text

To import a file you have created with another word processor, follow these steps:

1. At the Professional Write Main Menu, select the **Create/Edit** option.

2. When the Create/Edit screen is displayed, open the Files/Print menu by pressing F2 and select the **Get file** option. (You can bypass the menu selections by pressing Ctrl-G, if you prefer.)

3. When the directory box is displayed, type the path and file name of the file you want to import. (If you are unsure of the file's name, you can press Enter after typing the path and select the file from the list of files displayed.)

4. Press Enter. Professional Write then displays a Get File menu, asking you to choose the word processor you used to create the file.

5. Highlight the appropriate program and press Enter. Professional Write then displays a message, telling you that the file is being converted.

6. Professional Write then displays the file in the working copy.

Double-Spacing Text

If you want to double-space a section of text, follow these steps:

1. Highlight the area you want to double-space. (If you need to review highlighting procedures, see Chapter 3.)

2. Select the **Double space** option from the Text Block Operations menu.

Changing Margins

To set new margins for the document, follow these steps:

1. Open the Format menu by pressing F4.

2. Select the **Set left/right margin** option.

3. Next, select the **Insert new margins** option from the box that is displayed.

4. A line is displayed at the bottom of the screen, instructing you to position the cursor at the point on the ruler line where you want the left margin to be aligned and to type [. If you prefer, you can press F8 to display a window that enables you to enter a numeric left margin.

5. After you either type the indicator or enter the numeric margin setting, press Enter. Professional Write then automatically aligns to that margin any text you type.

Adding Tabs

To add tabs to your Professional Write document, follow these steps:

1. Position the cursor where you want the tab settings to take effect.

2. Open the Format menu by pressing F4.

3. Select the **Set tabs** option. A window is displayed, asking whether you want to insert new tabs or change existing tabs.

4. Select the **Insert new tabs** option.

5. Use → to move the cursor to the position on the ruler line where you want the tabs to be inserted.

6. Type *t* to set a text tab or *d* to set a decimal tab.

Changing Indentation

To change the indentation of text, follow these steps:

1. Mark the block to be indented. (Refer to Chapter 3 if you need to review highlighting blocks.) The Text Block Operations menu is displayed.

2. Choose the **Change indentation** option.

3. Use → to move the cursor to the place on the ruler line where you want the indentation to be placed.

4. Press Enter. Professional Write then automatically indents the section of text that you highlighted.

Saving the Document

If you have been working on a document and want to preserve it on disk, follow these steps:

1. Open the Files/Print menu by pressing F2.

2. Select the **Save working copy** option.

3. When the Filename box is displayed, type the name under which you want to save the file and press Tab.

4. After the Description prompt, enter a description of up to 40 characters, and press Tab.

5. After the `File type` prompt, type *n* and press Enter. Professional
   Write then saves the file.

Chapter Summary

In this chapter, you learned the basics of creating, formatting, and saving
files. From an elementary discussion of typing and cursor-movement keys,
you progressed to controlling margins, tabs, and indents; producing bulleted
lists and numbered steps; and saving Professional Write documents in a
variety of formats. In the next chapter, you learn to edit the document you
created and work with text and rectangular blocks.

5

Editing Documents

Most editing operations involve more than simple character-swapping and spell checking. Often, good editing requires flopping paragraphs around, and cutting, moving, and copying blocks of text.

So far in this book, you have learned about the various capabilities of Professional Write, tried your hand at a series of Quick Start exercises (Chapter 3), and entered a document of your own. In this chapter, you learn to work with the program's block editing features. In addition to the many examples in this chapter, at the end of the chapter you will find a Quick Start that takes you through all the editing procedures discussed. Before you get started with the steps involved in working with block editing, however, a few basic definitions are in order.

Working with Text Blocks

This section introduces you to working with text blocks and highlights important options that you will use as you work with regular text blocks and with rectangular text blocks.

Regular Blocks

What is a *regular* block of text? As you may have already seen, Professional Write offers you the option of making a distinction between a simple

Editing Q&A

If you are new to Professional Write or to computers in general, you may have a few questions about the whys and hows of block editing.

What is block editing? Block editing is simply that; editing procedures performed on blocks of text. In Professional Write, before you can copy, move, cut, paste, or change the format of text, you must highlight the section that will be affected by the operation. The section that you highlight is referred to as a *block*.

When can you edit a document? You can modify at any time any document you create with Professional Write. If you prefer to type the document and then save it, you can return later to edit your work.

Do you have to highlight a block before you can edit? Not in all cases. You can use the Backspace key and the insert and replace cursor modes to type over or remove any errors in the document. For major operations like deleting, copying, moving, or reformatting sections of text, however, you must first highlight the area as a text block.

What if you aren't happy with the editing changes you have made? As you may know, when you open a file (if it has been saved previously), Professional Write loads a *copy* of the file that is stored on disk. This copy is called the *Working Copy*. The changes that you make while you work on the file are not written out to the file on disk until you save the document; therefore, if you decide that you don't like the editing changes you have made, you can select **Erase working copy** from the Files/Print menu, and no changes will be made to the file on disk.

block of text and a *rectangular* block. Most paragraphs look rectangular in shape, however, so the rationale for using one type over the other may not be obvious at first.

A regular text block is a section of text that you highlight and work with as needed. This block, like the document, can be reformed, edited, and moved about as necessary. Each line ends with a *soft carriage return*, meaning that if you delete a few words in the middle of the block, the paragraph will reflow the text automatically to fill in the gaps. After the text reflows, the placement of the words and possibly the format of the block may be different.

A *rectangular block*, on the other hand, preserves the format of the block. Suppose, for example, that you have written a memo that includes two columns: one column lists the names of accounts, and the other column stores numeric values. You want to move the columnar material to a different place in the memo, but if you mark the text as a regular text block, Professional Write reflows the text and the program's wordwrap feature will destroy the format. To preserve the format and keep the columns in place, you mark this area as a rectangular block.

For many operations, unless you need to preserve the format of the block, you will want to use a regular text block. To highlight the block as a regular text block, choose the **Mark text** option from the Files/Print menu. After you choose this option, highlight the block, and press F10; the Text Block Operations menu is displayed automatically (see fig. 5.1). The options on this menu are available for regular text blocks. Table 5.1 highlights the options available on this menu. (The absence of a speed key combination indicates that no speed key is available for that option.)

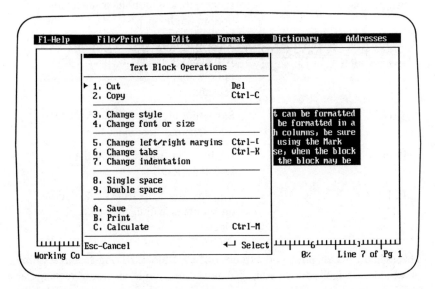

Fig. 5.1. *The Text Block Operations menu.*

▼
Table 5.1
Options on the Text Block Operations Menu

Option	Speed Key	Description
Cut	Del	Moves selected block to clipboard
Copy	Ctrl-C	Makes a copy of selected block and places copy on clipboard
Change style		Enables you to change the font style of the selected block
Change font or size		Enables you to change the font or font size of the selected block
Change left/ right margins	Ctrl-[	Enables you to change the right and left margins of the selected block
Change tabs	Ctrl-K	Enables you to change the tab settings for the block
Change indentation		Enables you to change the indentation for that block
Single space		If the block is double-spaced, this option single-spaces the text in the highlighted area
Double space		If the block is single-spaced, this option double-spaces the text in the selected area
Save		Saves the highlighted block of text as a separate document file
Print		Enables you to print only the selected block
Calculate	Ctrl-M	Enables you to perform calculations on numbers within the selected block

Throughout this chapter, you explore different block editing features, some of which are regular block editing features and some which are rectangular block editing features. Instruction is provided so that you know which type of block to use for which feature.

Rectangular Blocks

As mentioned, you use rectangular blocks when you want to keep the format of a particular area of text. To better illustrate this concept, consider figure 5.2. This figure shows a preview screen of the way this document will look in print.

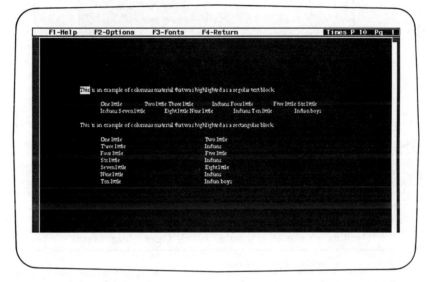

Fig. 5.2. *A block copied as a regular text block and as a rectangular text block.*

As you can see, the block on the top was marked as a regular text block before it was copied. The block on the bottom was marked as a rectangular block, and the format was preserved.

To mark a block as a rectangular block, you select the **Mark rectangle** from the Files/Print menu. Then, following the instructions that appear on the bottom of the screen, mark the block and press F10. The Rectangular Block Operations menu then appears (see fig. 5.3). Table 5.2 highlights the options available on this menu. (The absence of speed key combinations indicates that no speed key is available for that option.)

What Is the Clipboard?

Both tables 5.1 and 5.2 mention the use of the clipboard. The Professional Write clipboard is an unseen area of memory—not unlike a real clipboard—

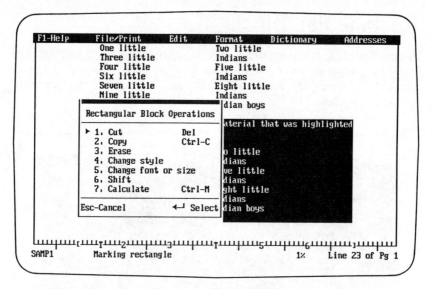

Fig. 5.3. *The Rectangular Block Operations menu.*

Table 5.2
Options on the Rectangular Block Operations Menu

Option	Speed Key	Description
Cut	Del	Cuts selected block to clipboard
Copy	Ctrl-C	Copies selected block to clipboard
Erase		Erases selected block and inserts spaces in place of erased text to preserve format
Change style		Enables you to change the style of the text in the block
Change font or size		Enables you to change the text font and size in the selected block
Shift		Enables you to move a block without disrupting the format
Calculate	Ctrl-M	Enables you to perform calculations on numeric values in the selected block

on which you temporarily place text items that you are moving, copying, or deleting. Following are some clipboard rules:

❑ The clipboard stores only one text item at a time.

❑ The text item remains on the clipboard until another text item is placed on the clipboard; then the second item overwrites the first. The item remains on the clipboard even when the file is saved and Professional Write is exited.

❑ You use the **Paste** command available from the Edit menu to place items from the clipboard into the document. A copy of the item placed on the clipboard remains there until another block of text overwrites it.

Cutting Text

Whether you are using a regular or rectangular text block, you use the **Cut** option when you want to move or delete text. When you use this option to move a block of text, you are actually performing a cut-and-paste operation, which, as you might imagine, also involves the use of the **Paste** option (available on the Edit menu).

Figure 5.4 shows a letter that an account representative with the Houston Rose Advertising Agency has written to a new client. After careful consideration, the employee decides to remove the second paragraph. Because there are no special formats to consider, this block can be marked as a regular text block.

To cut the paragraph from the document, follow these steps:

1. Begin highlighting the block by positioning the cursor at the beginning of the block and pressing Ctrl-T. (You also could select **Mark text** from the Edit menu.)

2. Use the arrow keys to move to the end of the paragraph and press F10. The Text Block Operations menu is displayed automatically.

3. Press Enter to select the **Cut** option, which is already highlighted (see fig. 5.5). You also can press the speed key, Del. Professional Write cuts the text from the document and places it on the clipboard. The text that follows the removed information moves up to fill its place.

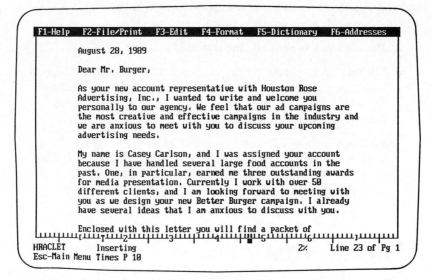

Fig. 5.4. *The letter before changes are made.*

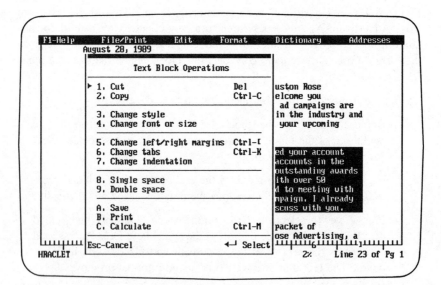

Fig. 5.5. *Cutting the text from the document.*

When you cut a block of text from a document, you are deleting the information that was in that place. For that reason, if you use **Cut** to remove items in a column of information, any columns to the right of the cut information will move to the left to fill the void left by the deletion. If you need to remove information from a column that will affect the format of other columns, mark the block as a rectangular block and select the **Erase** option from the Rectangular Block Operations menu. This option replaces the text you are erasing with spaces so that the format of the block does not change.

Pasting Text

The account representative looks at the document and cringes. No, he really needs that paragraph in the document somewhere; otherwise, how will the client know about his area of expertise? Perhaps it will fit better in another place.

To paste the text block back into the document, follow these steps:

1. Position the cursor where you want the text inserted.

2. Open the Edit menu by pressing F2 and select the **Paste** option. (You can bypass the menu selections and press the speed key combination, Ctrl-P, if you prefer.) Professional Write then places the text block back in the document at the cursor position.

If you want to move a block of text from one place to another, highlight the block, choose the **Cut** option, move the cursor to the point in the document you want the block to appear, and select **Paste** (from the Edit menu).

Copying Text

Suppose that our account representative is creating a series of letters, all in the same file. For example, he addresses client 1 on page 1, client 2 on page 2, and so on. Rather than create the same letter time and time again, he opts to copy pertinent sections from one page to the next.

To copy text, follow these steps:

1. Highlight the section to be copied. (If the block includes formats that you want to preserve, mark the block as a rectangular block.)

2. Select the **Copy** option (or press Ctrl-C). Professional Write places a copy of the text on the clipboard.

3. Move the cursor to the position where you want the text to be placed, and press Ctrl-P (or select **Paste** from the Edit menu). The text is copied to the desired location.

It doesn't matter whether you currently are using the replace or insert cursor when you paste text; Professional Write moves any text that follows the inserted text.

Working with Address Books

There is another solution to the problem just discussed. Instead of copying repeated information from one page to another, as the account representative did in the last example, you can create a form letter and merge information from an address book to fill in the names and addresses for you.

For example, without the address book feature, the account representative must mark the block of text he wants to copy and place that section on each letter he wants to create. Then he goes back and types in the addresses. This process takes up a significant amount of time and memory.

With Professional Write's address book feature, you can create a form letter—once—and have the program plug in names and addresses you have previously stored in an address book. This saves you quite a bit of typing time and preserves more room in your computer's memory. For more information about creating and working with address books and printing form letters, see Chapter 10.

Shifting Text

When you are working with a rectangular block of text, you have an option available to you that is not available when you are working with regular text block: **Shift**. The **Shift** option enables you to highlight and move left, right, up, or down a section of text for which you want to retain the format.

For example, the columns in the Houston Rose memo shown in figure 5.6 are a little off-center, and the writer wants to move the columns to the right.

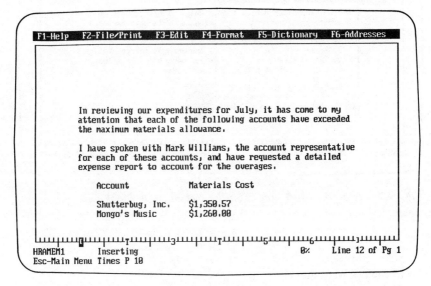

Fig. 5.6. *The memo before the columns are shifted.*

Follow these steps to shift a rectangular block of text:

1. Highlight as a rectangular block the text to be shifted. (Use **Mark rectangle** from the Edit menu or press Ctrl-R.)

2. When the Rectangular Block Operations menu is displayed, select the **Shift** option (see fig. 5.7).

3. Use the → key to move the block to the right. (You can use any of the arrow keys in a shift operation.)

Working with Fonts

It doesn't seem too long ago that, for the most part, you had no choice about the type of font you used in a document. If you were typing a letter

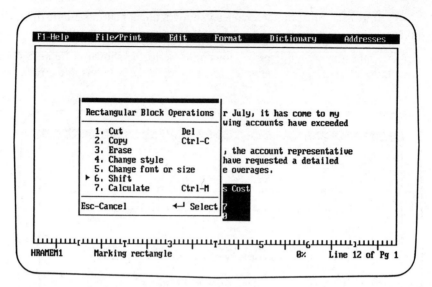

Fig. 5.7. *Using the **Shift** option on the Rectangular Block Operations menu.*

on your IBM Selectric, you perhaps had a choice of typeballs, but at best those choices were limited.

Thanks to the evolution of the printer, many users now have the choice of a variety of fonts, styles, and sizes. Table 5.3 lists the dot-matrix and laser printers for which Professional Write supports fonts. Not all printers support the same fonts: check your printer manual to find out more about your particular printer.

Table 5.3
Font Printers Supported by Professional Write

Type of Printer	Manufacturer	Model
Dot matrix	EPSON	LQ-800/1000
		LQ-500
		LQ-850/1050
		LQ-950
		FX-850/1054
		LQ-2500
		LQ-2550
	IBM	ProPrinter X24/XL24
		ProPrinter X24E/XL24E

Type of Printer	Manufacturer	Model
	IBM	QuickWriter
	Kyocera	
	OKIDATA	390 393 393C
	Panasonic	KX-P4450
	Texas Instruments	875/877
Laser	Apple	LaserWriters
	AST	TurboLaser /PS
	Hewlett-Packard	DeskJet
	Hewlett-Packard	LaserJet family
	NEC	Family of laser printers
	QMS	PS 800 +

Introduction to Fonts

What are fonts? A font is one set of characters (A through Z and all numeric and punctuation symbols) in a specific typeface, size, and style. For example, Helvetica 14-point bold is one font, and Avant Garde 8-point is another.

Who can use fonts? Users who have PostScript printers have the widest selection of fonts from which they can choose. However, the Hewlett-Packard LaserJet family of printers supports soft fonts and font cartridges, making quite a variety of fonts available. Additionally, some dot-matrix printers are able to print various fonts, but these generally have a poorer printer resolution than laser-printed fonts.

How does Professional Write know my printer supports fonts? When you use the Setup Menu to tell Professional Write which type of printer you have, the program loads the information about which fonts are supported. Always set up your font printer as Printer 1, however; Printer 2 does not provide font capability.

What are soft fonts? Soft fonts are fonts that are stored on disk. Not all laser printers support soft fonts, so check your printer's manual before you purchase any soft fonts. You specify where Professional Write can find the soft fonts, and the fonts are automatically downloaded at print time.

What's the difference between portrait and landscape orientation? Some fonts have a portrait orientation and some fonts have a landscape orientation. The only difference between these orientations is the way the text is printed on the page. Portrait prints the page in the normal 8 1/2-by-11-inch mode; landscape prints the page in a horizontal 11-by-8-1/2-inch mode.

How do I choose the font for the document? You specify the font you want to use when you first install your printer with the Setup Menu. However, you can change the font by using **Change font or size** from either the Text Block Operations menu or the Rectangular Block Operations menu.

For more information about installing and using fonts for your particular printer, see Chapter 7.

Changing Font and Font Size

Even though you tell Professional Write which font to use when you install your printer, you can change the font for a selected block of text or for the whole document, if you choose. Suppose, for example, that you are preparing a document for a client that, in addition to other information, shows a sample of ad copy. You can set off this ad copy by putting it in a different font.

To change the font and font size for a block of text, follow these steps:

1. Highlight the block of text for which you want to change the font or size.

2. On the Text Block Operations menu (or the Rectangular Block Operations menu, if you chose the **Mark rectangle** option), select **Change font or size**.

3. When the Select Font or Size menu is displayed, use the arrow keys to move the highlight to the font and size you want (see fig. 5.8).

4. Press Enter to select the font.

```
F1-He                                                                    sses
           ┌─────────────────────────────────────────────────────┐
           │                    Select Font or Size                │
           │                                                       │
           │   Font             Orientation   Point   Pitch   Styles│
           │                                                       │
           │   Courier          Landscape     14      8.5     N,B,I,BI│
           │   Times            Portrait      8       Prop.   N,B,I,BI│
           │   Times            Portrait      10      Prop.   N,B,I,BI│
           │ ► Times            Portrait      12      Prop.   N,B,I,BI│
           │   Times            Portrait      14      Prop.   N,B,I,BI│
           │   Times            Portrait      18      Prop.   N,B,I,BI│
           │   Times            Landscape     8       Prop.   N,B,I,BI│
           │   Times            Landscape     10      Prop.   N,B,I,BI│
           │                                                       │
           │   Selection: Times                                    │
           │                                                       │
           │   Regular font: Times P 10                            │
           │                                                       │
           │  Esc-Cancel            PgUp,PgDn-More        ↵ Select  │
           └──────┬──────────────────────────────┬─────────────────┘
                  │  C. Calculate      Ctrl-M     │ose Advertising, a
                  │                               │, and a standard
         ┗┻┻┻┻┻┛  │                               │┗┻┻┻┻┻┻┻6┻┻┻┻┻┻┻┻┻┻┻┛
         HRACLET  │                               │    2%     Line 30 of Pg 1
```

Fig. 5.8. *Selecting the font and size.*

When the document is displayed, the actual font and font size chosen are not displayed on-screen. If you want to get an idea of how the document will look when it is printed, you can use the **Preview working copy** option from the Files/Print menu.

Figure 5.9 shows how the document looks on-screen after the font is changed for the selected text block. In preview mode, you can see how the changed font will look on the printed page (see fig. 5.10).

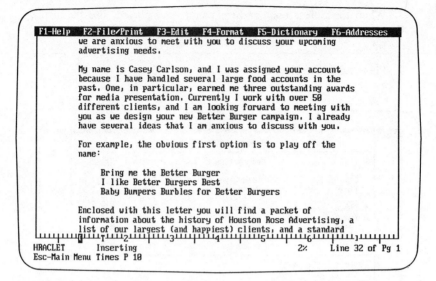

Fig. 5.9. *The document's appearance on-screen after the font is changed for the selected text block.*

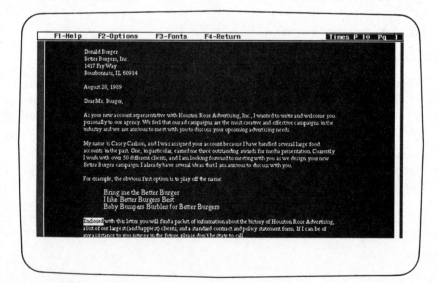

Fig. 5.10. *The document in preview mode.*

Tips for Working with Fonts

If your printer supports fonts, there are a few rules you should remember for creating effective documents:

Use size changes carefully. Don't overdo font size changes in your document. Usually, understated is better than over-stated, so don't use an 18-point font when a 14-point will do the job as well. It will give your document a cleaner look.

Don't mix more than two typefaces in one document. Resist the temptation to use too many different typefaces in one document. Usually, one or two typefaces is enough. For example, you could use Times for the body text of your document and Helvetica for the headings; but adding too many typefaces would make your document look more like graffiti than text. (Note the distinction between *typeface* and *font*: a *typeface* is a family of type, like Times, Helvetica, and New Century Schoolbook; a *font* is one specific typeface set that includes size and style, such as Times 12-point bold.

Remember that white space is important as a design element. When you consider the way your document looks, don't look at only the words. White space, and the way you use it, is as important as any sentence or heading on the page. Use the way the text is arranged to lead the reader's eye through the document; don't try to cram too much information into too little space.

Changing Text Style

Rather than changing the font of a particular passage of text, you may want to change the text style. Professional Write offers the following styles (in addition to normal style) for your text:

Boldface
Underline
Italic
Superscript
Subscript

You can select these styles by marking the section of text you want to change and changing the whole section, or by positioning the cursor on the word you want to change and pressing Ctrl-B (for boldface) or Ctrl-U (for underline). No other styles can be set by using speed key combinations.

To change the style of a block of text, follow these steps:

1. Highlight the block you want to change. (This can be either a regular text block or a rectangular text block.)

2. From the Text Block Operations menu (or the Rectangular Block Operations menu, if you chose **Mark rectangle** from the Edit menu), choose the **Change style** menu. The Style menu is displayed (see fig. 5.11).

3. Type the number of the style you want (you *cannot* select these options by using the arrow keys to move the highlight and pressing Enter) and press Enter.

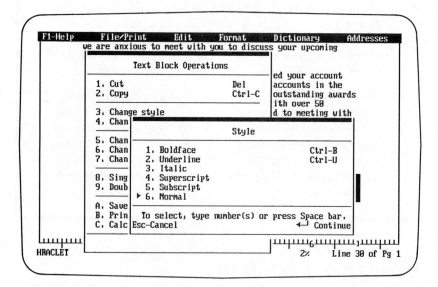

Fig. 5.11. *The Style menu.*

When the document is displayed, the block appears in a bolder type, but the actual style is not reflected. If you want to see how italic will look, for example, use the preview feature (available from the **Preview working copy** option in the Files/Print menu).

Using Boldface

You also have the option of changing the style from the Edit menu. If you want to highlight a word by making it boldface, you simply position the cursor on the word and press Ctrl-B (or you can open the Edit menu and select the **Boldface word** option, if you prefer).

The only problem with the boldface and underline features is that they are like in-laws; easy to get and hard to get rid of. Once you make a word bold, the only way to remove the boldface is to delete the word and then retype it. If you use the **Change style** options from one of the block operations menus, however, you can select the word (even a word can be a text block) and select **Normal** from the Style menu. This returns the style to the normal font without any deleting or retyping necessary.

Using Underline

The **Underline word** option is also available on the Edit menu. This option underlines the word at the cursor position. Instead of the word appearing as underlined on-screen, however, the word is shown as highlighted.

If you want to underline or boldface a series of words, you can press Ctrl-B (for boldface) or Ctrl-U (for underline) repeatedly. Each time you press one of the speed key combinations, Professional Write automatically performs the operation and moves the cursor to the next word so that you can repeat the keystroke, if you choose.

> If you want to underline the space between words, enter a *hard space* in place of a regular space by pressing Ctrl-space bar instead of just the space bar.

Using the Find-and-Replace Feature

Suppose that, as you are preparing a document about the founder of the Houston Rose Advertising Agency, you discover that you have made a horrible mistake: You have spelled the owner's name wrong. You have 10 minutes before the report is due. How can you go through all your files and change the name?

Professional Write offers a find-and-replace feature that will help you locate the error and fix it automatically. You can search for upper- or lowercase letters (or both), and you can include wild cards in your search.

A *wild card* is a character—or in this case, two periods—that tell Professional Write to find text with "any characters" in place of the periods. For example, consider the following items:

If you enter this	Professional Write finds
..ld	bold, old, fold, gold, and so forth
tr..	tree, tray, tribulation, trinket
..ea..	peach, tear, please, reasonable
..ment	parchment, torment, ferment

When you select the **Find & Replace** option from the Edit menu, the Find and Replace window is displayed. After the **Find:** option, enter the text (or a portion of the text and wild cards). Then press Tab to get to the **Ignore case (Y/N):** option and press Y if you want Professional Write to ignore the case of the characters. After the **Replace with:** prompt, enter the text you want Professional Write to insert in place of the found text. The **Manual or automatic (M/A):** option enables you to specify whether you want Professional Write to replace all occurrences of the text (automatic) or allow you to decide on a case by case basis which text strings you want to change.

Here's an example to make this concept a little clearer. Suppose that instead of including the name Walter Higgenmeyer in your documents about the history of Houston Rose, you accidentally used the name William Higgenmyer. The old guy's not a bad sport, but seeing his name published incorrectly 20 times in a historical document probably will not make his day.

To have Professional Write search for the phrase *William Higgenmyer* and replace it with *Walter Higgenmeyer*, follow these steps:

1. Position the cursor at the point from which you want to begin the search.

2. Open the Edit menu and select the **Find & Replace** option or press Ctrl-F. The Find and Replace box is then displayed (see fig. 5.12).

3. At the **Find:** prompt, type *William Higgenmyer* and press Tab.

4. After the **Ignore case (Y/N):** prompt, type *n* and press Tab.

5. After the **Replace with:** prompt, type *Walter Higgenmeyer* and press Tab.

Ignoring Case

As you know, you have the choice of telling Professional Write to search either by finding the text exactly as you enter it after the **Find:** prompt or by telling the program to ignore the case of the text. For example, this means that if you enter the word *Community* and answer N to **Ignore case**, Professional Write will find only the word **Community** with the first letter capitalized. Consider the following examples:

If you want to find	Ignore case	Finds
Macmillan	Y	macmillan
		MacMillan
		Macmillan
		MACMILLAN
		MaCmIlLaN, and
		so on
	N	Macmillan
random	Y	RANDOM
		Random
		random
		RaNdOm
		and so on
	N	random

To sum up, if you choose to ignore the case in a search procedure, Professional Write looks for the spelling only—not the capitalization of the word. You may get all kinds of results. If you need to find only a particular capitalization of a word (for example, *Community* when it is part of the phrase *Carmel Community Pool*, but not as the generic *community pool*), answer N to the **Ignore case** option.

6. After the **Manual or automatic (M/A):** prompt, type *a* to indicate that you want Professional Write to go through and change every occurrence of William Higgenmyer. (If you type *m* in response to this prompt, Professional Write stops at each occurrence and asks whether you want to go through with the replacement, as shown in figure 5.13).

7. Press Enter to begin the search. Professional Write makes the change as specified and tells you how many occurrences of the name were replaced (see fig. 5.14).

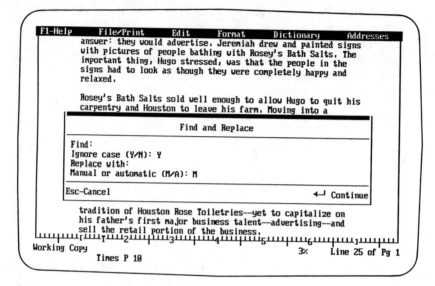

Fig. 5.12. *The Find and Replace box.*

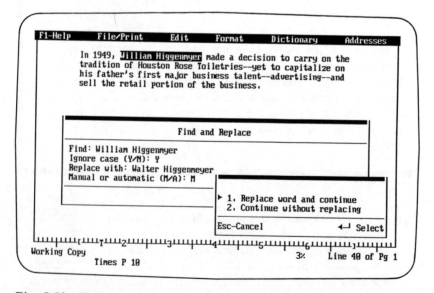

Fig. 5.13. *The program prompts you to choose whether you want to replace the text.*

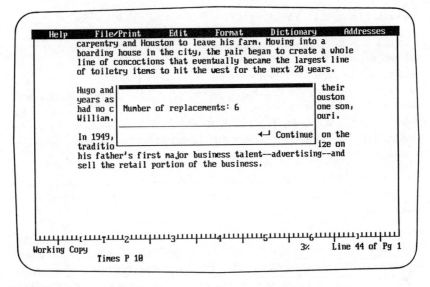

| Help | File/Print | Edit | Format | Dictionary | Addresses |

carpentry and Houston to leave his farm. Moving into a
boarding house in the city, the pair began to create a whole
line of concoctions that eventually became the largest line
of toiletry items to hit the west for the next 20 years.

Hugo and | | their
years as | | ouston
had no c | Number of replacements: 6 | one son,
William. | | ouri.

In 1949, | ↵ Continue | on the
traditio | | ize on
his father's first major business talent--advertising--and
sell the retail portion of the business.

Working Copy   3%   Line 44 of Pg 1
            Times P 10

*Fig. 5.14. Professional Write tells you how many times the text was
replaced.*

If you enter a word or phrase after the **Find:** prompt and Professional Write
cannot locate the word or phrase in the document, the program displays a
message telling you that no occurrences were found. You can then press
Enter to get back to the working copy.

> After you have stopped a search, you can have Professional Write
> continue the search (or search for the same text in another file) by
> pressing Ctrl-F. This automatically continues the search, without
> you specifying the options in the Find and Replace box.

Erasing Text

Inevitably, you will want to erase text. Whether you are doing away with a
word, line, block, or document, Professional Write offers you a variety of
features to use. In this section, you will learn to use each of these procedures to erase unwanted text.

Deleting a Word

Deleting a word is a simple procedure; you simply position the cursor on the word you want to delete, type Ctrl-W, and the word is gone. If you prefer, you can use the menu selection method by pressing F3 to open the Edit menu and selecting the **Delete word** option. The word is deleted and the cursor is automatically placed on the next word in the paragraph. To delete subsequent words, press Ctrl-W again for each word you want to delete. The paragraph is reformatted to compensate for the deletion of the word.

Use Ctrl-W (Delete word) with caution, however: once the word is gone, it's gone. There's no way to replace a word deleted with Ctrl-W short of retyping it.

Remember that, when all else fails, you can always bail out by erasing the working copy. As you know, the working copy is independent of the actual document file stored on disk, so any changes you have made in the current working copy to a file you have previously created and saved are not sent to the file on disk until you select **Save working copy** from the File/Print menu or press Ctrl-S.

To erase the working copy, choose the **Erase working copy** option from the File/Print menu. This option clears the screen and abandons any changes you have made to the current file. Remember, however, that the file remains intact on the disk so that you can make further modifications if necessary.

> You can use the find-and-replace feature to find and delete a word that is used repeatedly. Select **Find & Replace** from the Edit menu, enter the word you want to delete after the **Find:** prompt, and, after the **Replace with:** prompt, enter nothing. When you press Enter, Professional Write searches for the word, removes it, and replaces it with nothing, which in effect deletes the word throughout the document.

Erasing a Line

The command for erasing a line is just beneath the word deletion command on the Edit menu. It also works in a similar way. To delete a line, position the cursor on the line you want to delete and press Ctrl-L. If you choose, you can select the command from the Edit menu by opening the menu (with

F3), and selecting the **Delete line** option (see fig. 5.15). After you press Enter, the line is deleted.

```
F1-Help   F2-File/Print   F3-Edit   F4-Format   F5-Dictionary   F6-Addresses

Hugo's product,                                        e from
crushed rose pet                                       ld he call
attention to his    1. Insert blank line   Ctrl-I     g their old
standards? He an  ▶ 3. Delete line          Ctrl-L     nd the
answer: they wou    2. Delete word          Ctrl-W     inted signs
with pictures of                                       Salts. The
important thing,    4. Mark text            Ctrl-T     e in the
signs had to loo    5. Mark rectangle       Ctrl-R     appy and
relaxed.            6. Paste                Ctrl-P

Rosey's Bath Sal    7. Boldface word        Ctrl-B     to quit his
carpentry and Ho    8. Underline word       Ctrl-U     to a
boarding house i                                       te a whole
line of concocti    9. Draw lines                      gest line
of toiletry item                                       years.
                    A. Find & Replace       Ctrl-F

Hugo and Houston    B. Calculate            Ctrl-M     ng their
years as co-pres                                       Houston
had no children, but Hugo and his wife Marjorie had one son,
William. William was born in 1908 in St. Louis, Missouri.

Working Copy   Inserting                       3%    Line 25 of Pg 1
               Times P 10
```

Fig. 5.15. Selecting the Delete line option.

Deleting a Text Block

The procedure for deleting a text block is a bit safer than either the **Delete word** or the **Delete line** options. When you delete a text block, you are actually cutting it from the document and placing it on the clipboard. This way, you can recover the block if you decide that you shouldn't have deleted it.

To delete a text block, follow these steps:

1. Highlight the block you want to delete and press F10.

2. From either the Text Block Operations menu or the Rectangular Block Operations menu (depending on which type of block you selected), select the **Cut** option.

Professional Write deletes the block without any further intervention from you. If you decide that you need the block you just deleted, you can return it to the document by positioning the cursor at the appropriate point and selecting the **Paste** option from the Edit menu or by pressing Ctrl-P.

Erasing the Working Copy

When you load a document, Professional Write automatically places on-screen a copy of the document you choose. This copy is known as the *working copy*. You can perform various operations on the document, perhaps exit to the Professional Write Main menu, and when you select the **Create/Edit** option...there it is again.

How do you get rid of the working copy? What if you want to delete the file you are editing and display a blank document so that you can create another file? Easy. Just select **Erase working copy** from the Files/Print menu and press Enter. Professional Write erases the working copy and displays a blank document.

> It's not necessary to erase the working copy of a file if you are planning to load another file. To load another file, press Ctrl-G (or select **Get file** from the Files/Print menu). If you haven't saved the working copy, Professional Write warns you of this, and after you confirm your choice, loads the new file.

Deleting the File

With Professional Write, you also can delete a file you no longer need. To remove a file without exiting to DOS, select **Delete file** from the File/Print menu.

For example, suppose that you are working on one memo and realize that you never deleted an old memo sent to the same person. Without leaving the program, you can follow these steps to remove the unwanted file:

1. Open the File/Print menu by pressing F2.

2. Select the **Delete file** option by moving the highlight to that option and pressing enter or by typing *3*.

3. A window is displayed, asking for the path and file name of the file you want to delete. Enter the name of the file and press Enter. (If you do not know the name of the field, or if you want to delete several files, you can enter the path and press Enter. Professional Write then displays the directory screen and you can select the files to be deleted.)

4. A second window is displayed, warning you that the deletion of the file is final (see fig. 5.16). Press Enter to continue the procedure.

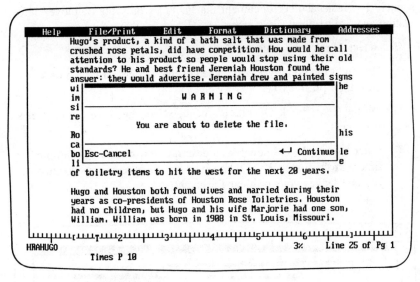

| Help | File/Print | Edit | Format | Dictionary | Addresses |

Hugo's product, a kind of a bath salt that was made from
crushed rose petals, did have competition. How would he call
attention to his product so people would stop using their old
standards? He and best friend Jeremiah Houston found the
answer: they would advertise. Jeremiah drew and painted signs

```
ui                                                           he
in        ┌─────────────────────────────────────────────┐
si        │              W A R N I N G                   │
re        ├─────────────────────────────────────────────┤
Ro        │       You are about to delete the file.      │  his
ca        ├─────────────────────────────────────────────┤
bo        │ Esc-Cancel                        ←┘ Continue│  le
li        └─────────────────────────────────────────────┘  e
```

of toiletry items to hit the west for the next 20 years.

Hugo and Houston both found wives and married during their
years as co-presidents of Houston Rose Toiletries. Houston
had no children, but Hugo and his wife Marjorie had one son,
William. William was born in 1908 in St. Louis, Missouri.

HRAHUGO   3%   Line 25 of Pg 1
        Times P 10

Fig. 5.16. *Professional Write asks you to confirm the deletion.*

Moving to Another Page

Not all documents are simple memos that you can pound out in a
quarter of an hour. You may be working with a variety of projects,
and for those that require many pages, you need to know how to
get from page to page. To move from one page to another, press
Ctrl-J.

Saving a Block as Another Document

The last operation addressed in this chapter concerns saving blocks of text
as individual documents. Suppose that you create a document that includes
financial information and a section announcing the promotion of several
employees. You now want to use the employee section in the company
newsletter, but the financial information is to be seen only by certain per-

sonnel. To create another document that includes only the employee information, you can follow these steps:

1. Select **Mark text** from the Edit menu.

2. Highlight the employee text, whether that is one paragraph or several; then press F10.

3. On the Text Block Operations menu, select the **Save** option (see fig. 5.17).

4. Enter a name for the new file, a description if necessary, and press Enter. Professional Write then saves the block as a new document file and leaves your original file intact.

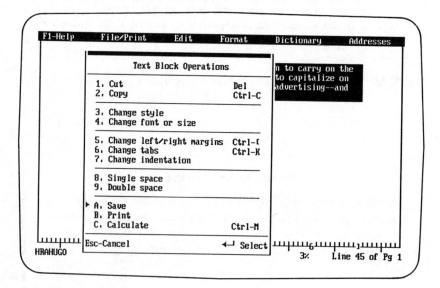

Fig. 5.17. *Using the* **Save** *option.*

Chapter 5 Quick Start: Editing

This Quick Start gives you a review of all the block editing procedures introduced in this chapter.

Cutting Text

To cut the paragraph from the document, follow these steps:

1. Begin highlighting the block by positioning the cursor at the beginning of the block and pressing Ctrl-T. (You also can select **Mark text** from the Edit menu, if you prefer.)

2. Use the arrow keys to move to the end of the paragraph and press F10. The Text Block Operations menu is displayed automatically.

3. Press Enter to select the **Cut** option, which is already highlighted. You can also press the speed key, Del. Professional Write then cuts the text from the document and places it on the clipboard. The text that follows the removed information moves up to fill its place.

Pasting Text

To paste the text block back into the document, follow these steps:

1. Position the cursor where you want the text to be inserted.

2. Open the Edit menu by pressing F2 and select the **Paste** option. (You can bypass the menu selections and press the speed key combination, Ctrl-P, if you prefer.) Professional Write places the text block in the document at the cursor position.

Copying Text

To copy text, follow these steps:

1. Highlight the section to be copied. (If the block includes formats that you want to preserve, mark the block as a rectangular block.)

2. Select the **Copy** option (or press Ctrl-C). Professional Write then places a copy of the text on the clipboard.

3. Move the cursor to the position where you want the text to be placed, and press Ctrl-P (or select **Paste** from the Edit menu). The text is then copied to the desired location.

Shifting Text

Follow these steps to shift a rectangular block of text:

1. Highlight as a rectangular block the text to be shifted. (Use **Mark rectangle** from the Edit menu or press Ctrl-R.)

2. When the Rectangular Block Operations menu is displayed, select the **Shift** option.

3. Use the → key to move the block to the right. (You can use any of the arrow keys in a shift operation.)

Changing Font and Font Size

To change the font and font size for a block of text, follow these steps:

1. Highlight the block of text for which you want to change the font or size.

2. On the Text Block Operations menu (or the Rectangular Block Operations menu, if you chose the **Mark rectangle** option), select **Change font or size**.

3. When the Select Font or Size menu is displayed, use the arrow keys to move the highlight to the font and size you want.

4. Press Enter to select the font.

Changing Text Style

To change the style of a block of text, follow these steps:

1. Highlight the block you want to change. (This can be either a regular text block or a rectangular text block.)

2. From the Text Block Operations menu (or the Rectangular Block Operations menu, if you chose **Mark rectangle** from the Edit menu), choose the **Change style** menu. The Style menu is then displayed.

3. Type the number of the style you want (you *cannot* select these options by using the arrow keys to move the highlight and pressing Enter) and press Enter.

Using Find and Replace

To use the find-and-replace feature, follow these steps:

1. Position the cursor at the point at which you want to begin the search.

2. Open the Edit menu and select the **Find & Replace** option or press Ctrl-F. The Find and Replace box is then displayed.

3. At the **Find:** prompt, type the text you want to search for.

4. After the **Ignore case (Y/N):** prompt, type *n* if you do not want to ignore case and y if you do.

5. After the **Replace with:** prompt, type the text—if there is any —that you want to replace the text with.

6. After the **Manual or automatic (M/A):** prompt, type *a* if you want the program to replace the text automatically or *m* if you want to have yea or nay power for each replacement.

7. Press Enter to begin the search.

Chapter Summary

In this chapter, you learned how to perform various editing operations such as highlighting text, moving, copying, deleting, or reformatting text. Additionally, you learned to use the find and replace feature and erase words, lines, documents, and files. In the next chapter, you build further on your word processing experience by learning to enhance your Professional Write documents.

6

Enhancing Documents

N ow that you have gotten the text into the document and have edited to your heart's content, what are you going to do to spruce it up? Does your report require headers and footers? Do you want to use the draw feature to highlight important items? Do you need to add page numbers or a cover page? This chapter shows you how to make your document more visually appealing by using some of the additional features in Professional Write.

Sprucing Up the Document

You don't need to enhance all the documents you create. Not everything needs a specialized touch, an interesting design, or an eye-catching layout. If you are typing a To Do list, for example, you don't really need to spruce it up. If you are writing a letter to your Aunt Mildred, you don't need to add any snazzy special effects, unless, of course, your Aunt Mildred has an eye for such things and would enjoy seeing the capabilities of the program.

With Professional Write, you can enhance your document in the following ways:

❏ Add a heading that repeats on every page of a report

❏ Insert a graph in a report at print time

❏ Draw boxes around important information

157

❑ Create a letterhead effect that highlights the name of your document or your company

❑ Design a unique memo style for your department

❑ Add automatic page numbering in the headers or footers of your document

❑ Use lines to help highlight or separate information segments

❑ Create callout boxes (also called *pull quotes*) to reinforce important information in the text

Consider, for example, figure 6.1. The document in the figure is just a plain and simple report—a title and some text. The person who created this report did add a bold style to the title, but has not used the different font capabilities to make the title a larger size. This document could use some dressing up in the way of changing the font and size of the title and section names.

Figure 6.2 shows the same report after it has been revised by a person armed with Professional Write. As you can see, the heading is now placed in a different font, and the white space around the heading has been used more effectively to highlight the report name. Boxes set off important information in the text.

Figure 6.3 shows page 2 of the report. A header has been added (the display of this header was suppressed on page 1), and a graph has been printed in the center of the page.

With Professional Write, you can do as much—or as little—as your needs dictate. The memo shown in figure 6.4 gives you an idea of how a simple design can make even your memos look a bit more professional.

In this chapter, you will see several different types of enhancements that you can use in your own documents. But don't limit yourself to those you see here; feel free to experiment and design documents that are tailored to the needs of your business tasks.

BrightStar Toys, Inc.   **1989 Annual Report**

1989 has been a record breaking year for BrightStar Toys, Inc. This report will detail the overall changes that have occurred in our company in the last 12 months; namely, the changes in staff, in housing, and in operations. Perhaps it would be quicker to list the areas that haven't changed!

Beginning on page two of this report, you will see material written by each of the departmental managers, summarizing the activities that have taken place in their departments during the last calendar year. The last three pages of the report are dedicated to future plans for 1990. Inserted inside the back cover of the report, you will find an Employee Response Card. Carrying on our tradition of the last 15 years, we ask you to fill out this card, listing your best and worst moments of the last year, and making any suggestions you might have for improvements in BrightStar's future. Thanks very much for your support during the last year.

New Hires/ New Promotions

As you know, BrightStar has added some very important people to our staff in the last year. In this section, you will be introduced to each of these people and find out a little more about their roles at BrightStar.

In Operations, Mary Lou Beasley was hired as a balance and distribution clerk. Coming from a ten-year employment with AT&T, Mary Lou brings BrightStar a solid understanding of employee needs and will assist Mark Homeston with payroll on a regular basis.

In Marketing, Roger Reynolds joins us from the prestigous Ridge, Watson, and Wheeler advertising firm in Boston, MA. Roger will be our Junior Marketing Manager and will be responsible for the Dinobots line, the CarGo line, and the Powerpuff Dolls.

Lindy Walker has also joined the Marketing department in order to use her copywriting skills to help us create some innovative new campaigns for this season's hottest toys. Welcome aboard, Lindy!

Janice Hopkins, Associate Production Director, has come to BrightStar from a fast-paced computer assembly company. She brings with her a fundamental understanding of both electronics and computer hardware and will greatly benefit the production lines of all our toys.

The Publications staff would like to announce the promotion of Summer Davidson to Desktop Publishing Director. In her new role, Summer will instruct and direct her staff to produce all materials previously typeset on our new desktop publishing systems. (Next year, you can expect to see the Annual Report done on desktop, as well!)

Other promotions/hires include the following:

> Roger Plotnik, promoted to 3rd Shift Supervisor
> Ann Raymond, promoted to Copywriter
> Lisa Mayfield, hired as Administrative Assistant
> Curtis VonBurg, hired as Sales Coordinator--West
> Randy Barnes, promoted to Packager
> Cindi Shooter, hired as Telemarketer

Sales Increases Nationwide

1989 has been a good year for BrightStar, as well. Because of a 15 percent nationwide sales increase, the company was able to pay larger profit sharing bonuses than has been the case in the past.

Our sales force has done a great job this year in getting the BrightStar lines out to the distributors and wholesalers. The Midwestern division ranked the highest in a recent sales promotion, with John Lancaster,

Fig. 6.1. The report in need of a makeover.

BrightStar Toys, Inc.

1989 Annual Report

1989 has been a record breaking year for BrightStar Toys, Inc. This report will detail the overall changes that have occurred in our company in the last 12 months; namely, the changes in staff, in housing, and in operations. Perhaps it would be quicker to list the areas that haven't changed!

Beginning on page two of this report, you will see material written by each of the departmental managers, summarizing the activities that have taken place in their departments during the last calendar year. The last three pages of the report are dedicated to future plans for 1990. Inserted inside the back cover of the report, you will find an Employee Response Card. Carrying on our tradition of the last 15 years, we ask you to fill out this card, listing your best and worst moments of the last year, and making any suggestions you might have for improvements in BrightStar's future. Thanks very much for your support during the last year.

New Hires/ New Promotions

As you know, BrightStar has added some very important people to our staff in the last year. In this section, you will be introduced to each of these people and find out a little more about their roles at BrightStar.

In Operations, **Mary Lou Beasley** was hired as a balance and distribution clerk. Coming from a ten-year employment with AT&T, Mary Lou brings BrightStar a solid understanding of employee needs and will assist Mark Homeston with payroll on a regular basis.

In Marketing, **Roger Reynolds** joins us from the prestigous Ridge, Watson, and Wheeler advertising firm in Boston, MA. Roger will be our Junior Marketing Manager and will be responsible for the Dinobots line, the CarGo line, and the Powerpuff Dolls.

Lindy Walker has also joined the Marketing department in order to use her copywriting skills to help us create some innovative new campaigns for this season's hottest toys. Welcome aboard, Lindy!

Janice Hopkins, Associate Production Director, has come to BrightStar from a fast-paced computer assembly company. She brings with her a fundamental understanding of both electronics and computer hardware and will greatly benefit the production lines of all our toys.

The Publications staff would like to announce the promotion of **Summer Davidson** to Desktop Publishing Director. In her new role, Summer will instruct and direct her staff to produce all materials previously typeset on our new desktop publishing systems. (Next year, you can expect to see the Annual Report done on desktop, as well!)

Other promotions/hires include the following:

Fig. 6.2. The report after enhancements have been added.

BrightStar Toys, Inc.
1989 Annual Report

* Lisa Mayfield, hired as Administrative Assistant
* Curtis VonBurg, hired as Sales Coordinator--West
* Randy Barnes, promoted to Packager
* Cindi Shooter, hired as Telemarketer

Sales Increases Nationwide

1989 has been a good year for BrightStar, as well. Because of a 15 percent nationwide sales increase, the company was able to pay larger profit sharing bonuses than has been the case in the past.

Our sales force has done a great job this year in getting the BrightStar lines out to the distributors and wholesalers. The Midwestern division ranked the highest in a recent sales promotion, with John Lancaster, Sales Manager, reaching the highest sales goal.

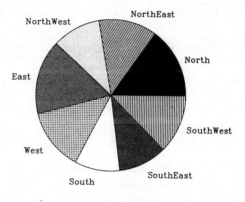

Fig. 6.3. *Page 2 of the enhanced report.*

From Our Super Shippers...

To: Maude Wilkins, Shipping Department
From: Roger Eberle, Operations
Date: 06/23/89
Re: Shipment of Dinobots

I received a call from Manufacturing this afternoon,
alerting me to a materials backorder that will
seriously delay the shipment of Dinobots currently
scheduled for 07/01/89.

Because the completion of the Dinobots is impossible
without these materials, we will have to communicate
this delay to our distributors.

Fig. 6.4. *An enhanced memo.*

Adding Headers and Footers

The terms *header* and *footer* may be familiar to you if you have prepared
reports with word processing programs before. Put simply, the *header* is
one or two lines of text that are printed at the top of the page that in some
way identify the document. For example, often the company name, report
title, and page number is included as part of the header. Similarly, the
footer is a text line printed at the bottom of the page, giving additional
information, such as the date, the volume number, or the sponsoring department. Figure 6.5 shows a report page that includes a header and footer.

Controlling Page Size

Before you add headers and footers to your document, you may want to
make sure that you have enough room to print them in the top and bottom
margins of your document. By default, Professional Write sets up the following margins for your documents:

Top margin: 6 lines
Bottom margin: 6 lines

Total page length: 66 lines

Generally, you can expect to get about six lines per inch, so the default
settings leave you approximately nine inches of text space on each page.

Houston Rose Advertising
History Unfolds...

capitalize on his father's first major business talent--advertising--and sell the retail portion of the business.

In 1888, not too many people were looking for an advertising agency. Lotions, potions, and sundries tended to sell themselves; medicine men pushed the fermented whiskey tonics in the suspicious-looking brown glass bottles. No one needed a company to represent their product--there just wasn't enough competition. If you had a product, you got attention. Only the rare wallflower was overlooked on the general store shelves.

On a dusty, dry day in July, 1888, Hugo Higgenmeyer had an idea for a new product. Unlike most others in his time, Hugo's product, a kind of bath salt that was made from crushed rose petals, did have competition. How would he call attention to his product so people would stop using their old standards? He and best friend Jeremiah Houston found the answer: they would advertise. Jeremiah drew and painted signs with pictures of people bathing with Rosey's Bath Salts. The important thing, Hugo stressed, was that the people in the signs had to look as though they were completely happy and relaxed.

Rosey's Bath Salts sold well enough to allow Hugo to quit his carpentry and Houston to leave his farm. Moving into a boarding house in the city, the pair began to create a whole line of concoctions that eventually became the largest line of toiletry items to hit the west for the next 20 years.

Hugo and Houston both found wives and married during their years as co-presidents of Houston Rose Toiletries. Houston had no children, but Hugo and his wife Marjorie had one son, William. William was born in 1908 in St. Louis, Missouri.

In 1949, William Higgenmyer made a decision to carry on the tradition of Houston Rose Toiletries--yet to capitalize on his father's first major business talent--advertising--and sell the retail portion of the business.

In 1888, not too many people were looking for an advertising agency. Lotions, potions, and sundries tended to sell themselves; medicine men pushed the fermented whiskey tonics in the suspicious-looking brown glass bottles. No one needed a company to represent their product--there just wasn't enough competition. If you had a product, you got attention. Only the rare wallflower was overlooked on the general store shelves.

On a dusty, dry day in July, 1888, Hugo Higgenmeyer had an idea for a new product. Unlike most others in his time, Hugo's product, a kind of bath salt that was made from crushed rose petals, did have competition. How would he call attention to his product so people would stop using their old standards? He and best friend Jeremiah Houston found the answer: they would advertise. Jeremiah drew and painted signs with pictures of people bathing with Rosey's Bath Salts. The important thing, Hugo stressed, was that the people in the signs had to look as though they were completely happy and relaxed.

Rosey's Bath Salts sold well enough to allow Hugo to quit his carpentry and Houston to leave his farm. Moving into a boarding house in the city, the pair began to create a whole line of concoctions that eventually became the largest line of toiletry items to hit the west for the next 20 years.

Hugo and Houston both found wives and married during their years as co-presidents of Houston Rose Toiletries. Houston had no children, but Hugo and his wife Marjorie had one son, William. William was born in 1908 in St. Louis, Missouri.

In 1949, William Higgenmyer made a decision to carry on the tradition of Houston Rose Toiletries--yet to capitalize on his father's first major business talent--advertising--and sell the retail portion of the business.

Company History Compiled and Published
by reVisions Plus, Inc., 1989

Fig. 6.5. *A report page with a header and footer.*

(That is, a one-inch margin at the top and bottom of the page leaves nine inches on which text will be printed.)

If you want to pick up a little extra space by cutting down on the margin settings, you can do so, but be careful. If you try to include headers and you reduce the number of lines in the top margin, Professional Write starts the text closer to the top of the page, possibly bumping into your header. Generally, if you reduce the top margin setting, use only one header line or no header at all.

> If you are printing on continuous-feed paper, you can set the number of lines (**Total page length**) to 0.

If you want to change the margins or page length settings, follow these steps:

1. Open the Format menu by pressing F4.

2. Select the **Set top/bottom margins & length** option. A window is displayed, showing the current settings (see fig. 6.6).

3. Position the cursor on the setting you want to change. (Move among the options by pressing Tab to go to the next setting or Shift-Tab to go the previous setting.)

4. When you are satisfied with the settings, press Enter.

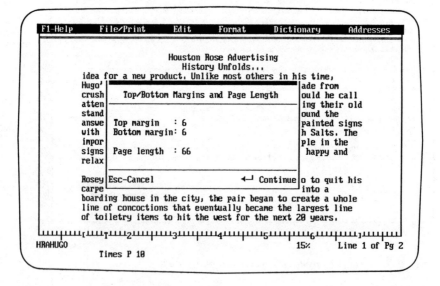

Fig. 6.6. Reducing the top margin.

Creating Headers

Now you are ready to enter a header for your document. Remember that you have the following options when you create headers:

❏ You can control the placement of the header (left-justified, right-justified, or centered)

❏ You can specify the style in which you want the header to be printed (bold, underline, italic, or normal)

❏ You can elect to print page numbers in the header (page numbering is discussed in the next section)

❏ You can change the font of a header (if your printer supports fonts)

❏ You can tell Professional Write to begin printing the header on a page other than page 1 (which enables you to create a title or cover page).

❏ You can enter a header of up to two lines, with 64 characters in each line.

When you create a header, you use the Header screen, which is displayed when you select **Set header** from the Format menu. The Header screen has several options with which you should be familiar (see fig. 6.7).

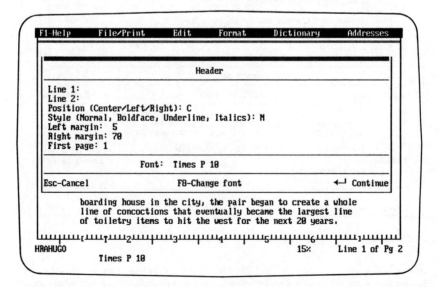

Fig. 6.7. *A window displays current margin settings.*

You type the text for the header after the prompts **Line 1:** and **Line 2:**. Professional Write accepts up to 64 characters (including spaces) in each header line. The **Position** prompt enables you to specify whether you want the header to appear centered (C), left-justified (L), or right-justified (R). All the options on the Header screen affect both lines of the header; for example, you cannot center header line 1 and right-justify header line 2. Both lines are treated together as one header.

The **Style** setting controls how the text is displayed on the screen. If your printer supports the styles, you can print the header in normal (N), boldface (B), underline (U), or italic (I) type. The **Left margin:** and **Right margin:** prompts enable you to enter custom margins for the header. For example, suppose that the margin of your document is set at 15 and 70, and you want the header to be positioned in the upper left corner of the screen, so that the left side of the header gives the appearance of hanging outside the margin. To do this, you can specify a left margin of 10, and Professional Write prints the header five spaces before the margin of the document (see fig. 6.8).

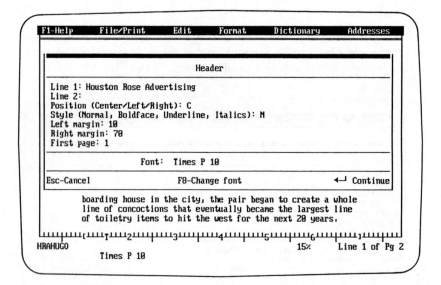

Fig. 6.8. The Header screen.

The **First page:** prompt on the Header screen enables you to specify the beginning page where you want the headers to be added. For example, suppose that you are creating a multipage report. The first page is a cover page; the second is a credits page that lists all the people whose work has gone into the report. The report actually begins on the third page. In this case, you don't want the header to appear on the first two pages, so after the **First page:** prompt, type *3*. Professional Write then knows to insert the header beginning on page three and continuing on subsequent pages throughout the document. Although headers are used most often to give readers information they need quickly about the document, such as the report name, company title, and page number, you can use headers for more unconventional things.

Suppose, for example, that you want to add some sort of a design element to a simple flier that you have just typed. You can use the header to spruce things up—even if it doesn't provide much useful information (see fig. 6.9).

HotShots * HotShots * HotShots * HotShots * HotShots * HotShots *
* HotShots * HotShots * HotShots * HotShots * HotShots * HotShots

If you could take your 35mm film to a quickie print shop and have them produce better quality pictures for less money, would you give that business a shot?

If your deadline was yesterday and a photo repro center offered to do your photos fast--for next to nothing--would you take a chance?

For a limited time only, bring **HotShots** your tired and worn out film and we'll turn it into something wonderful.

50 % off now through May 15th.

No charge for rush jobs between 10:00 and 2:00.

Fig. 6.9. *A different type of header.*

To add a header to your document, follow these steps:

1. Open the Format menu by pressing F4.

2. Select the **Set header** option. The Header screen is displayed.

3. Type the text you want to appear at the top line of the header after the **Line 1:** prompt. Professional Write enables you to type a header until the text reaches the right edge of the screen.

4. Press Tab to get to the **Line 2:** prompt.

5. Enter the text for line 2 if you want to include a second header line on your document. Press Tab after you finish typing the text at the **Line 2:** prompt.

6. After the **Position** prompt, tell Professional Write how you want the header to be positioned by typing *c* (for centered), *l* (for left-justified), or *r* (for right-justified). Remember that both header lines will be affected by the position you choose.

7. Indicate how you want the header to appear by typing *b* (for bold-face), *u* (for underline), or *i* (for italic) after the prompt. (N is the default, so if you want to select that option, simply press Tab to get to the next prompt.)

8. Enter a new margin for **Left margin:**, if you want, and press Tab.

9. Enter a new margin for **Right margin:**, if you want, and press Tab.

10. After the **First page:** option, type the number of the page on which you want the header to begin.

After answering all the prompts on the Header screen, you can press Enter to have Professional Write automatically add the headers for you. If your printer has font capability, however, there is one more option available to you: you can change the font of the header.

At the bottom of the Header screen, a line is displayed that tells you the name, orientation, and size of the current font. If you want to change that setting, press F8. Professional Write then displays the Select Font or Size window. To select a different font, simply press the up-arrow key (↑) or down-arrow key (↓) to move the highlight to the font you want and press Enter. You are returned to the Header screen, and Professional Write displays the new font in the **Font:** line at the bottom of the screen.

When you are happy with the settings in the Header screen, press Enter and Professional Write automatically places the header on every page of the document (see fig. 6.10).

Creating Footers

Entering a footer is almost identical to entering a header for your document. Remember that you have the following options when you are creating footers:

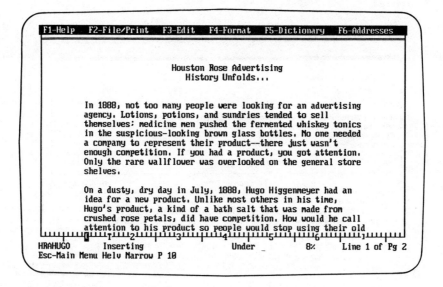

Fig. 6.10. Professional Write adds the header to the document.

❏ A footer can be two lines of 64 characters each. You may prefer, however, to limit the footer to one line so that your page does not look cluttered.

❏ You can print footers in bold, underline, italic, or normal style.

❏ You can add page numbers so that they print automatically in whatever numbering scheme you select.

❏ You can control the placement of the footer (left-justified, right-justified, or centered)

❏ You can change the font of the footer, if you want.

When you create or edit footers in Professional Write, you use the Footer screen (see fig. 6.11). As you can see, all the prompts on this screen are the same as those on the Header screen; the only difference is the name of the window.

Because the options on this screen are identical to those on the Header screen, there is no need to repeat them again here. To find out more about these options, refer to the preceding section ''Creating Headers.''

To add a footer to your document, follow these steps:

1. Open the Format menu by pressing F4.

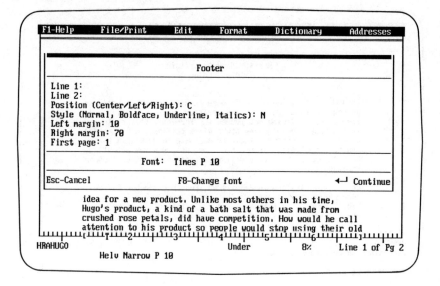

F1-Help   File/Print   Edit   Format   Dictionary   Addresses

Footer

Line 1:
Line 2:
Position (Center/Left/Right): C
Style (Normal, Boldface, Underline, Italics): N
Left margin: 10
Right margin: 70
First page: 1

Font: Times P 10

Esc-Cancel   F8-Change font   ←┘ Continue

idea for a new product. Unlike most others in his time,
Hugo's product, a kind of a bath salt that was made from
crushed rose petals, did have competition. How would he call
attention to his product so people would stop using their old

HRAHUGO   Under   8%   Line 1 of Pg 2
            Helu Narrow P 10

Fig. 6.11. The Footer screen.

2. Select the **Set footer** option. The Footer screen is displayed.

3. Type the text you want to appear in the top line of the footer after the **Line 1:** prompt. You can type a footer until the text reaches the right edge of the screen.

4. Press Tab to get to **Line 2:**.

5. Enter the text for line 2 if you want to include a second footer line on your document. Press Tab when you are finished with **Line 2:**.

6. Indicate how you want the header to appear by typing *b* (for boldface), *u* (for underline), or *i* (for italic) after the prompt. (N is the default, so if you want to select that option, simply press Tab to get to the next prompt.)

7. Enter a new margin for **Left margin:**, if you want, and press Tab.

8. Enter a new margin for **Right margin:**, if you want, and press Tab.

9. After the **First page:** option, type the number of the page on which you want the footer to begin.

After answering all the prompts on the Footer screen, you can press Enter to have Professional Write automatically add the footer for you. If your printer has font capability, however, there is one more option available to you: you can change the font of the footer.

At the bottom of the Footer screen, a line is displayed that tells you the name, orientation, and size of the current font. If you want to change that setting, press F8. Professional Write then displays the Select Font or Size window. To select a different font, simply press ↓ or ↑ to move the highlight to the font you want and press Enter. You are returned to the Footer screen, and Professional Write displays the new font in the **Font:** line at the bottom of the screen.

When you are happy with the settings in the Footer screen, press Enter and Professional Write automatically places the footer on every page of the document, beginning with the page specified in the **First page:** line.

Tips for Headers and Footers

Here's some advice for producing headers and footers that convey information in an effective way:

❑ Put the most important information in the header.

❑ Don't try to cram too much information into one line of a header or footer. Professional Write provides two lines for headers and footers, so break the line as needed to avoid cluttering the page.

❑ Vary the placement of headers and footers to highlight important information. For example, you may want to center the header (Houston Rose Advertising) so that the reader's eye is drawn first to that item; then position the footer starting at the left margin, so that the reader sees the less important information (December, 1989) last.

❑ You can give the header the appearance of being separated by a rule if you type a line of underscores (_) in header line 2. (To insert a line above a footer, type the underscores in footer line 1.)

Adding Page Numbers

When you are adding headers or footers to your document, you can have Professional Write automatically add page numbers, as well. You can choose from several different numbering schemes, and you can also specify the number of the page on which you want the numbering to begin.

When you add page numbers to the document, you include the number in asterisks, which in effect tell the program to "substitute the correct page number here." For example, when you type the header

Quarterly Report 1989, Page *2*

Professional Write prints the header starting on the page you specify after the **First page:** prompt, and inserts the page number 2 after the word *Page* in the header. On subsequent pages, Professional Write automatically inserts the correct page number between the asterisks. You can use almost any page numbering scheme you can come up with, but just remember one simple rule: place the actual page number—the number that will change from page to page—between asterisks. The program will then know to insert the correct page number in that space and, on each subsequent page, to increment the page number by 1.

If you enter this in a header	*Professional Write adds this on the first page*
Pg. *1*	Pg. 1
Page number: *14*	Page number: 14
Section/page number A-*3*	Section/page number A-3

Using the Draw Feature

Professional Write offers a feature that many other word processors do not: drawing capability. How many times have you wanted to draw a line on a document and resorted to typing a series of underscores or dashes? And what happens when you need vertical lines?

Professional Write's draw feature gives you another method of sprucing up your document. Figure 6.12 shows a document in which the draw feature has been used.

You can use the draw feature for a number of purposes:

❑ To highlight important information

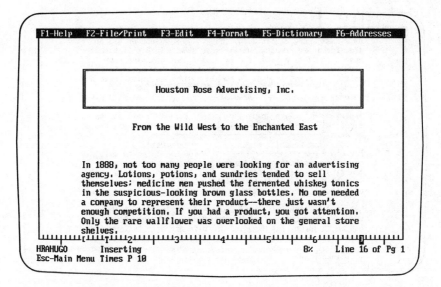

Fig. 6.12. Using the draw feature to enhance a document.

❏ To set off information that is different from the main flow of the text

❏ To serve as a design element for a heading or cover page

❏ To provide a border for text

The program enables you to choose the type of line you want to draw. When you select **Draw lines** from the Edit menu, the Drawing menu is displayed (see figure 6.13).

The draw feature does have limitations, however. Because Professional Write ''sees'' the line characters as if they were typical text characters, using draw can be tricky when you're working alongside various text items. You also may experience problems when you are drawing vertical lines that run the length of text, or when you are trying to draw a box around text.

Generally, as you will see later in this chapter (and also in Chapter 8), you can solve some of your unexpected draw problems either by using a monospace—rather than a proportional—font for the text in the document or by *not using* Font format (an option that you set on the Print Options menu, which is discussed fully in Chapter 8).

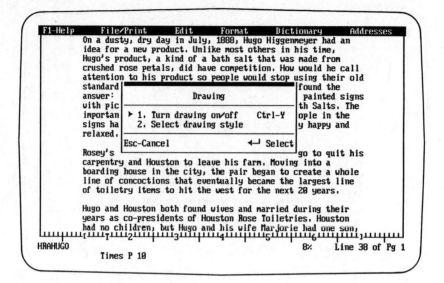

Fig. 6.13. The Drawing menu.

Drawing Lines

A line for a line's sake isn't very exciting, particularly if your document is rife with them. Use lines sparingly, and make sure that you have a reason for every line you use. In the example shown in figure 6.14, a line is used in the header to separate the heading from the text. Another vertical line has been added to help delineate a list of topics, providing a graphic effect.

To draw a line, follow these steps:

1. Position the cursor at the point in the document where you want the line to begin.

2. Open the Edit menu and select the **Draw lines** option.

3. Choose the **Turn drawing on/off** option. (You can press Ctrl-Y to bypass the menu selections, if you choose.) Professional Write returns you to the document. A Drawing indicator appears in the status line of the screen to let you know that the drawing feature has been activated.

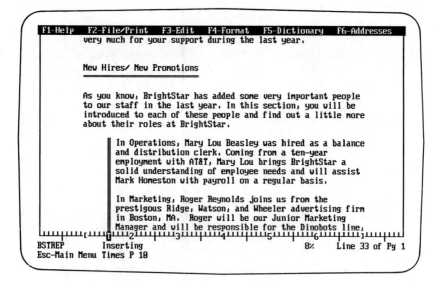

```
F1-Help  F2-File/Print  F3-Edit  F4-Format  F5-Dictionary  F6-Addresses
                   very much for your support during the last year.

                   New Hires/ New Promotions

                   As you know, BrightStar has added some very important people
                   to our staff in the last year. In this section, you will be
                   introduced to each of these people and find out a little more
                   about their roles at BrightStar.

                            In Operations, Mary Lou Beasley was hired as a balance
                            and distribution clerk. Coming from a ten-year
                            employment with AT&T, Mary Lou brings BrightStar a
                            solid understanding of employee needs and will assist
                            Mark Homeston with payroll on a regular basis.

                            In Marketing, Roger Reynolds joins us from the
                            prestigous Ridge, Watson, and Wheeler advertising firm
                            in Boston, MA.  Roger will be our Junior Marketing
                            Manager and will be responsible for the Dinobots line,
   |..|.|....|..|.|0.|..|.|..|2.|..|.|..3..|..|.|..4..|.|.|.|5.|.|.|.|6.|..|.|..|.|..|.|..|
   BSTREP         Inserting                              8%    Line 33 of Pg 1
   Esc-Main Menu Times P 10
```

Fig. 6.14. A document with lines used effectively.

4. Press the arrow key that will draw the line in the direction you want. For example, if you want the line to go to the right, press →. Professional Write adds a line character each time you press →. To draw a long line, you can press and hold the arrow key and Professional Write repeats the line character until you release the key.

5. When you are finished drawing the line, press Ctrl-Y to deactivate the draw feature.

Before you select the **Draw lines** option from the Edit menu, be sure to position the cursor at the point on-screen where you want the line drawing to begin. Once you make your selection from the Drawing menu, the draw feature is in effect, and any time you move the arrow keys, a line will be drawn. The draw feature remains active until you disable the feature by pressing Ctrl-Y or by selecting **Turn drawing on/off** from the Drawing menu.

Drawing with Arrow Keys

When you use Professional Write's drawing feature, you use the arrow keys to tell the program in which direction to draw the line. Use the following keys to help you draw with Professional Write:

Use this key	*To draw in this direction*
↑	Up one line
↓	Down one line
→	Right one character
←	Left one character
Home	Diagonally upward and one character to the left
PgUp	Diagonally upward and one character to the right
PgDn	Diagonally downward and one character to the right
End	Diagonally downward and one character to the left

Changing the Line Style

You can choose from three types of lines in Professional Write: a single line, a double line, or a heavy bar line. You can also create your own customized line (which is discussed in the next section).

To change the style of the line you are drawing, follow these steps:

1. From the Edit menu, select **Draw lines**.

2. When the Drawing menu is displayed, choose **Select drawing style** and press Enter. The Drawing Styles menu is displayed (see fig. 6.15).

3. Select the line style you want to use and press Enter.

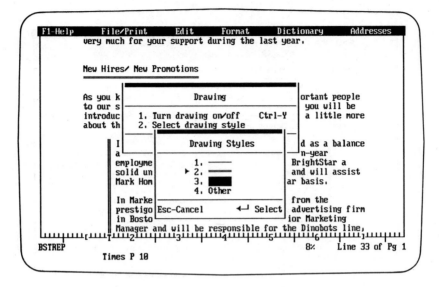

Fig. 6.15. *The Drawing Styles menu.*

Creating a Custom Line

With another option on the Drawing Styles menu, you can create your own line type. To create a custom line, follow these steps:

1. From the Edit menu, select **Draw lines**.

2. When the Drawing menu is displayed, choose **Select drawing style** and press Enter.

3. From the Drawing Styles menu, select **Other** and press Enter. A window is displayed, asking you to type the character you want to use as the character for the line (see fig. 6.16).

4. Type the character you want to use (the character can be any character on the keyboard) and press Enter. Professional Write then returns you to the document (with the draw feature activated) so that you can begin drawing.

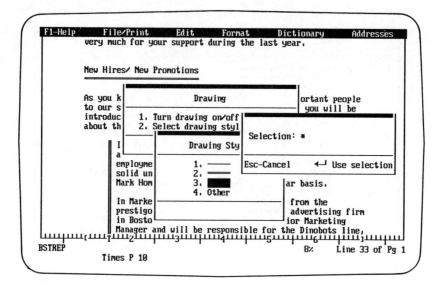

Fig. 6.16. *Creating a custom line.*

Erasing Lines

Until you get the hang of using the drawing feature, you may wind up occasionally adding lines where you don't want them. To erase a line, follow these steps:

1. Position the cursor where you want to begin erasing. (If drawing is still activated, press Ctrl-Y to turn it off before you move the cursor.)

2. Turn on drawing by pressing Ctrl-Y.

3. Press the Shift key and press the cursor-movement key that will move the cursor in the direction you want to erase.

4. Repeat step 3 as necessary to delete the line.

5. Press Ctrl-Y to turn off the drawing feature and return to normal mode.

> If you add or delete text that precedes the line in the document, Professional Write automatically moves the line if the text is altered.

Drawing Boxes

Drawing boxes is just a bit more complicated than drawing lines. To draw a box in Professional Write, follow these steps:

1. Position the cursor where you want to begin drawing the box.

2. Press Ctrl-Y to turn on the draw feature. (If you want to select the line style, select **Draw lines** from the Edit menu and then choose **Select drawing style**.)

3. Use the cursor-movement keys to draw the box. When you change directions (for example, if you had been pressing ↓ and you change to →), Professional Write draws the corner for you.

4. When the box is complete, press Ctrl-Y to deactivate the drawing feature.

If you are drawing a box around text, be sure you use a monospace—also called a *fixed pitch*—font. If you use a proportional font, because the characters take up varying amounts of space, the line you draw may not be straight—even though it appears that way on-screen. Figure 6.17 shows how a text box is printed when a proportional font is used. As you can see, the right edge of the box is out of alignment.

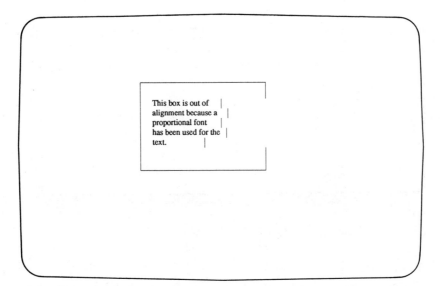

This box is out of
alignment because a
proportional font
has been used for the
text.

Fig. 6.17. The text box with a proportional font.

Working with text boxes can be tricky. You may need to experiment with the spacing inside the box—even if you use a fixed-pitch font. Also, when you are creating text boxes, the preview feature does not always display the box exactly as it will appear on-screen.

Creating a Cover Page

Now that you know how to use headers, footers, page numbering, and the drawing feature, you may want to enhance your document more by adding a cover page. Consider the sample cover page shown in figure 6.18.

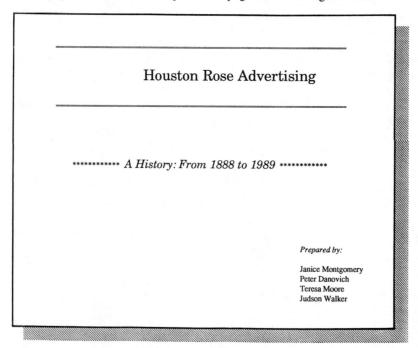

Houston Rose Advertising

************ *A History: From 1888 to 1989* ************

Prepared by:

Janice Montgomery
Peter Danovich
Teresa Moore
Judson Walker

Fig. 6.18. A sample cover page for a report.

This cover page is simply the first page of the document, but instead of showing the text of the report, certain sections—the title, subtitle, company name, and department—are highlighted to provide important information quickly. Further, the draw feature has been used to give the page some design.

To suppress page numbers and headers on this page, you choose **Set header** from the Format menu, and, when the Headers screen is displayed, type *3* after the **First page:** prompt. This causes Professional Write to suppress the header (and, therefore, the page number) until the third page of the document, where the header is really needed.

You create the text for this page as you would prepare any document. Simply move the cursor to the point on-screen where you want the text to begin and type the text. If you want to change the font of the text, you can select the text as a block (by pressing Ctrl-T, moving the cursor to the end of the block, and pressing F10) select the **Change font or size** option, and select the font you want from the Select Font and Size screen.

Importing Graphs

You can further enhance the document by adding graphs at print time. There is no way to display imported graphs on-screen, but you can insert a *GRAPH* command in the document to tell Professional Write to insert the graph at that point when the document is printed.

Figure 6.19 shows how you can use a *GRAPH* command to pull a graph into a document; figure 6.20 shows how the graph appears ''blocked out'' on the preview screen.

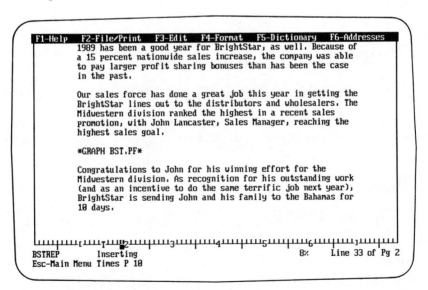

Fig. 6.19. A *GRAPH* command in a document.

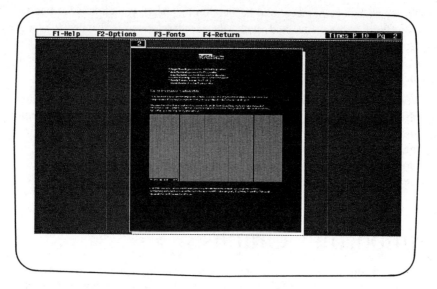

Fig. 6.20. The preview screen showing the placement of the graph.

For more information about compatible graph files and procedures that you can use to import graphs into Professional Write documents, see Chapter 8, "Previewing and Printing Documents."

Chapter 6 Quick Start: Enhancing the Document

This Quick Start provides you with procedures you can use to reinforce the information you have learned in this chapter.

Changing Margins and Page Length Settings

If you want to change the margins or page length settings, follow these steps:

1. Open the Format menu by pressing F4.

2. Select the **Set top/bottom margins & length** option. A window is displayed, showing the current settings.

3. Position the cursor on the setting you want to change. (Move among the options by pressing Tab to go to the next setting or Shift-Tab to go the previous setting.)

4. When you are satisfied with the settings, press Enter.

Adding a Header

To add a header to your document, follow these steps:

1. Open the Format menu by pressing F4.

2. Select the **Set header** option. The Header screen is displayed.

3. Type the text you want to appear as the top line of the header after the **Line 1:** prompt. You can type a header until the text reaches the right edge of the screen.

4. Press Tab to get to the **Line 2:** prompt.

5. Enter the text for line 2 if you want to include a second header line on your document. Press Tab when you are finished with **Line 2:**.

6. Indicate how you want the header to be positioned by typing b, u, or i after the prompt. (N is the default, so if you want to select that option, simply press Tab to go to the next prompt.)

7. Enter a new margin at the **Left margin:** prompt, if you want, and press Tab.

8. Enter a new margin at the **Right margin:** prompt, if you want, and press Tab.

9. After the **First page:** option, type the number of the page on which you want the header to begin.

Adding a Footer

To add a footer to your document, follow these steps:

1. Open the Format menu by pressing F4.

2. Select the **Set footer** option. The Footer screen is displayed.

3. Type the text you want to appear as the top line of the footer after the **Line 1:** prompt. You can type a footer until the text reaches the right edge of the screen.

4. Press Tab to get to **Line 2:**.

5. Enter the text for line 2 if you want to include a second footer line on your document. Press Tab when you are finished with **Line 2:**.

6. Indicate how you want the footer to be positioned by typing *b*, *u*, or *i* after the prompt. (N is the default, so if you want to select that option, simply press Tab to get to the next prompt.)

7. Enter a new margin for **Left margin:**, if you want, and press Tab.

8. Enter a new margin for **Right margin:**, if you want, and press Tab.

9. After the **First page:** option, type the number of the page on which you want the footer to begin.

Drawing a Line

To draw a line, follow these steps:

1. Position the cursor at the point in the document where you want the line to begin.

2. Open the Edit menu and select the **Draw lines** option.

3. Choose the **Turn drawing on/off** option or press Ctrl-Y.

4. Press the arrow key that will draw the line in the direction you want.

5. When you are finished drawing the line, press Ctrl-Y to deactivate the draw feature.

Changing Drawing Style

To change the style of the line you are drawing, follow these steps:

1. From the Edit menu, select **Draw lines**.

2. When the Drawing menu is displayed, choose **Select drawing style** and press Enter. The Drawing Styles menu is displayed.

3. Select the line style you want to use and press Enter.

Creating Custom Lines

To create a custom line, follow these steps:

1. From the Edit menu, select **Draw lines**.

2. When the Drawing menu is displayed, choose **Select drawing style** and press Enter.

3. From the Drawing Styles menu, select **Other** and press Enter.

4. Type the character you want to use (the character can be any character on the keyboard) and press Enter.

Erasing Lines

To erase a line, follow these steps:

1. Position the cursor where you want to begin erasing. (If drawing is still enabled, press Ctrl-Y to turn it off before you move the cursor.)

2. Turn drawing on by pressing Ctrl-Y.

3. Press the Shift key and press the cursor-movement key that will move the cursor in the direction you want to erase.

4. Repeat step 3 as necessary to delete the line.

5. Press Ctrl-Y to turn off the drawing feature and return to normal mode.

Drawing Boxes

To draw a box in Professional Write, follow these steps:

1. Position the cursor where you want to begin drawing the box.

2. Press Ctrl-Y to turn on the draw feature. (If you want to select the line style, select **Draw lines** from the Edit menu and then choose **Select drawing style**.)

3. Use the cursor-movement keys to draw the box. When you change directions (for example, if you had been pressing ↓ and you change to →), Professional Write draws the corner for you.

4. When the box is complete, press Ctrl-Y to deactivate the drawing feature.

Chapter Summary

In this chapter, you have seen a wide variety of features you can use to enhance your Professional Write documents. From a basic discussion of headers and footers to more specialized enhancement features like drawing lines and boxes, this chapter has given you many tips and suggestions for effectively designing and producing your enhanced Professional Write documents. In the next chapter, you will learn about installing and working with fonts. If your printer does not support font capability, you may want to skip the next chapter and proceed to Chapter 8, "Previewing and Printing Documents."

7

Understanding and Working with Fonts

Throughout this book, you have seen many references to fonts. In this short chapter, you will learn about the basics of understanding and working with fonts. Beginning with basic information (What are fonts? How do I know whether my printer supports fonts?), this chapter takes you through installation, selection, and troubleshooting operations that are necessary when you want to take advantage of the fonts supported by your printer.

As you know, not all printers support fonts. Professional Write mainly supports laser printer fonts, although fonts are available for some high-quality dot-matrix printers. (In other programs like PFS: First Publisher, dot-matrix fonts are offered that can produce a variety of different fonts on almost all dot-matrix printers but at a lower quality than those produced on a laser or high-quality dot-matrix printer.) If you are currently using a printer that does not support font capability and you have no access to a printer that does use fonts, you may want to skip this chapter and proceed to Chapter 8, "Previewing and Printing Documents."

Professional Write supports fonts for the following dot-matrix printers:

EPSON LQ-800/1000, LQ-500, LQ-850-1050, LQ-950, FX-850/1054
LQ-2500, LQ-2550

IBM ProPrinter X24/XL24, X24E/XL24E

187

IBM QuickWriter

Kyocera

OKIDATA 390, 393, 393C

Panasonic KX-P4450

Texas Instruments 875/877

Professional Write supports fonts for the following laser printers:

Apple LaserWriter family

AST TurboLaser /PS

Hewlett-Packard DeskJet (*Note:* This is an ink jet printer, not a laser printer, but its quality is significantly higher than dot-matrix quality. A full set of font cartridges is available for this printer.)

Hewlett-Packard LaserJet family

NEC family of laser printers

QMS PS 800 +

A Font Primer

This section introduces you to the basics of working with fonts. For more information on specific applications, like changing the font of a text block or specifying a header font, see the appropriate sections in other chapters.

What Are Fonts?

As you have learned elsewhere in this book, a *font* is one set of characters (A through Z and all numeric and punctuation symbols) in a specific typeface, size, and style. For example, Helvetica 14-point bold is one font, while Avant Garde 8-point is another.

All printers have some fonts built in. These are called *internal* fonts. Generally, these are not very high-quality fonts, providing perhaps a fixed-pitch or monospace font (like Courier) on some laser printers, or perhaps a line-printer font of some kind. Most printers have the capability of producing bold and underlined text, as well.

If you have a PostScript laser printer, you may have many more fonts available to you. For example, the QMS PS 800 + has 44 built-in fonts, including many fonts in the Times, New Century Schoolbook, Bookman, Palatino, and Avant Garde typefaces. Some dot-matrix printers support only one font (which appears as Normal font on the Select Font or Size screen), while others, like the EPSON LQ-2500, support several additional fonts from which you can choose.

How Do You Get Fonts?

You may be able to purchase more fonts for your laser printer. The type of font (and the packaging of the fonts) will depend on the type of printer you own. For example, if you use a Hewlett-Packard LaserJet or a DeskJet, you may be able to use font cartridges (small cartridges that you plug into your printer to give the printer additional font capability). You can also choose from a wide variety of *soft fonts*, which are fonts that are stored on disk and sent to your printer at print time. Not all laser printers support soft fonts, so check your printer's manual before you purchase any soft fonts.

Does Your Printer Support Fonts?

If you are unsure whether your printer supports fonts, you can do one of three things: you can look through the *Printer Manual* that was packaged with your Professional Write disks to find the capabilities of your particular printer; you can use the **Printer 1** option on the Setup menu to select your type of printer and see whether Professional Write asks you which font you want to use for the regular text; or you can look in your printer's manual.

> If your printer does not support fonts, Professional Write will not offer you the option of choosing a font for the document. If you highlight a block of text and try to change the font (by selecting **Change font or size** from the Text Block Operations menu), Professional Write displays the Select Font or Size screen with only one font—the current font—available. This font is shown as Normal font on the screen. You have no other options from which to choose.

If your printer supports fonts, you need to do several things:

1. Let Professional Write know that you have a printer that supports fonts.

2. Specify the type of fonts you want to use in your documents.

3. Know how to tell your printer at print time which fonts are being used.

The next few sections explain how to accomplish these things.

How Do You Install Fonts?

As you may recall from Chapter 2, you really don't install fonts; you tell Professional Write which printer you are going to use, and the program "knows" which fonts go with that printer. You set up the printer by following these steps:

1. Select **Setup** from the Main menu.

2. From the Setup menu, choose **Select printer 1**. When the printer screen is displayed, choose the printer that you will be using.

3. After you highlight and choose the printer you are using, press Tab to get to the right side of the screen, which lists the ports for your machine. If you need to change the port that is currently selected, move the highlight to that port and press Enter (see fig. 7.1).

4. If you are using a printer that supports fonts, Professional Write then displays the Select Regular Font screen. On this screen, you choose the font that will be used for the body text of your documents (see fig. 7.2).

5. If you are planning to connect your printer to a serial port (COM1 or COM2), Professional Write displays a Serial Port Settings screen that asks for some additional information about the way data will be sent to the printer.

6. Press Enter. Professional Write then returns you to the Main Menu.

Installing Font Cartridges and Soft Fonts

Professional Write supports a variety of soft fonts and font cartridges for the Hewlett-Packard LaserJet family of printers. Because these fonts are not built into the printer, you must tell Professional Write where to find them so that they can be found at print time.

When you choose a Hewlett-Packard printer from the Printers menu, a secondary menu is displayed, offering you the option of selecting a font car-

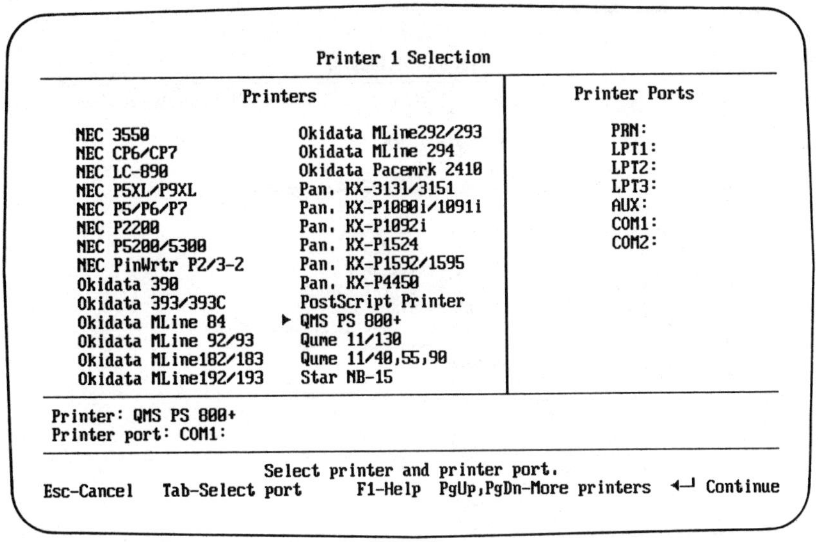

```
                        Printer 1 Selection

              Printers                        Printer Ports

   NEC 3550           Okidata MLine292/293        PRN:
   NEC CP6/CP7        Okidata MLine 294           LPT1:
   NEC LC-890         Okidata Pacemrk 2410        LPT2:
   NEC P5XL/P9XL      Pan, KX-3131/3151           LPT3:
   NEC P5/P6/P7       Pan, KX-P1080i/1091i        AUX:
   NEC P2200          Pan, KX-P1092i              COM1:
   NEC P5200/5300     Pan, KX-P1524               COM2:
   NEC PinWrtr P2/3-2 Pan, KX-P1592/1595
   Okidata 390        Pan, KX-P4450
   Okidata 393/393C   PostScript Printer
   Okidata MLine 84 ▶ QMS PS 800+
   Okidata MLine 92/93   Qume 11/130
   Okidata MLine182/183  Qume 11/40,55,90
   Okidata MLine192/193  Star NB-15

   Printer: QMS PS 800+
   Printer port: COM1:

                    Select printer and printer port,
   Esc-Cancel    Tab-Select port     F1-Help  PgUp,PgDn-More printers  ↵ Continue
```

Figure 7.1. *Selecting a printer.*

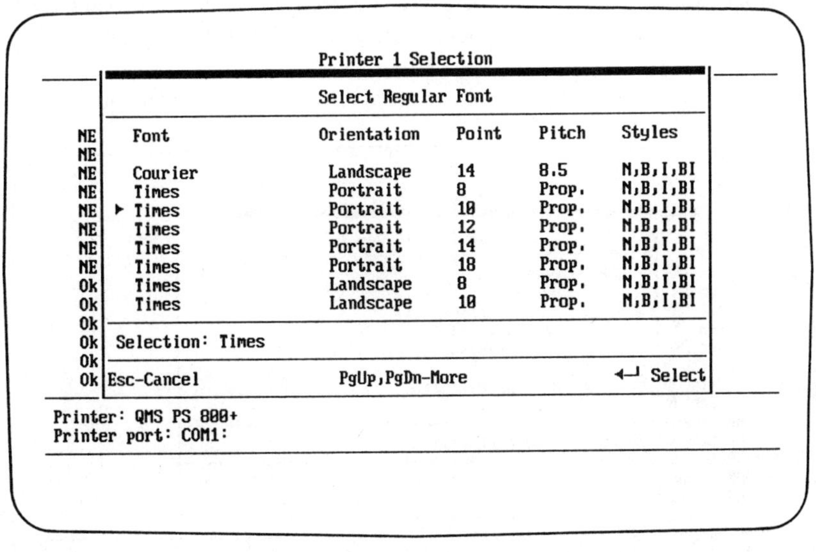

```
                        Printer 1 Selection

                      Select Regular Font

   NE
   NE
   NE    Font           Orientation    Point    Pitch    Styles
   NE
   NE    Courier        Landscape      14       8.5      N,B,I,BI
   NE    Times          Portrait       8        Prop.    N,B,I,BI
   NE  ▶ Times          Portrait       10       Prop.    N,B,I,BI
   NE    Times          Portrait       12       Prop.    N,B,I,BI
   NE    Times          Portrait       14       Prop.    N,B,I,BI
   NE    Times          Portrait       18       Prop.    N,B,I,BI
   Ok    Times          Landscape      8        Prop.    N,B,I,BI
   Ok    Times          Landscape      10       Prop.    N,B,I,BI
   Ok
   Ok    Selection: Times
   Ok
   Ok  Esc-Cancel              PgUp,PgDn-More              ↵ Select

   Printer: QMS PS 800+
   Printer port: COM1:
```

Figure 7.2. *Changing the font of a marked block of text.*

tridge or a soft font family for the printer, or changing the regular font or
the soft font directory. Depending on the model of printer you choose, the
name of the menu may be different from the one shown in figure 7.3.

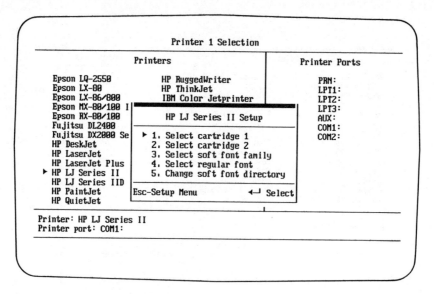

Figure 7.3. *The Hewlett-Packard LaserJet Series II Setup menu.*

If you are working with font cartridges, you need to select **Select cartridge
1**. The program then displays another menu with a list of cartridges available for that printer (see fig. 7.4). Highlight the one you plan to use and
press Enter. Professional Write then returns you to the Setup menu.

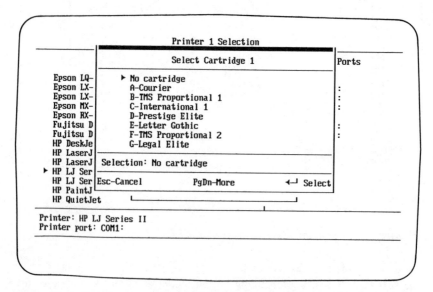

Figure 7.4. *Professional Write displays the cartridges available for your
printer.*

If you need to install soft fonts, choose **Select soft font family** from the Setup menu. Again, Professional Write displays the available soft fonts for the printer you chose (see fig. 7.5). Select the soft font family you will be using and press Enter.

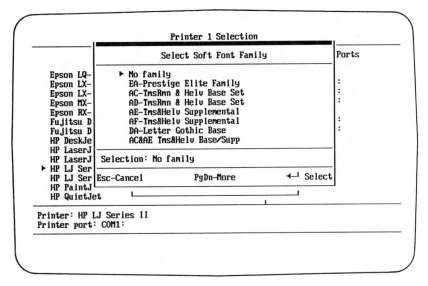

Figure 7.5. *The program lists available soft fonts.*

If you have stored the soft fonts in their own directory and want Professional Write to download them automatically at print time, you also need to tell the program where the fonts are stored. To do this, select **Change soft font directory** from the Setup menu. When the directory box is displayed, enter the path along which Professional Write will look to find the soft font files (see fig. 7.6).

Now that you have installed the cartridges and soft fonts for your printer, at print time you simply press *Y* to the **Download soft fonts: (Y/N)** option on the Print Options menu, and Professional Write does the rest.

What Is Orientation?

When working with fonts, *orientation* is the way in which the text is printed on the page. On the Select Font or Size screen (displayed either after you choose a laser printer on the Printers menu or after you select **Change font**

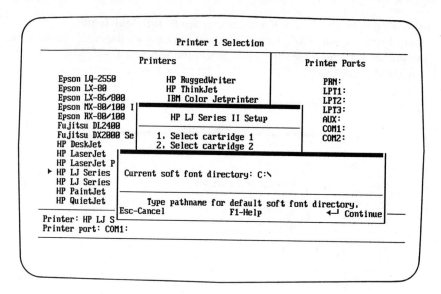

Figure 7.6. Changing the soft font directory.

or size from the text operations menus), you may see many fonts listed. Each of these fonts is shown as having either a portrait or landscape orientation.

Put simply, *portrait* orientation is used for documents that are printed the conventional way on 8 1/2-by-11-inch paper. Certain fonts are available in *landscape* mode, which means that you can turn the paper and print the document lengthwise across the now 11-by-8 1/2-inch paper. Landscape orientation is useful for a variety of documents, such as handouts, training materials, and advertising fliers.

Remember that you must use portrait fonts when you use portrait mode and landscape fonts for landscape mode; otherwise, your printer may hang up, continue printing a series of blank pages, or both.

How Do You Choose Fonts for Your Document?

As you already know, when you choose a printer that supports fonts from the Printers screen, the Select Font or Size screen is displayed so that you can choose the font you want to use as the basic font for the text in your document. What happens, however, if you want to change the font of a particular paragraph?

To change the font for a block of text, simply highlight the block, press F10, and select **Change font or size** from the Text Block Operations menu that is displayed (see fig. 7.7). When the Select Font or Size window appears, choose the font you want to use and press Enter.

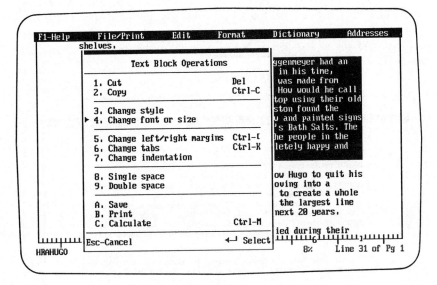

Figure 7.7. Changing the font of selected text.

You can also change the font being used for headers or footers you have specified by pressing F8 after you type the header or footer. (For more information about headers and footers, see Chapter 6.)

> If you want to change the style of a block of text but you want to retain the font and size you have chosen, highlight the block, press F10, and select **Change style** from the Text Block Operations menu that is displayed.

How Do Fonts Appear On-Screen?

The font that you see on the screen will always look the same, whether you choose 18-point bold New Century Schoolbook or 10-point Times. If you choose a block of text and assign it a font different from the one currently used as the document default font, that block will appear highlighted on the screen, but the font of the characters will not appear different. Professional Write uses a standard 10-point font as the on-screen display font, giving you 10 characters per inch, no matter what size the font will be when it is printed. (Hence, again, the need for the preview feature.)

You can tell what font has been chosen for a particular block of text by positioning the cursor in that block and looking at the status line at the bottom of the screen. In that line, you see the name of the font, the orientation, the size, and any style (such as boldface or italic) that has been chosen for the font (see fig. 7.8).

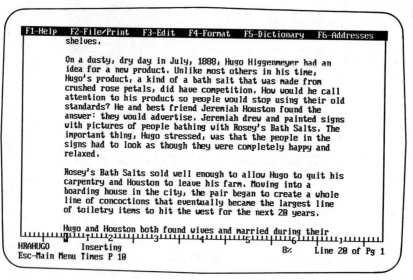

Figure 7.8. *Determining which font has been used.*

What Is Font Format?

When you get ready to print, you will see on the Print Options menu a selection called **Font format**. How does choosing this setting affect your document as it prints?

Typing *5* after the **Print style:** option on the Print Options menu tells Professional Write that you want the file to be printed in font format. Put simply, *font format* prints font characters in their correct sizes and styles while preserving the margins you have set for the document. The result may be a document that is different from the one you saw in preview mode; font format may wrap lines and change the form of paragraphs in order to preserve your margins.

Without font format, however, your document would appear as you see it on the Create/Edit screen. This means that even though you use a proportional font that could fit more characters on a line than the on-screen font, the lines will break at the places shown on-screen, giving you a document with shorter, choppier lines. It's best to use font format if you are working with proportional fonts in your documents. Figure 7.9 shows how a document appears when printed without font format; figure 7.10 shows the same document printed when font format has been selected.

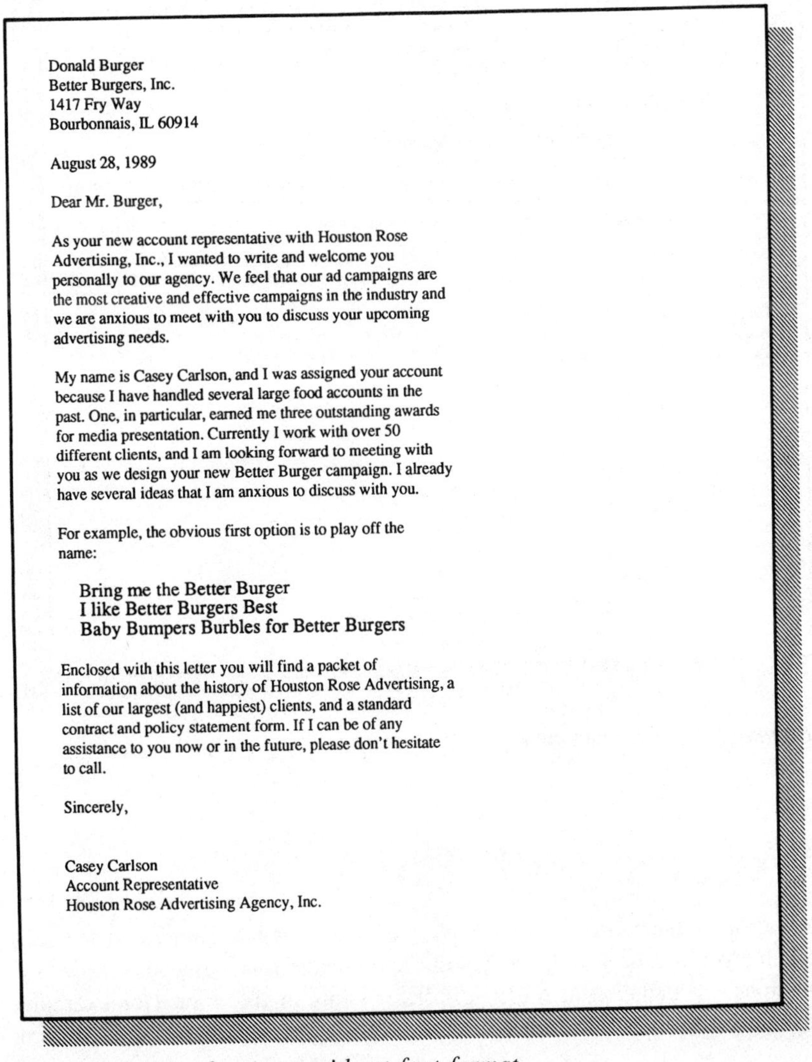

Donald Burger
Better Burgers, Inc.
1417 Fry Way
Bourbonnais, IL 60914

August 28, 1989

Dear Mr. Burger,

As your new account representative with Houston Rose
Advertising, Inc., I wanted to write and welcome you
personally to our agency. We feel that our ad campaigns are
the most creative and effective campaigns in the industry and
we are anxious to meet with you to discuss your upcoming
advertising needs.

My name is Casey Carlson, and I was assigned your account
because I have handled several large food accounts in the
past. One, in particular, earned me three outstanding awards
for media presentation. Currently I work with over 50
different clients, and I am looking forward to meeting with
you as we design your new Better Burger campaign. I already
have several ideas that I am anxious to discuss with you.

For example, the obvious first option is to play off the
name:

Bring me the Better Burger
I like Better Burgers Best
Baby Bumpers Burbles for Better Burgers

Enclosed with this letter you will find a packet of
information about the history of Houston Rose Advertising, a
list of our largest (and happiest) clients, and a standard
contract and policy statement form. If I can be of any
assistance to you now or in the future, please don't hesitate
to call.

Sincerely,

Casey Carlson
Account Representative
Houston Rose Advertising Agency, Inc.

Figure 7.9. The document without font format.

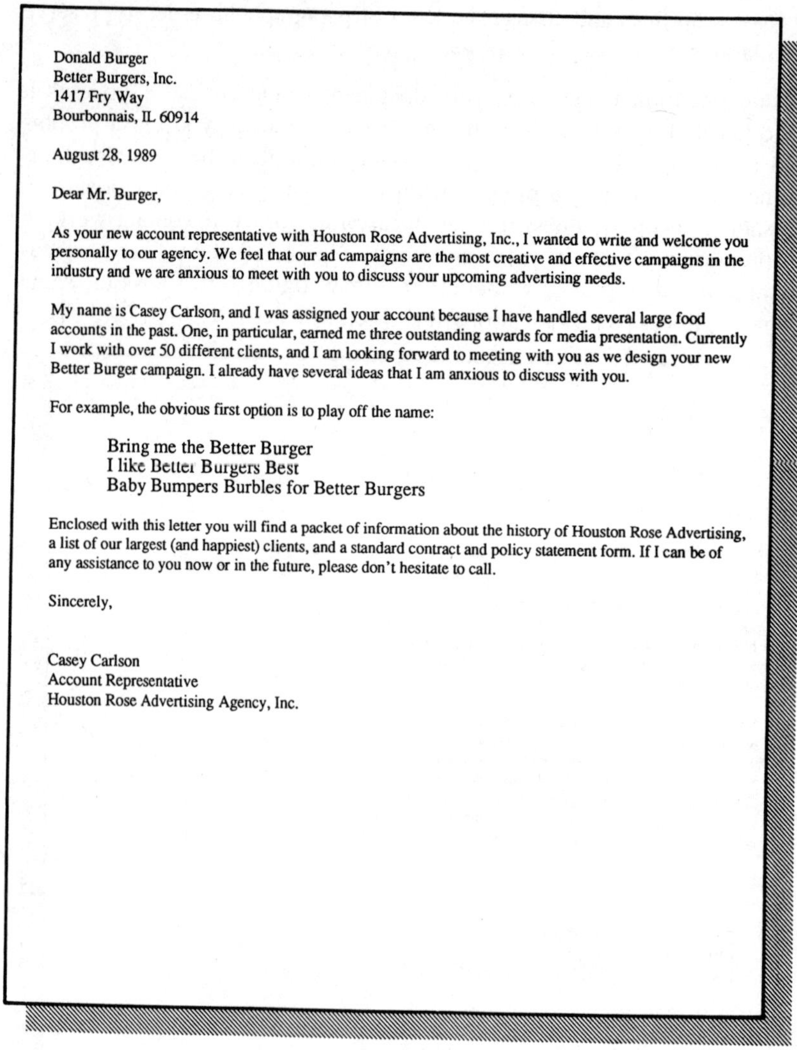

Donald Burger
Better Burgers, Inc.
1417 Fry Way
Bourbonnais, IL 60914

August 28, 1989

Dear Mr. Burger,

As your new account representative with Houston Rose Advertising, Inc., I wanted to write and welcome you personally to our agency. We feel that our ad campaigns are the most creative and effective campaigns in the industry and we are anxious to meet with you to discuss your upcoming advertising needs.

My name is Casey Carlson, and I was assigned your account because I have handled several large food accounts in the past. One, in particular, earned me three outstanding awards for media presentation. Currently I work with over 50 different clients, and I am looking forward to meeting with you as we design your new Better Burger campaign. I already have several ideas that I am anxious to discuss with you.

For example, the obvious first option is to play off the name:

       Bring me the Better Burger
       I like Better Burgers Best
       Baby Bumpers Burbles for Better Burgers

Enclosed with this letter you will find a packet of information about the history of Houston Rose Advertising, a list of our largest (and happiest) clients, and a standard contract and policy statement form. If I can be of any assistance to you now or in the future, please don't hesitate to call.

Sincerely,

Casey Carlson
Account Representative
Houston Rose Advertising Agency, Inc.

Figure 7.10. The document with font format.

Working with Fonts

In various other places in this book, you have seen references to the procedures you use to install, work with, and change fonts. Because those discussions are included at the appropriate points in the book (for example, changing the font of a block of text is discussed in Chapter 5, "Editing

---

Using *FORMAT* Commands

Occasionally, you may be working with a document for which you want to use the font format only sparingly. For example, perhaps in some parts of the document you want the margins to appear as they are shown on-screen, and in other parts you want the font format to be in effect. You can insert *FORMAT* commands directly into the document so that Professional Write knows where to turn font format on and off.

In the blank line before the place where you want the font format to begin, type the following line:

   FORMAT YES

Remember to enclose the command in asterisks. If you prefer, you can abbreviate the command as *f y*. (*Note:* Professional Write recognizes this command whether you use uppercase or lowercase.)

At the point where you want the font format to end, position the cursor in the blank line and type the following line:

   FORMAT NO

Again, you can abbreviate the command as *f n*, if you choose.

Documents''), the explanation of fonts may seem fragmented. For the sake of completeness, this section includes the various procedures you will use as you set, modify, and work with fonts in your Professional Write documents.

Specifying the Regular Font

As you may recall, when you first install Professional Write, you tell the program what printer you are planning to use by selecting **Setup** from the Main Menu and **Select printer 1** from the Setup Menu. After you choose the printer you want from the Select Printer 1 screen and press Enter, Professional Write ''sees'' whether you have chosen a printer that supports fonts. If you have chosen a font printer, the program displays the Select Regular Font screen. On this screen, you choose the font you want to use as the regular text in your Professional Write documents. Position the highlight on the font you want and press Enter.

Changing Fonts

You have a couple of options for changing the font once you have specified the regular font. If you are sure that you want to change the font you have chosen for all your Professional Write documents, you can change the font you have selected for the regular font. If you want to make a more limited change and modify only the font selected for a portion of the document, you can change the font for a selected block of text. Lastly, if you want to change all occurrences of a specific font you have used, you can use the **Change a font** option (available in preview mode) to change all places where the font you specify has been used.

Changing the Regular Font

You can change the regular font at any time by returning to the Setup Menu and repeating the process you used to select the regular font as part of the printer installation procedure.

Changing the Font for a Text Block

You may, however, want to change only a portion of a document to another font. In this case, you highlight the block you want to change, press F10, and select the **Change font or size** option from either the Text Block Operations menu or the Regular Block Operations menu. When the Select Font or Size menu is displayed (this is the same menu as the Select Regular Font menu—except that it has a different name displayed at the top), choose the font you want by moving the highlight to the font and pressing Enter.

When you return to the document, the block you changed will appear bold-faced on-screen (the actual font chosen will not be displayed), and the status line at the bottom of the screen will display the name, size, and orientation of the font that is active for that block.

Changing the Font from within Preview

From within preview, you can change fonts in the following instances:

❑ The current line

❑ All subsequent lines in the same font

❑ All occurrences of the specified font in the working copy

To change a font in preview mode, follow these steps:

1. Make sure that the document is displayed in close-up view. (If it is not, press Alt-V.)

2. Position the cursor so that it is placed in the section with the font you want to change.

3. Open the Fonts menu by pressing F3.

4. Choose the **Change a font** option. (You also can press Alt-F if you want to bypass the menu selections.) Preview automatically highlights the text that is in the same font as the font at the cursor position. Then, without further intervention from you, Professional Write displays the Select Font or Size screen.

5. Choose the font you want and press Enter.

6. Professional Write then asks whether you want to change all occurrences of the font to the font you specified. Press N if you want only to change the currently highlighted block.

7. Press Enter, and Professional Write replaces the highlighted font with the new font.

In the next section, you will be introduced to some of the common problems and solutions involved in working with fonts.

Troubleshooting Font Problems

If everything doesn't work perfectly the first time you print the document, don't worry. Once you get the procedure worked out for your particular printer, printing will be a breeze.

The discrepancy between the way the document appears in the Create/Edit screen and the way it looks when printed is disheartening for some new users; that is why getting familiar with using preview mode is important. By examining—and modifying, if necessary—your document in preview mode, you can cut much revision work out of your word processing time.

Remember, however, that even preview mode is an approximate display of the final product. Your document may still look different than you expect.

For more information about fonts and special print considerations for your particular printer, consult the *Printers* manual that was packaged with your Professional Write disks.

Box Problems

One of the most common font problems is actually a drawing problem:

> "This text box I created with the drawing feature looked straight on the screen, but when I printed the document, the right edge of the box was all over the place."

If you are drawing a box or adding lines around text, you need to use a monospace (fixed-pitch) font so that all the lines are the same length, and the right edge of the box aligns properly.

This problem is caused by the variable widths of the characters in proportional fonts (see fig. 7.11). For example, in a proportional font, the letter W takes up more room than the letter i. With a monospace font, each letter takes up the same amount of space.

> When you are creating a text box, use a fixed-pitch font for the text so that the right edge of the box aligns properly.

Line Problems

A second common problem again involves the use of the drawing feature and fonts:

> "I drew a line down the left edge of the document and it appeared correct on-screen, but when I printed the document, parts of the line wound up in the middle of the paragraph."

This problem is caused by font format. Once you draw a line in the document, Professional Write sees the line characters as it sees any other character in the document. When you press Enter, the line moves down. When you position the cursor and press Del, you delete a section of the line.

When font format is active, the program may rewrap lines and reformat paragraphs in order to conform to the margins you have set for the document. In this particular case, when Professional Write reformatted the paragraph, it didn't recognize the line characters as being part of a line and reformatted all the characters to fit the margins. Therefore, parts of the line got mixed in with the text in the paragraph.

To fix this problem, make sure that when the Print Options menu is displayed, you do not select **Font format** in the **Print Styles:** section.

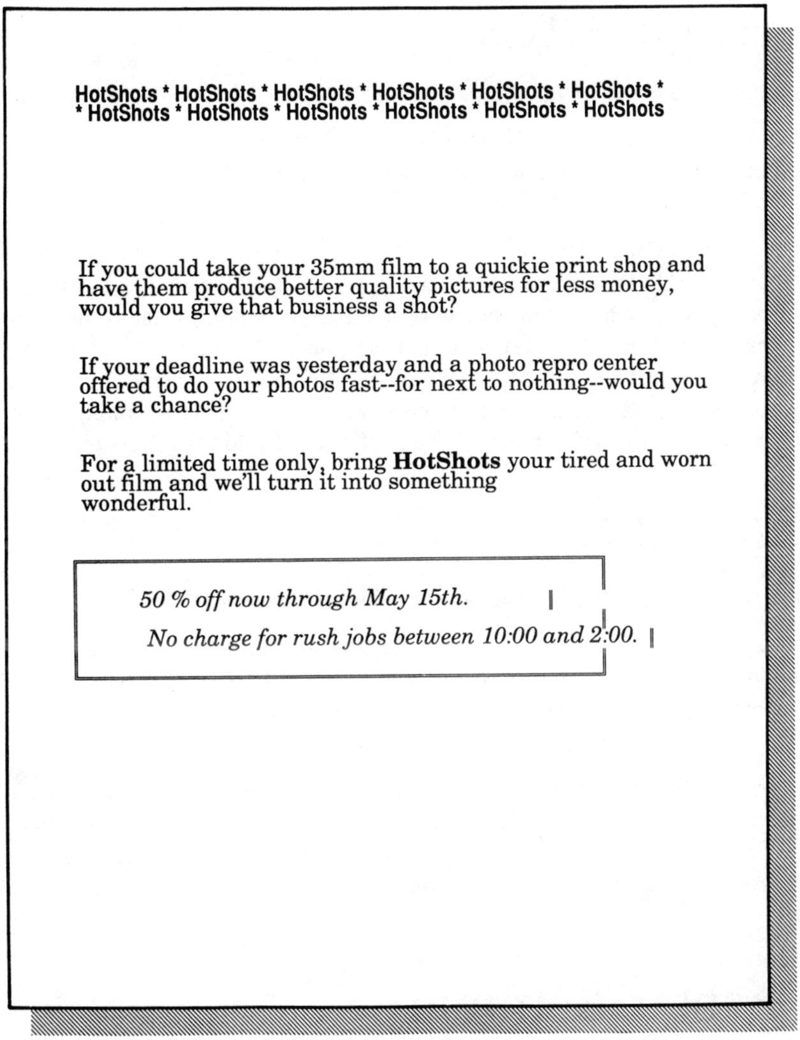

HotShots * HotShots * HotShots * HotShots * HotShots * HotShots *
* HotShots * HotShots * HotShots * HotShots * HotShots * HotShots

If you could take your 35mm film to a quickie print shop and
have them produce better quality pictures for less money,
would you give that business a shot?

If your deadline was yesterday and a photo repro center
offered to do your photos fast--for next to nothing--would you
take a chance?

For a limited time only, bring **HotShots** your tired and worn
out film and we'll turn it into something
wonderful.

> *50 % off now through May 15th.*
>
> *No charge for rush jobs between 10:00 and 2:00.*

Figure 7.11. *A box printed out of alignment.*

If you have added lines or boxes to your document, try turning
Font format off if the lines in your document print incorrectly.

Uncentered Text

Another problem involves the positioning of text:

> "After entering a title for my report, I selected **Center text** from the Format menu. The title looked centered on-screen, but when I printed it, it was too far to the right."

If a section of text that you specified to be centered turns out to be off-center, return to the document and check whether you had added any spaces before the text. When Professional Write centers the text, it takes into consideration any characters on that line. If you had pressed the space bar before you typed the text and centered the line, the program centered the text and space characters. The difference on the screen may be minimal, but when printed, you notice that the spaces throw the title off the center point.

Crowded Text

One common problem involves the spacing of large fonts:

> "I used a large font to highlight the title and subtitle of my report, and the titles looked fine in preview, but when I printed the document, the lines of text were too close together."

Because larger fonts take up more space than smaller fonts, you may need to arrange for more room between lines when you use larger fonts. To solve the spacing problem, double-space the text by selecting **Double space** from the Text Block Operations menu or by choosing **Turn double spacing on/off** from the Format menu before you type the text.

Chapter Summary

In this chapter, you learned the basics about fonts: how to find out whether your printer supports them; how to tell Professional Write which fonts you want to use; and how to troubleshoot font problems.

In the next chapter, you learn to turn your Professional Write document into a final, printed copy by using the preview and printing features.

8

Previewing and Printing Documents

T o this point, you have learned to create, edit, and enhance Professional Write documents. In this chapter, you learn how to use the program's preview capability and how to print your document.

Professional Write's preview feature enables you to see approximately how your document will look when it is printed—complete with font changes, formats, and special effects like imported graphs.

Why Do You Need Preview?

Some word processing programs boast what they call WYSIWYG (pro-nounced *wizzy-wig*) displays. WYSIWYG is an acronym for ''what you see is what you get,'' meaning that in those programs, what you see on-screen is what you get in print.

Because Professional Write supports a wide range of fonts, the Create/Edit screen does not give you an accurate representation of the final, printed document. The text shown on the Create/Edit screen is comprised of stan-dard 10 point characters, while the text, when printed, may be anywhere from 8 to 18 points in whatever typeface you specify.

Because the text on the Create/Edit screen is always the same size even though the printed characters may be larger or smaller, users of the program need a way to see how the document will look when it is printed. Otherwise, how do you know, for example, how much room is required for a heading that is to be printed in 18-point Helvetica? Or 8-point Avant Garde? Hence the creation of the preview feature, new with Professional Write 2.1. The preview feature shows you the effects of all the different fonts, sizes, and styles. You can also get an idea of the formats, margins, indentations, and lines you have added to the document.

For example, figure 8.1 shows a typical document in the Create/Edit mode. Figure 8.2 shows the same document in preview mode. Although difficult to see in the reduced figure size used in this book, the title and the headlines are in a larger font.

Understanding Preview

The purpose of preview is to give you an on-screen idea of how the document will look when it is printed. Preview shows you the placement of text, the style of headlines, the style and size of titles, the position of imported graphs, the approximate margins, and the page breaks of your document.

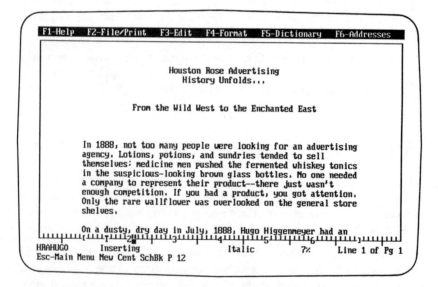

Fig. 8.1. A typical document in the Create/Edit screen.

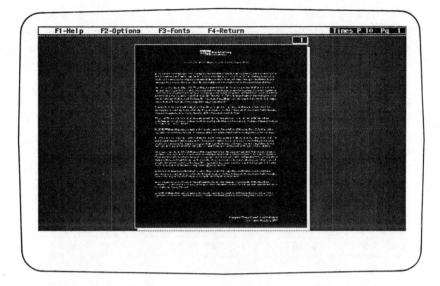

Fig. 8.2. The preview screen for the document.

If you select Font format when you specify the **Print style:** option on the Print Option menu (just before printing), the format of the text may differ from the display in preview mode.

From within preview, you can do the following things:

❑ Change the view from a full-page to a close-up view or vice versa

❑ Change the font for a section or word

❑ Set the print styles for the document

❑ List the fonts used in the document

❑ Change the size of the displayed page

❑ Display a list of all available fonts

The Preview Menu Bar

Before you begin previewing your documents, you need to become familiar with the different options and menus available in preview mode. As you may know, you activate the preview feature by selecting **Preview working copy** from the File/Print menu. (You can also do this by pressing the speed key combination Ctrl-O.)

With the preview mode comes a new menu bar, as shown in figure 8.3. The menus on this bar—Options, Fonts, and Return—are described in the following sections. On the far right end of the menu bar appear the current page number and the name, size, and orientation of the font at the cursor position.

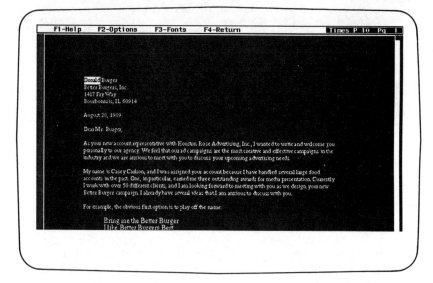

Fig. 8.3. The preview menu bar.

You open menus on the preview menu bar by pressing the function key next to the menu name:

Press	To open
F1	Help
F2	Options menu
F3	Fonts menu
F4	Return menu

All menu items have speed keys, so you can bypass the menu selections completely if you want. As you begin to use preview, you may want to open the menus and select the options so that you can get familiar with the placement and function of each option. As you become proficient with the preview feature, you may want to use the speed keys to get around faster. Table 8.1 shows all the speed keys available for preview mode.

Table 8.1
Speed Keys Available with Preview Mode

Speed Key	Option	Menu
Alt-V	Change view	Options
Alt-S	Set print style	Options
Alt-P	Change paper size	Options
Alt-F	Change a font	Fonts
Alt-D	List fonts in document	Fonts
Alt-A	List available fonts	Fonts
Esc	Return to current position	Return
Alt-X	Return to starting position	Return

The Options Menu

On the Options menu, the options for changing the view, print styles, and paper size are displayed (see fig. 8.4). Table 8.2 highlights the selections on the Options menu.

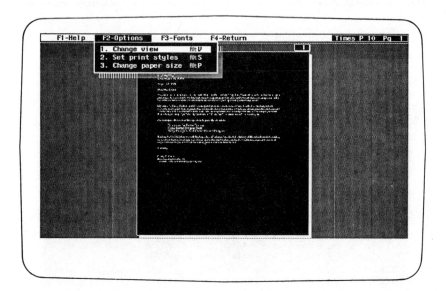

Fig. 8.4. The Options menu.

Table 8.2
Options on the Options Menu

Option	Speed Key	Description
Change view	Alt-V	Enables you to change from a full-page (or two-page) view to a close-up view of the document
Set print styles	Alt-S	Similar to this option on the Print Options menu, enables you to choose from a variety of text styles
Change paper size	Alt-P	Enables you to change the size of the paper displayed in preview; does not affect the printed page

The Fonts Menu

The Fonts menu provides you with options for determining which fonts can be used for your document and for changing fonts, if necessary (see fig. 8.5). Table 8.3 describes the options available on this menu.

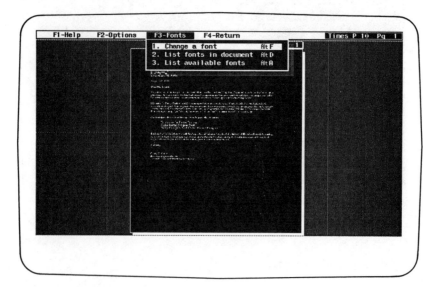

Fig. 8.5. The Fonts menu.

Table 8.3
Options on the Fonts Menu

Option	Speed Key	Description
Change a font	Alt-F	Enables you to change the font you have chosen for a particular block of text
List fonts in document	Alt-D	Enables you to list all fonts used in the current document
List available fonts	Alt-A	Enables you to list all currently available fonts supported by your printer

The Return Menu

As you might expect, the Return menu is responsible for returning you to the document after you have used preview (see fig. 8.6). Table 8.4 highlights the options available on the Return menu.

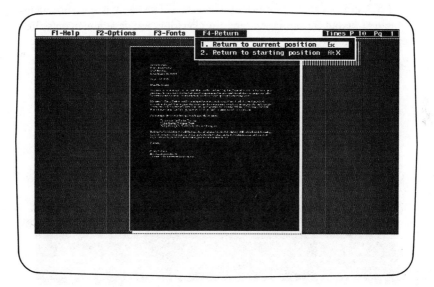

Fig. 8.6. The Return menu.

▼
Table 8.4
Options on the Return Menu

Option	Speed Key	Description
Return to current position	Esc	Returns you to the document at the place where the preview cursor appears in the view
Return to starting position	Alt-X	Returns you to the beginning of the document

Understanding Views

When you first start preview, the document is shown in a full-page view, meaning that the entire page is displayed on the screen. You probably cannot make out individual characters because of the size of the text.

Full-Page View

Figure 8.7 shows a document in full-page view. This view is good for gauging the text layout of the screen, and for checking any design elements, like lines or indents.

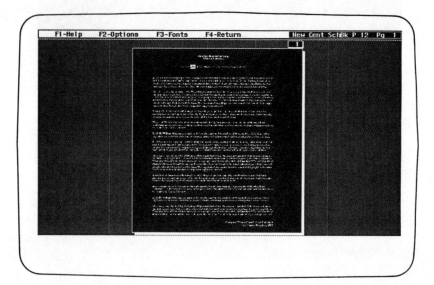

Fig. 8.7. A full-page view in preview.

When a document is first displayed in preview, it appears in the full-page view, with the first page of the document shown alone on the screen. When you press PgDn, a second page is placed next to the first (see fig. 8.8). Each time you press PgDn, another page is added to the right side of the screen, and the previous left page is moved off the screen.

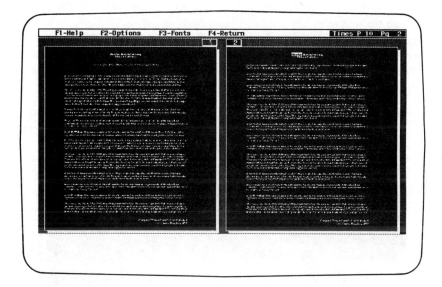

Fig. 8.8. *Two pages in full-page view.*

You cannot edit or modify font selections while the document is displayed in full-page view. However, while you are using the full-page view, you can do the following things:

❏ Change print styles

❏ List available fonts

❏ Use the option in the Return menu to go back to the document you are previewing

If you want to change the font you have used or look at the text in the document, you need to change to a close-up view.

Close-Up View

You can change to the close-up view in one of two ways: by opening the Options menu and selecting **Change view**; or by pressing the speed key combination, Alt-V.

After you change the view, the top of the document is shown in the screen with all the font sizes and attributes displayed (see fig. 8.9). *Note:* Although the font *sizes* are represented accurately in the close-up screen, the actual font—such as Times, Helvetica, and so on—is not shown. Professional Write uses a standard proportional on-screen font to represent the font chosen.

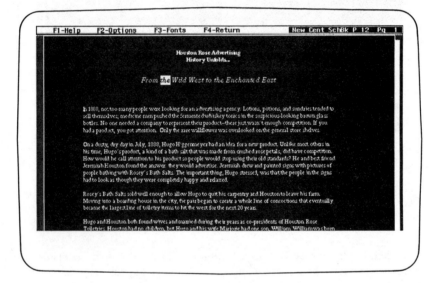

Fig. 8.9. *The font sizes are shown in close-up view.*

When you are using the close-up view, you can do the following tasks:

❏ Change the font chosen for a section or a word

❏ Modify the selected print style

❏ Display a different paper size

❏ Return to the document

The following sections describe how to move the cursor in both full-page and close-up views and explain further how to perform operations from within preview.

Using the Word Cursor

When you are in normal Create/Edit mode, the cursor takes the shape of either a small flashing underscore (which means you are in replace mode) or a character-sized flashing box (which means you are in insert mode). In preview mode, the cursor becomes the size of the word at the cursor position, hence the name *word cursor*.

Actually, the word cursor functions more as a pointer than a cursor. Although you cannot edit the word at the cursor position, you can determine which font the word has been assigned (the font name, size, and orientation are displayed in the upper right corner of the screen), and you can use the cursor as a marker to show Professional Write where to return in the document.

Table 8.5 lists the cursor-movement keys for moving the word cursor in both full-page and close-up views.

Table 8.5
Keys for Moving the Word Cursor

Use This Key	To Move This Direction
↑	Up one line
↓	Down one line
→	Right one word
←	Left one word
Home	Beginning of line
End	End of line
PgUp	Full-page: Previous page Close-up: Previous screen
PgDn	Full-page: Next page Close-up: Next screen
Ctrl-PgUp	Previous page
Ctrl-PgDn	Next page

Using Preview

This section highlights the steps involved in using the many features of preview. As you know, you can begin preview by selecting **Preview working copy** from the File/Print menu or by pressing Ctrl-PrtSc at any point in the program.

Changing the View

After you activate preview, the first page of the document is shown in full-page view. To change the view, follow these steps:

1. Position the word cursor in the portion of the document you want to view. (Remember that in a close up view, Professional Write can display only a portion of the page at one time.)

2. Open the Options menu by pressing F2.

3. Select the **Change view** option. (You can also press Alt-V to bypass the menu selections, if you prefer.)

4. Press Enter. Professional Write then displays the document in close-up view. If you want to view a different section of the document, use the cursor-movement keys (refer to table 8.5).

To change back to a full-page view, press Alt-V.

Modifying the Previewed Document

The modifications you can make to the previewed document are limited, but you can change the print style or the paper size of the document.

Changing Print Styles

On the Print Options menu, a **Print style:** setting is displayed. You also can change the print style from within preview mode. You can choose from the following print styles:

❏ Normal

❏ Justified

❏ Compressed

❏ Letter-quality

❏ Font format

You can select more than one print style. For example, you may want to choose items 1 and 5 (**Normal** and **Font format**), so that the text is printed normally but in font format. When you use font format, however, the **Compressed** and **Letter-quality** styles may not have any effect. Chapter 7 provides more information about using **Font format** in your documents.

To change the print style you have selected for the document, follow these steps:

1. When preview is active, open the Options menu by pressing F2.

2. Select the **Set print styles** option. (You can bypass the menu selections by pressing Alt-S, if you choose.) The Print Styles menu is then displayed. Any styles you have previously selected on the Print Options menu will be highlighted.

3. On the Print Styles menu, type the number(s) of the style(s) you want to use. (In this case, type *3*.)

4. Press Enter. Professional Write then updates the file and displays the preview page with the new style in effect (see fig. 8.10.).

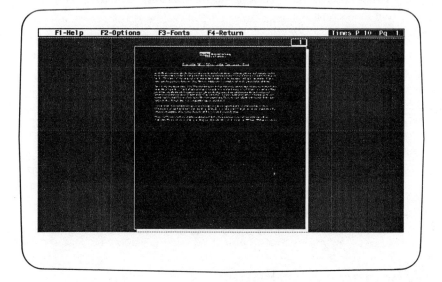

Fig. 8.10. *The preview screen after a new style is selected.*

To remove print styles, open the Options menu and select **Set Print Styles**. When the Print Styles menu is displayed, either type the number of the selected style (this disables the style), highlight the style and press Enter, or move the highlight to the style and press the space bar.

Changing the Displayed Paper Size

As you know, you can modify the paper length setting in Professional Write so that you can print on a variety of paper sizes. When you preview a page, Professional Write defaults to a standard 8 1/2-by-11-inch page. The **Change paper size** option on the Options menu enables you to change the size of the page you view.

Changing the paper size of the previewed document does not affect the way the document is printed. To change the paper size for printing, choose the **Set top/bottom margins & length** option from the Format menu.

To change the paper size of the displayed document, follow these steps:

1. When the document is being displayed in preview mode, open the Options menu by pressing F2.

2. Select the **Change paper size** option. (You can also press Alt-P to bypass the menu selections, if you prefer.) The Paper Size menu is then displayed (see fig. 8.11).

3. On the Paper Size menu, select the paper size to which you want to change the preview display. (In this case, select **Legal**.)

4. Press Enter. Professional Write then shows the document in the new paper size you have chosen (see fig. 8.12).

Working with Fonts

This section introduces you to the options for working with fonts while in preview mode. From within preview, you can examine current font choices, change fonts, list all fonts used in the document, and list all available fonts.

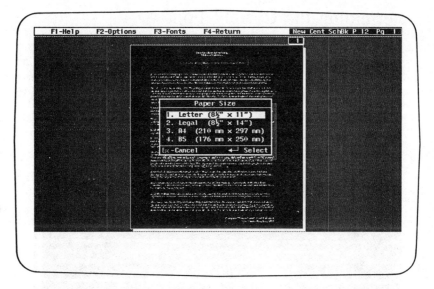

Fig. 8.11. The Paper Size menu.

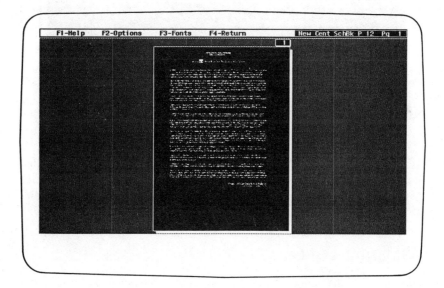

Fig. 8.12. The document displayed in the new paper size.

Determining the Current Font

As mentioned earlier in this chapter, the word cursor in part functions as a pointer, enabling you to move to certain areas of the document to determine which font has been assigned to the text. To find out what font is used for a specific text block, simply move the word cursor to that section and look in the upper right corner of the screen (see fig. 8.13).

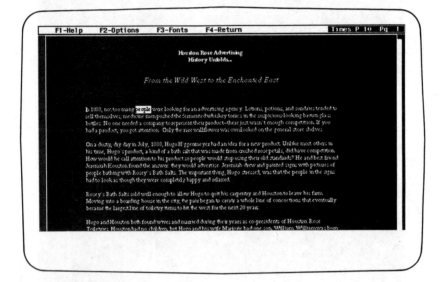

Fig. 8.13. *Finding the current font.*

As you can see, the word cursor in figure 8.13 is positioned on a word that is assigned the font Times P 10. This tells you that the current font for that block is in the Times typeface, has a portrait orientation, and 10-point sized type. (For more about orientation and fonts, see Chapter 7.)

Changing Fonts

You also have the option of changing the font at the cursor position. From within preview, you can change fonts in the following instances:

❑ The current line

❑ All subsequent lines in the same font

❑ All occurrences of the specified font in the working copy

To change a font in preview mode, follow these steps:

1. Make sure that the document is displayed in close-up view. (If it is not, press Alt-V.)

2. Position the cursor so that it is placed in the section with the font you want to change.

3. Open the Fonts menu by pressing F3.

4. Choose the **Change a font** option. (You can also press Alt-F if you want to bypass the menu selections.) Professional Write highlights the text that is in the same font as the font at the cursor position and then displays the Select Font or Size screen (see fig. 8.14).

5. Choose the font you want and press Enter.

6. Professional Write then asks whether you want to change all occurrences of the font to the font you specified. Press N if you want only to change the currently highlighted block.

7. Press Enter, and Professional Write replaces the highlighted font with the new font.

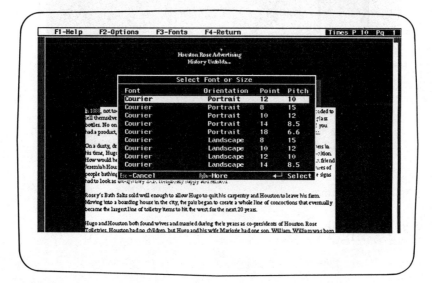

Fig. 8.14. *All text in the same font as the font at the cursor position is highlighted.*

Listing Fonts in a Previewed Document

With preview, you can also list all the fonts used in the document you are previewing. To list the fonts that have been assigned to the document in the working copy, follow these steps:

1. Open the Fonts menu by pressing F3.

2. Choose the **List fonts in document** option by highlighting the option and pressing Enter or by typing the number to the left of the option. (You also can press Alt-D to bypass the menu, if you prefer.)

Professional Write then displays a list of fonts in the document (see fig. 8.15). If any of the fonts in the document are not supported by the printer you have installed with Professional Write, an asterisk (*) is displayed beside the font name.

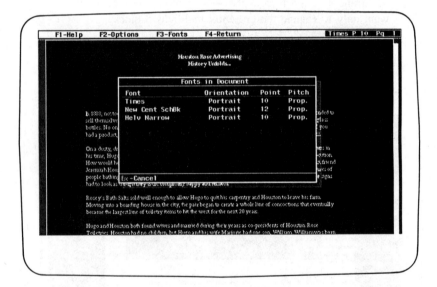

Fig. 8.15. *Displaying a list of fonts in the document.*

Listing Available Fonts

Another list shows all the fonts that are supported by your printer. To display all fonts that your printer is capable of producing, follow these steps:

1. Open the Fonts menu by pressing F3.

2. Select the **List available fonts** option. (You can press Alt-A to get around the menu selections, if you want.)

3. Press Enter. Professional Write then lists all fonts supported by your printer.

> You can also display a list of available fonts by pressing F8 when the Print Options menu is displayed.

Returning to the Document

The last set of options available in preview concerns the task of returning to the document. Depending on which section of the document you want to display, you use one of the two options in the Return menu.

Returning to the Current Position

As mentioned earlier in this chapter, the word cursor functions as a type of pointer that can be used to help you move back to the document at a particular place. For example, suppose that you want to return to page 2, paragraph 3 of the document you are currently previewing. When you are ready to return to the Create/Edit screen, follow these steps:

1. Position the word cursor on the word that you want to return to.

2. Open the Fonts menu by pressing F3.

3. Select the **Return to current position** option.

4. Press Enter. Professional Write then returns you to the working copy at the place where the word cursor was positioned in preview.

Returning to the Beginning of the Document

You also can return to the beginning of the working copy. Similar to the other return option, when you want to go back to the Create/Edit screen, follow these steps:

1. Open the Fonts menu by pressing F3.

2. Select the **Return to starting position** option.

3. Press Enter. Professional Write then returns you to the beginning of the working copy.

Printing Documents

The last major topic of this chapter involves printing the documents you have created. Before you begin, here are a few reminders:

❏ If you have access to two printers, make sure that your printer with font capability is set up as printer 1.

❏ If you are using soft fonts, copy the soft fonts to your Professional Write directory so that the program will be able to locate the files at print time.

❏ Check to make sure that the printer you are going to use supports all the fonts in the document. (You can do this by pressing F8 when the Print Options menu is displayed or by using the **List fonts in document** option, available from preview's Font menu.)

❏ Make sure that you have used the Setup Menu to tell Professional Write which type of printer you are using.

❏ Check your printer to make sure that the paper has been inserted and aligned properly and that the printer is on-line and ready to receive and print information.

A Review of Printer Setup

As you may recall from Chapter 2, setting up your printer is as simple as telling Professional Write which printer you will be using. Once you choose your printer type from the Printers screen, the program does the rest.

Here is a quick recap of the printer setup procedure (for more information, review "Setting Up Printer 1" in Chapter 2):

1. When the Main Menu is displayed, select **Setup**.

2. From the Setup Menu, choose **Select printer 1**.

3. Select the printer you want to use. Press Tab to get to the right side of the screen if you want to change the printer port specified.

4. If you are using a printer that supports fonts, a screen is displayed, asking which font you want to use as the default font. Choose a font by highlighting it and pressing Enter.

5. If you have chosen a serial port, another screen is displayed, asking you to verify that the correct settings are assigned to that port. Press Enter.

6. After you press Enter, you are returned to the Main Menu. Professional Write now recognizes the printer you plan to use as Printer 1. (You can also repeat this procedure for Printer 2, if you like.)

Getting a Quick Printout

If you are like many people, when you are down to the wire and you need to print something fast, the quality of the printing becomes less important. Professional Write enables you to print a document quickly and, although it is not pretty, it is fast.

To get a quick, draft printout, follow these steps:

1. When the document is displayed on the screen, press Ctrl-O. (You could open the File/Print menu and select the **Print working copy** option if you had more time.)

2. When the Print Options menu is displayed, glance at the **Print to:** line to make sure that the file will be sent to the correct printer. (If the wrong printer number is shown, move the cursor to that option by pressing Tab and type the correct number.)

3. Press Enter. Professional Write then prints the document quickly, with no frills included.

Figure 8.16 shows an example of a quick printout. Later in this chapter, you will learn to use different options to change the look of this printout.

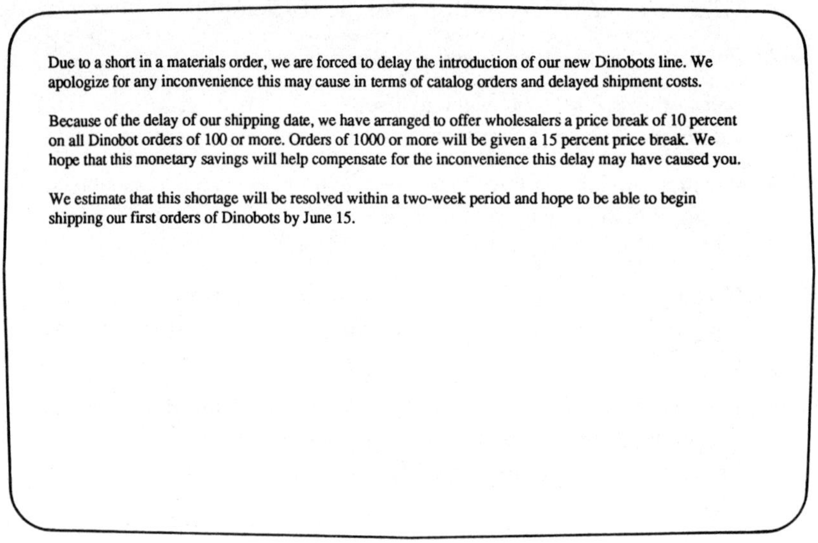

Due to a short in a materials order, we are forced to delay the introduction of our new Dinobots line. We apologize for any inconvenience this may cause in terms of catalog orders and delayed shipment costs.

Because of the delay of our shipping date, we have arranged to offer wholesalers a price break of 10 percent on all Dinobot orders of 100 or more. Orders of 1000 or more will be given a 15 percent price break. We hope that this monetary savings will help compensate for the inconvenience this delay may have caused you.

We estimate that this shortage will be resolved within a two-week period and hope to be able to begin shipping our first orders of Dinobots by June 15.

Fig. 8.16. *A quick printout.*

Understanding the Print Options Screen

You use the Print Options screen to communicate your print choices to Professional Write. On this screen, you specify the number of copies you want to print, the print range, what type of paper you will be printing on, whether you want the text indented, what type style you want to use, to what peripheral you want the information sent, and whether any soft fonts need to be downloaded (see fig. 8.17).

> On the Print Options screen, press Tab to move the cursor to the next option on the screen, and press Shift-Tab to move to a previous option.

The sections that follow introduce each of the options available on the Print Options screen.

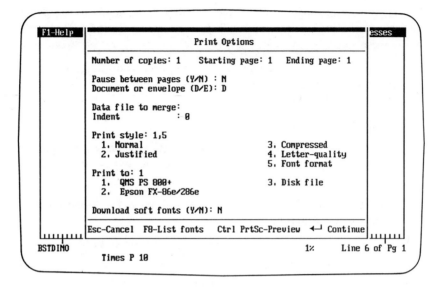

```
┌─────────────────────────────────────────────────────────────┐
│ F1-Help │                                         esses │
│         │              Print Options                    │
│         │                                               │
│         │ Number of copies: 1    Starting page: 1  Ending page: 1 │
│         │                                               │
│         │ Pause between pages (Y/N) : N                 │
│         │ Document or envelope (D/E): D                 │
│         │                                               │
│         │ Data file to merge:                           │
│         │ Indent        : 0                             │
│         │                                               │
│         │ Print style: 1,5                              │
│         │   1. Normal              3. Compressed        │
│         │   2. Justified           4. Letter-quality    │
│         │                          5. Font format       │
│         │ Print to: 1                                   │
│         │   1.  QMS PS 800+        3. Disk file         │
│         │   2.  Epson FX-86e/286e                       │
│         │                                               │
│         │ Download soft fonts (Y/N): N                  │
│         │                                               │
│         │ Esc-Cancel  F8-List fonts  Ctrl PrtSc-Preview  ← Continue │
│ BSTDINO │                              1%    Line 6 of Pg 1 │
│         │     Times P 10                                │
└─────────────────────────────────────────────────────────────┘
```

Fig. 8.17. *The Print Options screen.*

Printing Multiple Copies

The first option on the Print Options screen enables you to specify the number of copies you want to print. The default setting is 1; that is, Professional Write assumes that you want to print only one copy, unless you enter a different value after the **Number of copies:** option.

If you are printing a document that is more than one page long, when you tell Professional Write to print multiple copies, the program prints one entire document first; then the second copy of the entire document; then the third, and so forth. This saves you the trouble of collating the document after all the copies are made.

Selecting Pages for Printing

You don't always want to print the entire document. For example, suppose that you are working on a 30-page document and you have revised pages 4 and 5. Instead of printing the entire document you can print only the pages that have been changed.

To specify a print range, you use the **Starting page:** and **Ending page:** options on the Print Options menu. To print selected pages of a document, follow these steps:

1. Make sure that the document you want to print is displayed on the screen. (If not, select **Get file** from the File/Print menu—or press Ctrl-G—and select the file you want.)

2. Open the File/Print menu by pressing F2.

3. Select the **Print working copy** option. (If you prefer, you can press the speed key combination, Ctrl-O, to bypass the menu selections.)

4. When the Print Options screen is displayed, press Tab to move the cursor to the **Starting page:** option.

5. Type the page number of the first page you want to print (in this case, *4*).

6. Press Tab to get to the **Ending page:** option.

7. Type the page number of the last page in the range (in this case, *5*).

8. Specify other options as necessary (these other options are explained in subsequent sections of this chapter).

9. When you are ready to print the document, press Enter.

Specifying Pages for Print Ranges

Although Professional Write enables you to use all sorts of page numbering schemes (such as 2-1, 2-2, 2-3 or A.1, A.2, A.3, and so on), when you are specifying the pages for the **Starting page:** and **Ending page:** options on the Print Options menu, be sure to use the actual page numbers of the document.

Because you assign the page numbers only in the header or footer, Professional Write will not recognize anything other than a ''normal'' page number as an accepted value for the print range. To find the number of a particular page, look in the status line at the bottom of the screen.

Working with Pages

Another variable to consider is the type of paper you will be printing on. Will you be feeding the paper through sheet by sheet, or will you use continuous-feed (connected) paper?

The **Pause between pages:** option on the Print Options menu enables you to have Professional Write stop after printing one page so that you can insert and align the next sheet of paper before the program begins printing again. Generally, you will answer Y to this option only when you are using single-sheet paper, like letterhead, on a printer that does not have an automatic paper feed.

Working with Envelopes

The next option on the Print Options screen, **Document or envelope:**, enables you to specify whether you are printing on a regular sheet of paper or an envelope. The default setting is D (document), so unless you are planning to print an envelope, you don't need to change the setting for this option.

Professional Write can pull the address from letters you write and print the address on an envelope without any extra typing from you. To tell the program to create an envelope, follow these steps:

1. Open the document for which you want to print the envelope. Make sure that an address has been included at the top of the file, in standard business-letter form. (The program will ''know'' to print this address on the envelope.)

2. Press Ctrl-O to display the Print Options screen.

3. Press Tab until the cursor is positioned after the **Document or envelope** option.

4. Type *e*.

5. Place the envelope in the printer. (The printhead should be positioned at the top edge of the envelope.)

6. Make sure that the printer is on-line and ready.

7. Press Enter.

Merging Information

The **Data file to merge:** option enables you to merge a data file with the file you are printing. For example, when you are printing form letters by using the information from an address book file, you specify the name of the address book file so that Professional Write knows where to find the information.

More information about merge printing documents is explained in Chapter 10, ''Creating and Working with Address Books.''

Changing Margins at Print Time

The **Indent:** option enables you to change the indentation of the document when you print. Perhaps you only occasionally print on company letterhead, but when you do, you need to move the document to the right to make room for the design of the stationery. Instead of getting into the document and changing the margins, you can specify an indentation at the **Indent:** setting on the Print Options menu.

To change the indentation at print time, follow these steps:

1. Open the document you want to print.

2. Press Ctrl-O to display the Print Options menu.

3. Press Tab until the cursor is positioned after the **Indent:** setting.

4. Type a number indicating the indentation you want. (For best results, estimate to 1/10 of an inch. For example, entering *4* would indent the document 4/10 of an inch.)

5. Change other options as necessary.

6. Press Enter to begin printing.

If you save the document after you change the print options, Professional Write will save the indentation you specified.

Selecting Printing Styles

As you know, you have the option of specifying several styles for Professional Write documents. Depending on the capabilities of your printer, you can take advantage of the various styles by using the **Change style** option on the Text Block Operations menu or by specifying the style you want on the Print Options menu. The print styles available to you are:

❑ Normal

❑ Justified

❑ Compressed

❑ Letter-quality

❑ Font format

The first setting, **Normal**, is Professional Write's default, causing your printer to print in the normal mode for that particular printer.

Justified prints your document so that all text on the right margin aligns to the same point; that is, spaces are added between words so that all lines end at the same character position.

Justification seems to be a personal or professional preference item: either you like it, or you don't. The advocates of justification claim it makes the page look more professional, more uniform. The detractors complain that justification is harder to read for long stretches. However, if you want the entire document to be justified, type *2* after the **Print style:** option.

> If you want to justify only a portion of text, you can use the special print command *JUSTIFY*. For more information, read the section "Using Special Print Commands," later in this chapter.

The **Compressed** type style prints the letters closer together and slightly smaller, which makes them appear darker. Printing in compressed mode enables you to print more letters on a line, but sometimes output is more difficult to read.

The **Letter-quality** option pertains to dot-matrix printers only. When you choose **Letter-quality**, the print head strikes the paper more times for each letter, which results in a clearer, better-looking printout. Use **Letter-quality** when you need to make a document look as good as possible and you don't have access to a laser printer.

The **Font format** option is discussed in Chapter 7. Refer to the appropriate sections of that chapter for more information.

Sending Print Files to Disk

Most programs provide some means of printing a file to disk, and Professional Write is no exception. In the last option on the Print Options menu, you can choose where you would like to send the data. You can send the data one of three places:

❏ To the printer you specified as Printer 1

❏ To the printer you specified as Printer 2

❏ To a file

Figure 8.18 shows the **Print to:** option as it appears when Professional Write is set up to accept a QMS PS 800+ as Printer 1 and an EPSON FX/286E as Printer 2. The printers shown on your Print Options screen will depend on the printers you have installed for your system. If you want to print a document to a file so that you can print it later or, perhaps, take it to another computer and print it, you can specify *3* after the **Print to:** option to tell Professional Write to send the document to a file. When you press Enter to print the file, Professional Write displays a screen, prompting you to enter a name for the file. After you type the name and press Enter, the program displays a brief message telling you that the file is being printed to the disk.

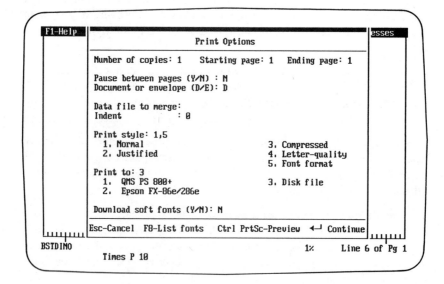

*Fig. 8.18. The **Print to:** settings.*

Working with Soft Fonts

The last option on the Print Options menu involves the use of soft fonts. As you may recall, *soft fonts* are fonts that are stored on disk and are sent—or downloaded—to your printer at print time. If you plan to use soft fonts with Professional Write, you need to do the following:

1. Set up as Printer 1 the printer you plan to use soft fonts with.

2. Copy the soft fonts to the directory in which you store your Professional Write program files.

3. Press Y after the **Download soft fonts:** option on the Print Options menu.

> If you will be working with many soft fonts, you may want to set up a new subdirectory beneath the directory that stores your Professional Write program files. For example, if your program files are stored in the C:\WRITE directory, you may want to create the subdirectory C:\WRITE\FONTS to store your soft fonts.
>
> If you create a separate directory for the soft fonts, be sure to tell Professional Write that such a directory exists. To do this, you need to go through the Setup menu and change the soft font directory. For more instruction on this procedure, refer to ''Setting Up for Soft Fonts,'' in Chapter 7.

After you type *y* for the **Download soft fonts:** option and press Enter, Professional Write downloads the fonts and starts the printing process.

Special Print Commands

This section covers the special print commands that you can insert in your files before you print them. These commands enable you to join files, control the justification of the files, perform several formatting operations, add graphs, begin a new page, or change the print style.

The special print commands that you can embed in Professional Write documents are:

JOIN
JUSTIFY
GRAPH
NEW PAGE
PRINTER
FORMAT
RIGHT
CENTER

Some basic rules apply to all these print commands:

❏ Always place a print command on a blank line immediately preceding the line in which you want the command to take effect.

❏ Be aware that some commands stand alone (*JOIN*, *GRAPH*, *NEW PAGE*), while others require companion commands (*FORMAT YES*/ *FORMAT NO*, *JUSTIFY YES*/ *JUSTIFY NO*).

❏ Know that the *NEW PAGE* command may affect the document differently than you expect if you use font format.

The *JOIN* Command

Suppose that you have been working on several modules of a document, which will eventually be used as one complete document. This document has grown to massive proportions, and for both size limitations and editing reasons, you have divided the file into several small chunks.

You can use the *JOIN* command to add the files together at print time, rather than copying all the files into one before printing. Figure 8.19 shows how the *JOIN* command is inserted in the file at the point where the file is to be joined.

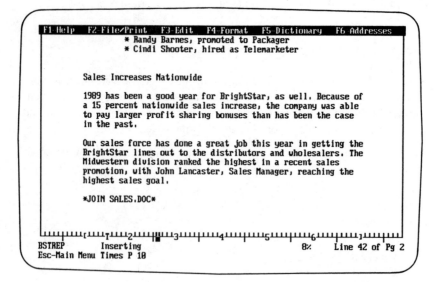

*Fig. 8.19. Using the *JOIN* command.*

If you plan to join two or more files, check the headers, footers, and print style you have specified for the documents to make sure that the styles are consistent. If no header or footer has been selected for the documents being joined to the first one, those documents take on the header and footer style of the first document.

You can join more than one file to the first file, if you want. However, you cannot place a *JOIN* command in a file that has been joined to another file. For example, suppose that you want to add documents 2 and 3 to document 1. The equation would look something like this:

Document1 + document2 + document3 = printed result

When you are using the *JOIN* command to instruct Professional Write to print all these files together, you open Document 1, go to the end of the file, and enter

JOIN document2
JOIN document3

Note: In this example, *document2* and *document3* are meant to represent file names. When you use the *JOIN* command, be sure to enter the exact spelling of the file name you want to join to the first document.

The *JUSTIFY* Command

Justification can be a useful tool for setting off a section of text that you want to emphasize. Professional Write gives you an option that enables you to justify a portion of text, rather than the entire document. To justify a section of text, you use the special print command *JUSTIFY*. If you want to turn the justification on and then off again, enter two forms of the command, as shown in figure 8.20.

The *GRAPH* Command

You use the *GRAPH* command to insert a graph in a document at print time. Professional Write can accept graphs created in several other programs produced by Software Publishing Corporation:

❏ PFS: First Choice (if the graph is saved in Professional Write format with the extension .PF)

❏ Harvard Presentation Graphics (in PFS: WRITE format)

❏ Harvard Graphics (save the graph as a picture file)

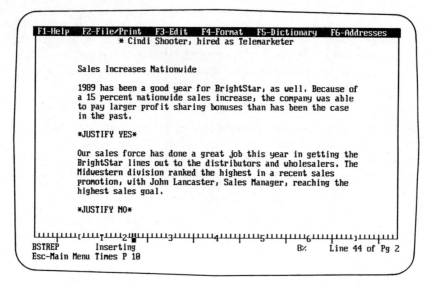

F1-Help   F2-File/Print   F3-Edit   F4-Format   F5-Dictionary   F6-Addresses
                    * Cindi Shooter, hired as Telemarketer

        Sales Increases Nationwide

        1989 has been a good year for BrightStar, as well. Because of
        a 15 percent nationwide sales increase, the company was able
        to pay larger profit sharing bonuses than has been the case
        in the past.

        JUSTIFY YES

        Our sales force has done a great job this year in getting the
        BrightStar lines out to the distributors and wholesalers. The
        Midwestern division ranked the highest in a recent sales
        promotion, with John Lancaster, Sales Manager, reaching the
        highest sales goal.

        JUSTIFY NO

        BSTREP   Inserting   8%   Line 44 of Pg 2
        Esc-Main Menu Times P 10

Fig. 8.20. Using the *JUSTIFY* command.

❏ PFS: First Graphics (in Professional Write format)

❏ PFS: GRAPH Version B (print the graph to disk)

❏ Professional Plan (in Professional Write format)

Like the other special print commands, you enter the *GRAPH* command
at the point in the document where you want the graph to be printed. Use
the form

    GRAPH graphname

where *graphname* is the name of the file. Be careful not to add spaces between the beginning asterisk and the command or the file name and the
closing asterisk. You can, however, abbreviate the command to the form

    g graphname

Professional Write adds lines to accommodate the graph; you don't need to
press Enter several times to leave enough room. If you want to see how
much room the graph will use, press Ctrl-PrtSc to activate the preview feature; Professional Write shows the placement of the graph as a solid gray
block (see fig. 8.21).

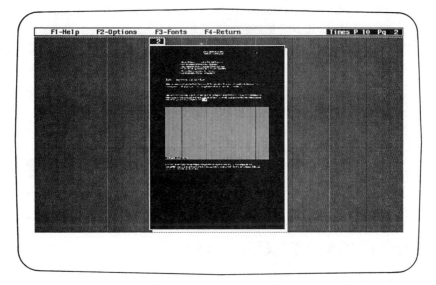

Fig. 8.21. *A graph blocked out in preview.*

If you position a *GRAPH* command in such a way that Professional Write does not have enough room to insert the graph on the page, the program will move the graph (and any text that follows the *GRAPH* command) to the next page.

The *NEW PAGE* Command

As you might expect, the *NEW PAGE* command inserts a new page in the line after the command. You can use this command, for example, when you have just ended one section of a document and you want to begin the next section at the top of a new page. To use the *NEW PAGE* command, simply position the cursor on the blank line above the place where you want the new page to begin and type *new page*.

You can also abbreviate the command as *n*, if you like. Appearances can be deceiving, however, because although you have entered the *NEW PAGE* command at the correct point, it may not appear to do anything. The line number at the bottom of the page doesn't change and you don't see the double-bar that indicates a completed page. How do you know that you have, in fact, started a new page?

The *NEW PAGE* command isn't obvious until you use preview or print the document. Bear in mind, however, that even if you use preview, your document still may look different if you print the file in font format.

The *PRINTER* Command

You use the *PRINTER* command to send printer control codes to your printer. Depending on your printer's capabilities, you may not need to use this command at all. Generally, *PRINTER* commands are used in pairs; one to turn on the feature (such as boldface, double-wide printing, over-strike type, and so on), and the other to turn the feature off. For more about the printer control codes that can be used with your printer, consult your printer's manual.

The *FORMAT* Command

As you may recall from Chapter 7, font format is a print style that you specify on the Print Options menu. This format tells Professional Write to reformat the paragraphs as necessary to accommodate the proportional font you have used. If you choose not to use font format, the program preserves the margins you have chosen and keeps the document in the same basic shape as it appears on screen, whether or not you have used a proportional font.

The *FORMAT* command enables you to turn on and off the font format feature. For example, suppose that in your document you have created a two-column list of clients and distributors in a certain region. If you leave font format on, the list is reformatted as though it were a paragraph, and the tabs and indents are garbled. If you turn font format off, the format of the list is preserved, but the regular paragraphs in the document may look too narrow.

To solve this problem, you can insert a *FORMAT YES* command in the first line of the document. (The line should be blank.) Then, in the blank line preceding the two-column list, enter a *FORMAT NO* command. Finally, in the blank line after the list, enter *FORMAT YES*. This pre-serves the format of the list and still gives you the effect you want for the paragraphs in the document. (*Note:* You can abbreviate these commands as *f y* and *f n*, if you choose.)

The *RIGHT* Command

Use the *RIGHT* command to right-justify the line that follows the command. For this command, you don't need a ''partner'' to turn off the justification; it works only for one line. If you like, you can abbreviate the *RIGHT* command as *r*.

The *CENTER* Command

Similar to the *RIGHT* command, the *CENTER* command centers the line that follows the command. You enter this command on the blank line preceding the line you want to center. Because *CENTER* works only for the line that follows the command, you do not need a companion command to disable the feature. You can abbreviate the *CENTER* command as *c*. Figure 8.22 shows a document with the necessary commands to print the main title centered and the subtitle right-justified. Figure 8.23 shows the document after it is displayed in preview mode.

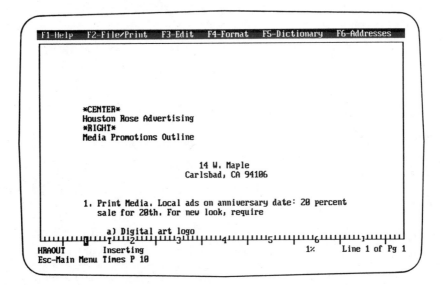

Fig. 8.22. *Using the *CENTER* and *RIGHT* commands.*

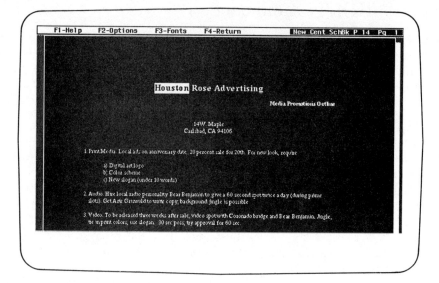

Fig. 8.23. *The effects of the *CENTER* and *RIGHT* commands.*

Chapter 8 Quick Start: Previewing and Printing

This section highlights many of the procedures you have learned in this chapter.

Changing the View

After you activate preview, the first page of the document is shown in full-page view. To change the view, follow these steps:

1. Position the word cursor in the portion of the document you want to view. (Remember that in a close-up view, Professional Write can display only a portion of the page at one time.)

2. Open the Options menu by pressing F2.

3. Select the **Change view** option. (You can also press Alt-V to bypass the menu selections, if you prefer.)

4. Press Enter. Professional Write then displays the document in close-up view. If you want to view a different section of the document, use the cursor-movement keys.

Changing Print Style

To change the print style you have selected for the document, follow these steps:

1. When preview is active, open the Options menu by pressing F2.

2. Select the **Set print styles** option or press Alt-S.

3. On the Print Styles menu, type the number(s) of the style(s) you want to use.

4. Press Enter. Professional Write then updates the file and displays the preview page with the new style in effect.

Changing Paper Size

To change the paper size of the displayed document, follow these steps:

1. When the document is being displayed in preview mode, open the Options menu by pressing F2.

2. Select the **Change paper size** option or press Alt-P.

3. On the Paper Size menu, select the paper size to which you want to change the preview display.

4. Press Enter. Professional Write then shows the document in the new paper size you have chosen.

Changing a Font

To change a font in preview mode, follow these steps:

1. Make sure that the document is displayed in close-up view. (If it is not, press Alt-V.)

2. Position the cursor in the section with the font you want to change.

3. Open the Fonts menu by pressing F3.

4. Choose the **Change a font** option or press Alt-F.

5. Choose the font you want and press Enter.

6. Professional Write then asks whether you want to change all occurrences of the initial font to the font you specified. Type *n* if you want to change only the currently highlighted block or *y* if you want to change all occurrences of that font.

7. Press Enter, and Professional Write replaces the highlighted font with the new font.

Listing the Fonts in the Working Copy

To list the fonts that have been assigned to the document in the working copy, follow these steps:

1. Open the Fonts menu by pressing F3.

2. Choose the **List fonts in document** option by highlighting the option and pressing Enter or by typing the number to the left of the option. (You also can press Alt-D to bypass the menu, if you prefer.)

3. Press Enter. Professional Write then displays a list of fonts in the document. If any of the fonts in the document are not supported by the printer you have installed with Professional Write, an asterisk (*) is displayed beside the font name.

Listing Printer-Supported Fonts

To display all fonts that your printer is capable of producing, follow these steps:

1. Open the Fonts menu by pressing F3.

2. Select the **List available fonts** option. (You can press Alt-A to get around the menu selections, if you want.)

3. Press Enter. Professional Write then lists all fonts supported by your printer.

Returning to the Current Position

When you are ready to return to the Create/Edit screen, follow these steps:

1. Position the word cursor on the word that you want to return to.

2. Open the Fonts menu by pressing F3.

3. Select the **Return to current position** option.

4. Press Enter. Professional Write then returns you to the working copy at the place where the word cursor was positioned in preview.

Returning to the Beginning of the Document

Similar to the other return option, when you want to go back to the beginning of the document, follow these steps:

1. Open the Fonts menu by pressing F3.

2. Select the **Return to starting position** option.

3. Press Enter. Professional Write then returns you to the working copy at the beginning of the document.

Getting a Quick Printout

To get a quick printout, follow these steps:

1. When the document is displayed on the screen, press Ctrl-O.

2. When the Print Options menu is displayed, glance at the **Print to:** line to make sure that the file will be sent to the correct printer. (If the wrong printer number is shown, move the cursor to that option by pressing Tab and type the correct number.)

3. Press Enter. Professional Write then prints the document quickly, with no frills included.

Printing Selected Pages

To print selected pages of a document, follow these steps:

1. Make sure that the document you want to print is displayed on the screen.

2. Open the File/Print menu by pressing F2.

3. Select the **Print working copy** option or press Ctrl-O.

4. When the Print Options screen is displayed, press Tab to move the cursor to the **Starting page:** option.

5. Type the page number of the first page you want to print.

6. Press Tab to get to the **Ending page:** option.

7. Type the page number of the last page in the range.

8. Specify other options as necessary.

9. When you are ready to print the document, press Enter.

Printing Envelopes

To tell the program to create an envelope, follow these steps:

1. Open the document for which you want to print the envelope. Make sure that an address has been included at the top of the file, in standard business-letter form. (The program will "know" to print this address on the envelope.)

2. Press Ctrl-O to display the Print Options screen.

3. Press Tab until the cursor is positioned after the **Document or envelope** option.

4. Type *e*.

5. Place the envelope in the printer. (The printhead should be positioned at the top edge of the envelope.)

6. Make sure that the printer is on-line and ready.

7. Press Enter.

Changing Indentation

To change the indentation at print time, follow these steps:

1. Open the document you want to print.

2. Press Ctrl-O to display the Print Options menu.

3. Press Tab until the cursor is positioned after the **Indent:** setting.

4. Type a number indicating the indentation you want. (For best results, estimate to 1/10 of an inch. For example, entering *4* indents the document 4/10 of an inch.)

5. Change other options as necessary.

6. Press Enter to begin printing.

Chapter Summary

In this chapter, you have been introduced to an important new feature in Professional Write 2.1: previewing. The new preview feature enables you to see on-screen how your document looks—with all the correct font sizes and styles, page breaks, and graph positions—before you print. Additionally, you learned to find your way through the Print Options menu and determine which type of print settings will best meet your needs. In the next chapter, you learn more about Professional Write's special features: the dictionary, thesaurus, and calculator.

Part III

Professional Write Special Features

Includes

Special Features: The Dictionary, Thesaurus, and Calculator

Creating and Working with Address Books

Using Macros

Special Features: The Dictionary, Thesaurus, and Calculator

To this point in the book, you have learned to use the built-in features of Professional Write to create, edit, and print your documents. Perhaps you have added lines and boxes to your documents. Maybe you have created a cover page and added headers and footers.

In addition to all the features you have used thus far, Professional Write offers you three additional tools for ensuring the accuracy of your work. In this chapter, you will learn to use the dictionary, the thesaurus, and the calculator.

Working with the Dictionary

Remember the last time you searched desperately through the dictionary to find a word you hardly ever use? Or, have you ever looked at the word *piece* so many times you can't remember when *i* comes before *e*?

249

If you had been using Professional Write, you could have simply and calmly had the program check the spelling for you. Just like that.

Dictionary at a Glance	
Number of words available for checking:	77,000
Number of words that can be entered in a custom dictionary:	5,000
Number of custom dictionaries allowed:	Unlimited

What Is the Dictionary?

Professional Write's dictionary is really a spelling checker; it does not provide you with the part of speech, usage, and definition of every word you check. Rather, the dictionary scans through your document, ''reading'' all the words and looking for misspellings.

The dictionary will find the following errors in your text:

❑ Misspelled words

❑ Typos

❑ Double words (such as ''the car that that you bought'')

❑ Odd capitalization

You can create your own customized dictionary to store words that you use often in your documents. For example, if you write computer books for a living, you may often use acronyms like IBM, CGA, EGA, and VGA in your text. Because you write about these items day after day, you know what the acronyms stand for, but Professional Write will stop at each one, displaying the Irregular Capitalization menu and suggesting that perhaps you would like to change the words. To get around having to answer the Irregular Capitalization menu repeatedly, you can create your own dictionary of words that are unique to your uses. Then, when you have Professional Write use your customized dictionary, the program will be able to concentrate on finding words that really are misspelled or capitalized erroneously.

Using the Dictionary

The procedure for using the dictionary is easy. Simply follow these steps:

1. Position the cursor at the point you want to begin spell checking the document. (*Note:* If you want to check the whole document, position the cursor at the top of the file. Otherwise, Professional Write will check the document only from the cursor position to the end of the document, and, depending on the placement of the cursor, an important part of the text may go unchecked.)

2. Open the Dictionary menu by pressing F5.

3. Select the **Proof to end of document** option and press Enter (see fig. 9.1). If you prefer, you can press the speed key combination, Ctrl-V, to bypass the menu selections.

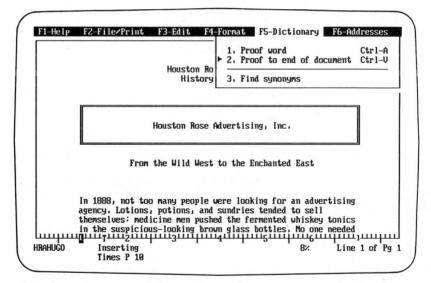

Fig. 9.1. *Starting the dictionary.*

Professional Write then begins checking the document. When a word is encountered that needs further checking, the program highlights the word and displays a screen alerting you of the problem. Figure 9.2 shows the Questionable Word menu, which is displayed when Professional Write finds a possibly misspelled word.

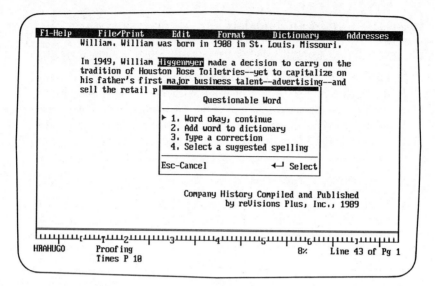

Fig. 9.2. The Questionable Word menu.

If Professional Write has highlighted the word simply because it was not found in the program's dictionary, you can select option 1, **Word okay, continue**, and Professional Write will continue checking the document. If the word is one that you use frequently in your work, you can add the word to your personal dictionary by selecting option 2, **Add word to dictionary**.

If the word is misspelled and you know the correct spelling, you can choose option 3, **Type a correction**, and Professional Write will display a screen displaying the found word and prompting you to enter the correct spelling. When you type the correct spelling and press Enter, the program corrects the word and continues checking the document.

If you know that the word is spelled incorrectly but you are unsure of the correct spelling, you can have Professional Write display a list of alternative spellings for the highlighted word. Figure 9.3 shows the screen that is displayed when **Select a suggested spelling**, option 4, is chosen.

Checking One Word

You also have the option of quickly checking the spelling of the word at the cursor position. When the cursor is positioned on (or in the space after) the word, open the Dictionary menu and select the **Proof word** option. (You

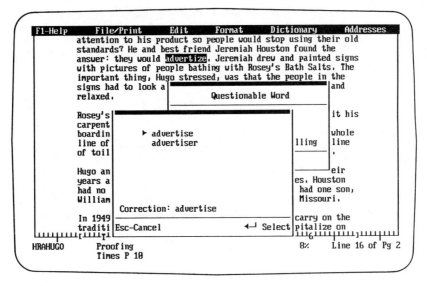

Fig. 9.3. Listing alternative spellings.

can instead press Ctrl-A, if you prefer.) Professional Write then checks the accuracy of the word and, if a problem is found, provides you with a menu displaying the options you can use to correct the word.

What Is a Personal Dictionary?

When you tell Professional Write to add a word to the dictionary, the program automatically adds the word to your personal dictionary. Your personal dictionary file, called PERSONAL.SPC, is created by Professional Write to store any words that you choose to add when you are checking a document.

Suppose that as you are checking your company's history, you run across the following words that you elect to add to the dictionary:

Hugo
Higgenmeyer
Jeremiah
Rosey's
Marjorie

When the Questionable Word screen is displayed, you choose the **Add word to dictionary** option for each word to add it to your personal dictionary. From that point on, Professional Write no longer stops on the words that have been added.

Looking at the Personal Dictionary

You can open the personal dictionary as you would any other Professional Write document file. The file is named PERSONAL.SPC, and you retrieve it by selecting **Get file** from the File/Print menu (or by pressing Ctrl-G), typing the file name, and pressing Enter. The personal dictionary is then displayed on the screen (see fig. 9.4).

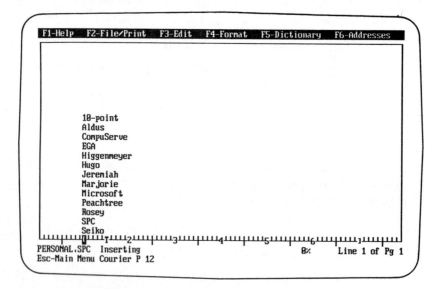

Fig. 9.4. *The personal dictionary file.*

You can add words to the dictionary after you open the file, if you like. Remember to enter only one word on each line. Also keep in mind that Professional Write will recognize a word only if you use the exact spelling in the document, so if you are entering a word that is capitalized in several ways, you may want to enter the word in all forms in which it might appear.

If you use a hard disk system, you have enough room to create a personal dictionary of up to 5,000 words. If you are using your floppy disk to store the file (use the Dictionary Disk), you are limited to about 500 words. If space is a problem, you can divide the dictionary into two or more personalized dictionaries. There is no limit to the number of dictionaries you can create, but you can only use one personal dictionary at a time.

> To add words directly to your personal dictionary, press Ctrl-G, type the file name PERSONAL.SPC, and press Enter. When the file is displayed in the working copy, type the words you want to add. Remember, however, to enter only one word on each line.

Creating Additional Personal Dictionaries

As mentioned in the preceding section, there is no limit to the number of personal dictionaries you can create. But here is the catch: Professional Write will recognize only one dictionary at a time, and that dictionary must be named PERSONAL.SPC.

Suppose that you are responsible for creating reports that are unique to four different departments:

❑ Sales

❑ Development

❑ Returns

❑ Production

Ideally, you can create a dictionary for each department so that Professional Write recognizes words that are specific to that department.

Because Professional Write recognizes only the dictionary named PERSONAL.SPC, you must always make sure that the dictionary you want to use is given that name.

Perhaps an example will help illustrate this concept. Suppose that the four different dictionaries previously mentioned are named SALES, DEVELOP, RETURNS, and PROD, respectively. When you know that you are going to work on the sales report, you need to rename the SALES dictionary as PERSONAL.SPC so that Professional Write will be working with the words you entered for that department. Then, when you are finished with that report, you rename PERSONAL.SPC as SALES so that you can name another PERSONAL.SPC when it becomes necessary.

You can rename the file one of two ways: by using the DOS command RENAME, or by opening the file and saving it under another name.

To use DOS to rename the file, follow these steps:

1. Exit Professional Write.

2. When the DOS prompt is displayed (C› if you have a hard disk, and A› if you use a floppy disk based system), type the following command line (assuming that the file you want to rename is named SALES):

   REN SALES PERSONAL.SPC

3. Press Enter.

When you want to rename PERSONAL.SPC as SALES, simply reverse the procedure by typing *ren personal.spc sales* at the DOS prompt.

If you want to rename the file from within Professional Write, you can follow these steps:

1. Start Professional Write.

2. Open the SALES dictionary file.

3. Select the **Save working copy** option from the File/Print menu.

4. Enter the name PERSONAL.SPC as the file name under which you want to save the file.

5. When Professional Write warns you that a file exists with that name, press Enter to continue the procedure.

Now a copy of SALES has been named PERSONAL.SPC, so Professional Write will recognize the dictionary when you proofread the document. The next time you want to use a different dictionary, you can use this procedure to overwrite the dictionary (SALES) that is named PERSONAL.SPC. Remember, however, that if you add any words to the dictionary while you are working on the document, you should use the **Save working copy** option to also save a copy of the dictionary to the original SALES file; otherwise, any changes you make to the file will be overwritten when you save the next dictionary under the name PERSONAL.SPC.

Using the Thesaurus

Professional Write offers another feature to help you enliven your documents. The thesaurus feature of Professional Write offers you synonyms for hard-to-find words or words that are used too often.

To use the thesaurus, follow these steps:

1. Place the cursor on the word for which you want to find a synonym. (You can also place the cursor in the space after the word.)

2. Open the Dictionary menu by pressing F5.

3. Choose the **Find synonyms** option. Professional Write displays a list of synonyms available for the word at the cursor position (see fig. 9.5). If the word has more than one meaning, Professional Write displays a list of alternative words for each usage.

4. Select the word you want to use by moving the highlight to that word and pressing Enter.

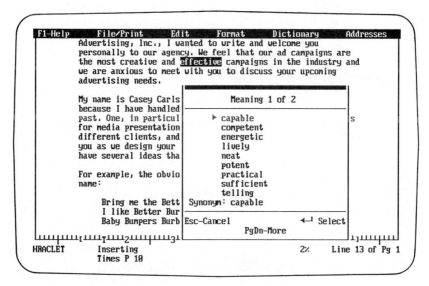

Fig. 9.5. *Displaying available synonyms.*

The following list gives you an idea of the types of synonyms Professional Write chooses for words you select.

If you choose	Professional Write displays
community	common, cooperative, group, joint, partnership, public[1]
shortcut	alternative, bypass, cutoff, time-saver

[1] These items were offered for the first meaning of "community." Professional Write provides synonyms for four different meanings.

adventurous	audacious, aweless, bold, brave, cool, courageous, daring, dauntless, fearless
vivacious	active, animated, brisk, lively, spirited, sportive, sprightly
boring	cheerless, dreary, dull, monotonous, sorrowful, tedious, tiresome, uninteresting, wintry

Using the Calculator

Another feature of Professional Write helps you ensure the mathematical accuracy of the information in your document. Professional Write gives you a means of performing calculations and inserting the results directly into your document. You don't even need to retype the values or the operators.

Figure 9.6 shows you a document in which calculations are necessary. To begin calculating, you have two options:

❏ You can select **Calculate** from the Edit menu (or press Ctrl-M), or

❏ You can highlight the block, press F10, and choose **Calculate** from the block operation menu.

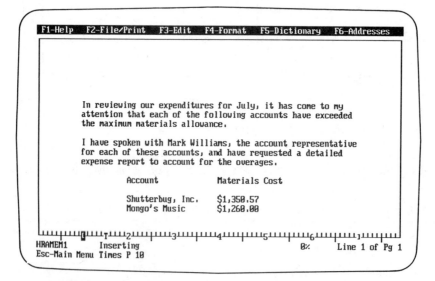

Fig. 9.6. The document on which a calculation will be performed.

In this example, a simple calculation needs to be done. The two numbers, $1,350.57 and $1,260.00, need to be added. To have Professional Write do this calculation, follow these steps:

1. Position the cursor on the first digit of the top number.

2. Press Ctrl-T to activate a block operation.

3. Press → and the ↓ until the numbers are highlighted.

4. Press F10.

5. When the Text Block Operations menu is displayed, select the **Calculate** option. The Calculator is then displayed, with the values—and the result—already entered (see fig. 9.7). Professional Write assumed that you wanted to add the numbers.

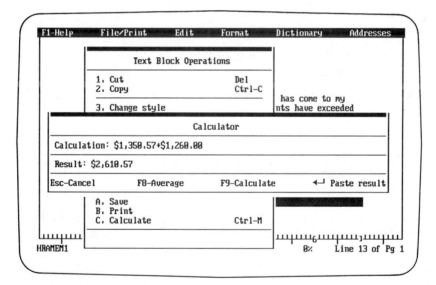

Fig. 9.7. *Professional Write added the numbers.*

Pasting the Result into the Document

You can paste the result of your calculation directly into the document, if you want. After you come up with the result you seek, press Enter to paste the value into the document. After you press Enter, you are returned to the document, and a direction at the bottom of the screen instructs you to move the cursor to the place you want the result to be pasted and press Enter. After you do so, the result is pasted in place.

Averaging Values

You also can have Professional Write average a column of numbers for you. For example, consider a lengthy column of numbers that represents the monthly sales of all licensed Dinobot dealers. The person producing a report has been asked to find the average income of all Dinobot dealers across the country.

To have Professional Write figure the average, follow these steps:

1. Position the cursor on the first digit of the topmost value.

2. Press Ctrl-T to activate the block operation.

3. Use the arrow keys to highlight the entire column of numbers.

4. Press F10 to mark the end of the block.

5. On the Text Block Operations menu, select **Calculate** (or press Ctrl-M, if you prefer to bypass the menu selections).

6. When the Calculator is displayed, press F8. Professional Write figures the average.

If you choose, you can press Enter to have Professional Write paste the average into the document.

Performing More Complex Calculations

Unfortunately, not all calculations are as simple as adding and averaging. What happens, for example, when you need to divide one number by another and add the remainder to four percent of another?

Like all true calculators, Professional Write operates with an *order of precedence*, or set of rules by which an equation is calculated. For example, when you have a calculation like

$$4.5 * 3 \char`^ 2$$

You need to know which calculation is performed first. The order of precedence provides a rule that says multiplication (*) is performed after exponentiation (^). So the calculation, when performed in accordance with the order of precedence, is

$$4.5 * 3 \char`^ 2 = 40.5$$

because 3 squared equals 9, and 9 multiplied by 4.5 equals 40.5. Table 9.1 lists the order of precedence followed by Professional Write.

Table 9.1
Calculation Order of Precedence

Operator	Order	Example
^ or *	1st	2 * 3 ^ 2 = 18
− (negative)	2nd	−4 + 25/5 = 1
* and /	3rd	3 + 10 * 2 + 1 = 24
+ and −	4th	2 + 2 − 2 − 1 = 1

You can type equations directly into the **Calculation:** field of the Calculation screen. If an equation is already entered, you can type over or modify it as necessary (see fig. 9.8). After you make changes, press F9 to recalculate the equation. If you want to paste the result after you are finished, press Enter.

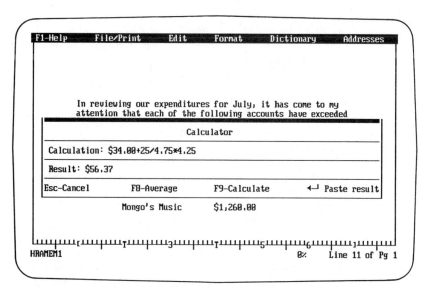

Fig. 9.8. *Entering a more complex calculation.*

Chapter 9 Quick Start

This Quick Start highlights the procedures you have learned in this chapter for working with the dictionary, the thesaurus, and the calculator.

Using the Dictionary

To use the dictionary, follow these steps:

1. Position the cursor at the point you want to begin spell checking the document. (*Note:* If you want to check the whole document, position the cursor at the top of the file. Otherwise, Professional Write will check the document only from the cursor position to the end of the document, and, depending on the placement of the cursor, an important part of the text may go unchecked.)

2. Open the Dictionary menu by pressing F5.

3. Select the **Proof to end of document** option and press Enter. If you prefer, you can press the speed key combination, Ctrl-V, to bypass the menu selections.

If you want Professional Write to spell check only the word at the cursor position, select **Proof word** from the Dictionary menu, or press Ctrl-A.

Using the Thesaurus

To use the thesaurus, follow these steps:

1. Place the cursor on the word for which you want to find a synonym. (You can also place the cursor in the space after the word.)

2. Open the Dictionary menu by pressing F5.

3. Choose the **Find synonyms** option. Professional Write displays a list of synonyms available for the word at the cursor position. If the word has more than one meaning, Professional Write displays a list of alternative words for each usage.

4. Select the word you want to use by moving the highlight to that word and pressing Enter.

Using the Calculator

To use the calculator, follow these steps:

1. Position the cursor on the first digit of the top number.

2. Press Ctrl-T to activate a block operation.

3. Press the arrow keys until all the numbers are highlighted.

4. Press F10.

5. When the Text Block Operations menu is displayed, select the **Calculate** option. The Calculator is then displayed, with the values—and the result—already entered. Professional Write assumes that you want to add the numbers. If you want to subtract, multiply, or divide, type the calculation in the Calculator field.

Averaging Values

To have Professional Write compute averages, follow these steps:

1. Position the cursor on the first digit of the topmost value.

2. Press Ctrl-T to activate the block operation.

3. Use the arrow keys to highlight the entire column of numbers.

4. Press F10 to mark the end of the block.

5. On the Text Block Operations menu, select **Calculate** (or press Ctrl-M, if you prefer to bypass the menu selections).

6. When the Calculator is displayed, press F8. Professional Write figures the average.

Chapter Summary

In this chapter, you learned about three special features that help ensure the accuracy of your Professional Write documents. Basic introductions and procedures for the dictionary, thesaurus, and calculator were explained. The next chapter teaches you to use yet another special feature of Professional Write in "Creating and Working with Address Books."

10

Creating and Working with Address Books

Is your Rolodex dog-eared? Have the names of your contacts changed so many times that you have written names on top of names on top of names?

Maintaining a database—any kind of database—requires a considerable amount of work and consistency. Whether you are responsible for keeping track of the names and addresses of all Dinobots distributors on the West coast or you maintain the employee roster to make sure that everyone gets an invitation to the company Christmas bash, entering and keeping up with all that information requires more than a little involvement and upkeep.

If you are using a manual filing system (the big ivory cabinet with the little manila folders), updating just one file requires that you go to the cabinet, look in the correct alphabetical drawer, search through the folders (while keeping your fingers crossed that the folder was filed in the correct place), remove the folder, find the sheet you need to update, paint correction fluid over the changed information, and type the new information on that sheet.

That's quite a bit of work to update one record.

If you had entered the information into a Professional Write address book, you could simply open the address book file, tell Professional Write which file you need, and change the information, right there on-screen, with no wasted steps (or correction fluid).

265

You can create and use an address book for any type of information that requires the storage of names, addresses, and other miscellaneous information. Here are a few ideas for address book uses:

❏ Keeping track of a client list

❏ Employee information

❏ Prospective customers

❏ Manufacturer information

❏ An interview roster

❏ Personal phone list

In this chapter, you will learn to create your own address books, enter and work with information, and print address book information. Before you begin, however, a few introductions are in order.

What Is an Address Book?

An address book, in Professional Write, is a type of mini-database. Okay, you say, but what's a database?

Whether you know it or not, you have worked with databases in the past. Your friendly Yellow Pages is a type of database: a listing of names and phone numbers of area businesses organized in some particular order.

A *database* can be anything from a shoebox full of receipts to an elaborate software program designed to record every data item about people, from their height to their IQ. Any collection of information organized in some fashion can be considered a database.

The address book feature of Professional Write enables you to create your own database of names, addresses, and other important information about people you contact in your work. The information about each person (or company) is known as a *record*. This can save you hours of lookup time when you are sending out a thousand form letters or calling the top 200 Dinobots distributors. Having the information in an address book, and, therefore, at your fingertips, makes finding the information so easy that it's almost effortless.

You also can incorporate the information in the address book into form letters or regular correspondence letters, without having to retype the information. With a few simple commands, you can tell Professional Write to plug the information in at the point you specify, without any further intervention from you.

How Do You Use an Address Book?

You create and use address books by using the Addresses menu, located at the far right side of the menu bar (see fig. 10.1). This menu provides you with all the options you need to create address books and enter, find, and copy individual addresses. Table 10.1 provides an overview of the various options on the Addresses menu. (*Note:* There are no speed key combinations available for the options on this menu.)

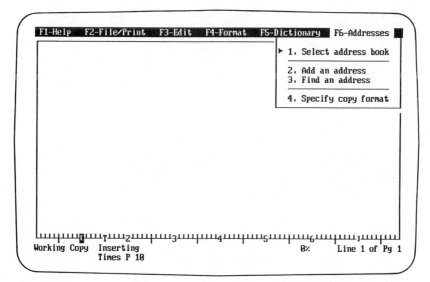

Fig. 10.1. The Addresses menu.

Figure 10.2 shows one record from a typical address book that contains customer information.

As you can see from this record, the title of the address book is displayed at the top of the screen. Almost every line in the record begins with an identifier, telling you what type of information to enter on that line. This identifier in which you type the information is known as the *field*. For example, the first field on-screen is the Title field. When you open the address book, the cursor is positioned in the Title field; all you need to do is begin typing

Table 10.1
Options on the Addresses Menu

Option	Description
Select address book	Chooses the address book with which you want to work
Add an address	Adds an address to an existing address book
Find an address	Enters search criteria and locates a specific record
Specify copy format	Selects the copy format that you want to use to incorporate address book information into other Professional Write documents.

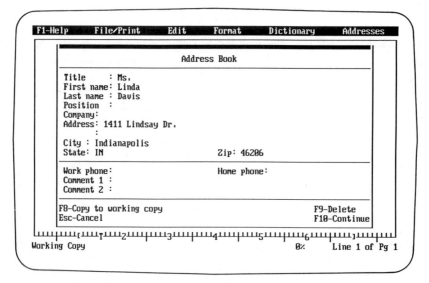

Fig. 10.2. A typical address book record.

to enter the information in the field. To get to the next field (First name), press Tab.

Table 10.2 shows the keys you use to maneuver around the Address Book screen.

Table 10.2
Cursor-Movement Keys in the Address Book

Key	Moves the cursor
Tab	To the next field
Shift-Tab	To the previous field
↑	Up one line
↓	Down one line
→	Right one character
←	Left one character
Ctrl- →	Right one word (in same field)
Ctrl- ←	Left one word (in same field)

Creating Address Books

In this section, you will learn to plan, open, and enter information into your Professional Write address book. As you begin with this hands-on learning phase, keep the following rules in mind:

❏ You can have any number of address books (as much as your computer's memory can support)

❏ You cannot change the fields that are displayed on the Address Book form, although it is up to you how you enter the information.

❏ You do not have to fill in every field for every record; you can use only the fields that your needs require.

❏ On a hard disk system or on a 3 1/2-inch disk, an address book can store up to 2,000 records.

❏ If you're using 5 1/4-inch disks, your address book can store up to 1,000 records.

Opening the Address Book File

The first step in creating an address book is to create the address book file. To do this, follow these steps:

1. Start Professional Write.

2. When the Main menu is displayed on-screen, select the **Create/ Edit** option.

3. On the Create/Edit screen, press F6 to open the Addresses menu.

4. Choose the **Select address book** option. Professional Write displays a screen telling you that ADDRESS.SPC is the address book being used (see fig. 10.3).

5. Backspace over the file name ADDRESS.SPC and type the name you want to assign to your address book.

6. Press F7. The program provides a screen on which you can enter a description of the file. (The description is optional, but it can help you find the file you need when your data directory starts to get crowded.)

7. Type a description to help you remember the contents of the file (see fig. 10.4).

8. Press Enter. The first blank record of your new address book is displayed (see fig. 10.5).

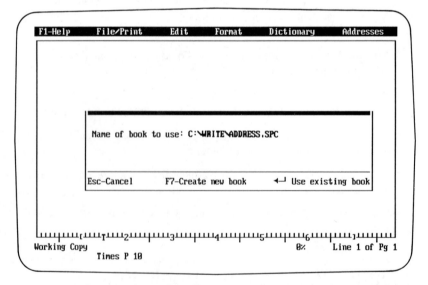

Fig. 10.3. Professional Write tells you which address book is being used.

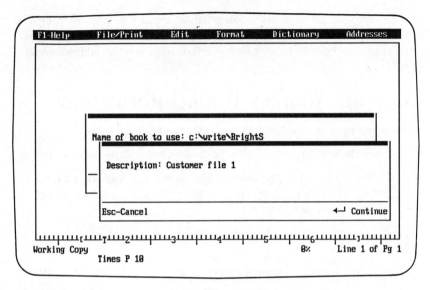

```
F1-Help       File/Print    Edit      Format      Dictionary      Addresses




      ┌──────────────────────────────────────────┐
      │ Name of book to use: c:\write\BrightS     │
      │                                           ┌──────────────────────┐
      │    Description: Customer file 1           │                      │
      │                                           │                      │
      │                                           │                      │
      │ Esc-Cancel                          ◄─┘ Continue                 │
```

Fig. 10.4. Entering a description for the address book file.


```
F1-Help       File/Print    Edit      Format      Dictionary      Addresses
      ┌──────────────────────────────────────────────────────────┐
      │                    Address Book                           │
      │    Title    :                                             │
      │    First name:                                            │
      │    Last name :                                            │
      │    Position  :                                            │
      │    Company:                                               │
      │    Address:                                               │
      │          :                                                │
      │    City :                                                 │
      │    State:                    Zip :                        │
      │                                                           │
      │    Work phone:               Home phone:                  │
      │    Comment 1 :                                            │
      │    Comment 2 :                                            │
      │                 Enter new information.                    │
      │ Esc-Cancel                               F10-Add          │
```

Working Copy
    Times P 10

Fig. 10.5. The first blank record of the new address book.

As you can see, the Address Book window appears to pop up over the working copy of the document. The cursor is positioned after the first field (Title) and you are now ready to enter information into the address book.

Entering Address Book Information

To enter information into the address book, follow these steps:

1. From the working copy, open the Addresses menu by pressing F6.

2. If you want to use the current file, select the **Add an address** option. (If you need to open another file first, use the **Select address book** option first.)

3. Position the cursor in the field to which you want to add information.

4. Type the information for the field.

5. Press Enter or Tab to go to the next field.

6. Continue entering information in the fields as necessary.

7. When you finish entering all necessary information in the address book record, press F10 to add the record to the address book file and to display a blank record.

> If you make a mistake while you are entering information, use the Backspace or the Del key to remove the incorrect letter. Then retype the correct text.

Working with Address Books

As mentioned earlier in this chapter, after you have the information in the Professional Write address book, you need to know how to work with it. After you have entered records, you can perform the following tasks:

❏ Search for specific records

❏ Modify (edit) records

❏ Copy records

❏ Print records

❏ Import records into a document

Searching for Records

To start a search procedure, you use the **Find an address** option in the Addresses menu. You then tell Professional Write how it can locate the records you want by entering instructions on the search form. This section explains how to use the search feature and shows you how to enter search criteria and wild cards.

What Is the Search Form?

You tell Professional Write to locate certain records by entering information on the search form. But what does it look like; how will you know it when you see it?

The search form actually looks just like a blank Address Book form, except that the line Enter search instructions is displayed at the bottom of the form.

To display the search form, select **Find an address** from the Addresses menu.

Entering Search Instructions

The concept of using search instructions is simple. When you want to find a particular record, you enter a word that you want to look for in a particular field. Perhaps an example will explain this better than an abstract explanation.

Suppose that you have been entering address book information that records the names and addresses of clients in the midwest. After entering a variety of records, you realize that you have been typing the ZIP code for a town in Illinois incorrectly; instead of 60814, as you have been entering, the correct ZIP code is 60914.

You need to go through all the records and find the ones that have the incorrect ZIP code so that you can change the information. Manually searching through hundreds of records would be a tedious job. Wouldn't it be nice to have the program do it for you?

To have Professional Write find the information, select **Find an address** from the Addresses menu. The search form is displayed. Because you need to find all the records that have 60814 entered in the Zip field, you press Tab nine times to position the cursor in the Zip field. Then, to tell Professional Write to find that ZIP code, you type *60814* and press F10 (see fig.

10.6). The status line at the bottom of the search form tells you to press F10 to find the address.

Professional Write then displays the first record found that has 60814 entered in the Zip field (see fig. 10.7). You can page through additional records that match the search instructions by pressing PgDn. If you want to see a previous record, you can return to it by pressing PgUp.

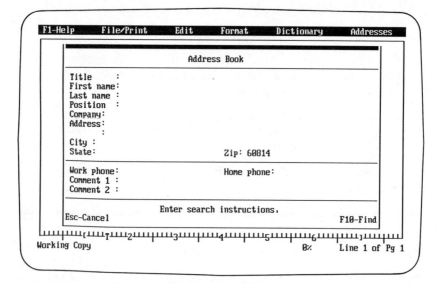

Fig. 10.6. Entering the search instruction.

This type of searching results in an exact match; in other words, Professional Write finds only those records that match exactly the information you specified in the field. (The program ignores differences in capitalization, however.) In the preceding example, the program wouldn't have found a record with 60714 entered in the Zip field; only records with 60814 were retrieved.

Using Wild Cards

Another type of search is available to you if you are uncertain about the values in the fields of the records you want to find. Suppose, for example, that you want to display the records of all customers who have a last name beginning with the letter B. By using what's known as a *wild card search*, you can have Professional Write locate all the records with a word beginning with B in the Last Name field.

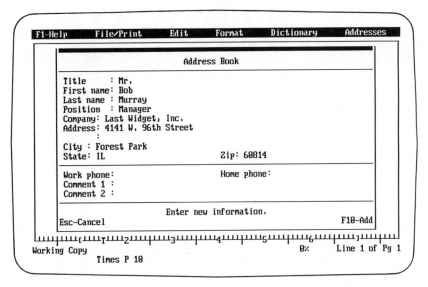

```
┌─────────────────────────────────────────────────────────────────┐
│ F1-Help      File/Print      Edit      Format      Dictionary      Addresses │
│  ┌──────────────────────────────────────────────────────────┐  │
│  │ ▬▬▬▬▬                                                      │  │
│  │                      Address Book                          │  │
│  │   Title    : Mr.                                           │  │
│  │   First name: Bob                                          │  │
│  │   Last name : Murray                                       │  │
│  │   Position  : Manager                                      │  │
│  │   Company: Last Widget, Inc.                               │  │
│  │   Address: 4141 W. 96th Street                             │  │
│  │         :                                                  │  │
│  │   City : Forest Park                                       │  │
│  │   State: IL                    Zip: 60814                  │  │
│  │  ────────────────────────────────────────────────────     │  │
│  │   Work phone:              Home phone:                     │  │
│  │   Comment 1 :                                              │  │
│  │   Comment 2 :                                              │  │
│  │  ────────────────────────────────────────────────────     │  │
│  │                 Enter new information.                     │  │
│  │   Esc-Cancel                              F10-Add          │  │
│  └──────────────────────────────────────────────────────────┘  │
│  ‖‖‖‖[‖‖‖‖‖T‖‖‖2‖‖‖‖‖3‖‖‖‖‖4‖‖‖‖‖5‖‖‖‖‖6‖‖‖‖‖‖7‖‖‖‖‖‖        │
│  Working Copy                          0%     Line 1 of Pg 1      │
│           Times P 10                                             │
└─────────────────────────────────────────────────────────────────┘
```

Fig. 10.7. *Professional Write displays the first record that matches the search instructions.*

Professional Write provides a *wild-card* symbol (..) that you can use in place of letters (or numbers) of which you are unsure. Perhaps you know what the letters are, but you do not want to take the time to type them. Whatever the reason, you can use the wild-card symbol to tell Professional Write to "substitute any characters here." The following list gives you some examples of search instructions that use the wild-card symbol:

Enter this	In this field	To find this
B..	Last name	Bennington Bip bazooka Buffoon
..an	First name	Dan Stan LeeAn Sean Fran
(317)..	Work phone	(317)846-7722 (317)575-9900 (317)632-6501
Pres..	Position	President

Figure 10.8 shows a wild-card search being initiated. After you press F10 to begin the search, Professional Write finds and displays the first record that meets the search instructions. To view other records, press PgDn.

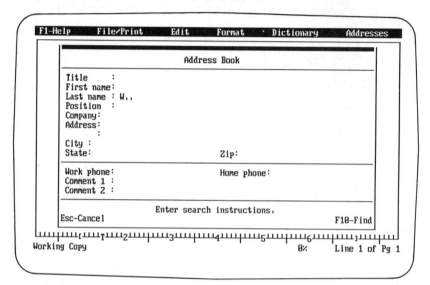

Fig. 10.8. *Entering a wild-card search instruction.*

After Professional Write locates the records you want, page through the records by pressing PgDn to display subsequent records and PgUp to display previous records.

Editing Address Book Information

You now know how to enter information into address books and how to search for and display the information you want. Now you need to know what to do with that information.

After the record is displayed, you can edit it as you would any other document. Use the cursor-movement keys (listed in table 10.2) to move the cursor to the field you want; then type over the text as necessary or make other editing changes. To delete the information in a field, press Ctrl-E.

After you make your changes, press F10 to save the record.

Deleting Records

Occasionally, you will need to weed out your address book file. Information changes, people come and go, and products and companies come and go, as well. When you need to delete a record in the address book, follow these steps:

1. Use the search form to locate the record(s) you want to delete.

2. Press the F9 key. Professional Write warns you that you are about to delete the record (see fig. 10.9).

3. Press Enter. The record on-screen is deleted, and the next record found according to the search instruction is displayed.

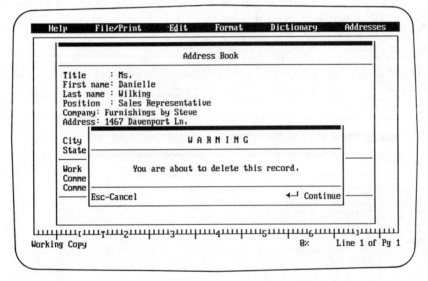

Fig. 10.9. Professional Write warns you about deleting the record.

Using Address Book Information in Form Letters

Do you always know a form letter when you see one? A badly copied letter with names and addresses typed in tells the recipient "We wanted to get this information to you, but your patronage is not worth enough time to merit a personal letter." And yet, from a business standpoint, you may not have the time or the personnel to make every letter you send out a piece of personal correspondence.

Professional Write enables you to produce form letters that don't look like form letters. In addition, because the program pulls information from existing records in your address book, you can literally create one hundred form letters in the time it takes you to type one personalized letter.

Creating the Form Letter

The whole secret to creating a form letter and merging information lies in the way you create the form. The form that you create—called the *form letter model*—stores the basic information that will be printed on every letter. Also on the form letter model are the *field identifiers*, which tell Professional Write where to place the data from the address book fields that it merges with the document.

For example, figure 10.10 shows the address book from which data is placed in the form letter. Figure 10.11 shows how the field identifiers are placed in the form letter model so that the information is merged correctly.

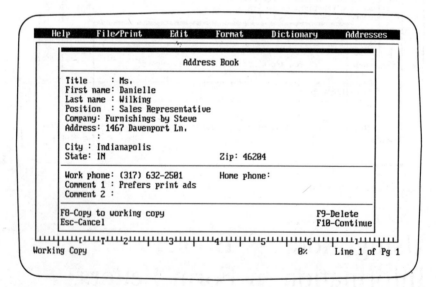

Fig. 10.10. The address book from which data is pulled.

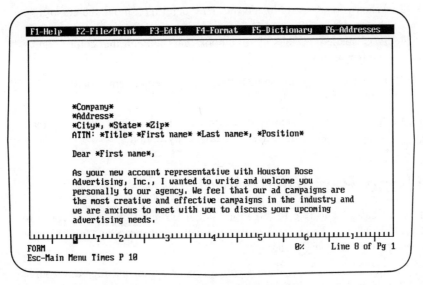

```
 F1-Help   F2-File/Print   F3-Edit   F4-Format   F5-Dictionary   F6-Addresses



       *Company*
       *Address*
       *City*, *State* *Zip*
       ATTN: *Title* *First name* *Last name*, *Position*

       Dear *First name*,

       As your new account representative with Houston Rose
       Advertising, Inc., I wanted to write and welcome you
       personally to our agency. We feel that our ad campaigns are
       the most creative and effective campaigns in the industry and
       we are anxious to meet with you to discuss your upcoming
       advertising needs.

 FORM                                            0%      Line 8 of Pg 1
 Esc-Main Menu Times P 10
```

Fig. 10.11. The form letter with field identifiers.

Understanding Field Identifiers

There are a few rules you should remember regarding the use of field identifiers:

❏ Field identifiers are taken from the field names used in the address book.

❏ Enclose all field identifiers in asterisks (*).

❏ Use the same number of spaces and words in the field identifier that you used as the field name in the address book.

❏ Place punctuation outside the asterisks (such as *City*, *State* *Zip*).

❏ Do not type the colon after the field identifier.

❏ You can enter more than one field identifier on a line, but remember that the length of the data in some fields may be longer than others.

To create the form letter model, follow these steps:

1. Compose the document in the usual way, as you would any other letter in Professional Write.

2. When you are ready to add the field identifiers, move the cursor to the proper position and type an asterisk, the field name (exactly as it is spelled in the address book but without the colon), and another asterisk.

3. Press Enter to go to the next line, and proceed to enter field identifiers as necessary.

4. After you finish creating the form letter model, open the File/Print menu and select the **Save working copy** option.

Using Position Indicators

In some cases, you need to tell Professional Write exactly where you want the information to be inserted so that the data aligns properly. For example, consider the following paragraph:

BrightStar Toys, Inc., thanks you for your comments regarding our *Comment 1* line, and we hope that you continue to be pleased with your investments in BrightStar products.

In this address book, you record the names, addresses, and comments of customers who write in about toys they have purchased. If the customer has a positive comment, you place the name of the toy purchased in the Comment 1 field; if the response is negative, you place the toy's name in the Comment 2 field. This way, you can create two different form letters based on the customer's response to your products, and you have a way of searching for the products that receive the least favorable comments.

Position indicators help you tell the program how to position the information. Because *Comment 1* in the example is included in a paragraph, you need to tell the program to treat the identifier as text. To do this, you add the indicator (T) after the field identifier, such as

Comment 1 (T)

Professional Write then formats the text around the field identifier and places the incoming data in the correct place.

Other position indicators are (L) for when you are merging information with preprinted forms and need to align the information carefully, and (R) for when you are merging information into columns of numbers.

Copying Address Book Information

Another address book use involves having Professional Write address your letterhead for you. If you are tired of typing all those repetitive addresses, you can use the address book program to plug in the addresses for you automatically.

For example, suppose that you want to paste the information from the address book record shown in figure 10.12 into a document. To copy the information into the document without retyping it, follow these steps:

1. Open the document into which you want to paste the information.

2. Open the address book by choosing **Select address book** from the Addresses menu (if the address books isn't already active).

3. When the first record of the address book is displayed, select **Find an address**. The search form is then displayed.

4. Type the search instructions and press F10 to begin the search.

5. When Professional Write displays the correct address, press F8 to paste the information into the document. Professional Write then removes the address book from the screen and displays the document with the address in place (see fig. 10.13).

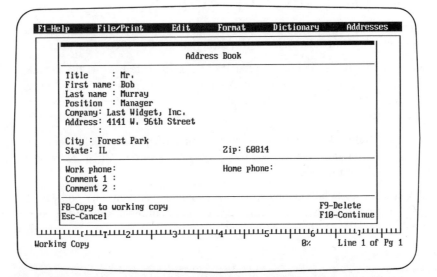

Fig. 10.12. *You can paste information from the address book into a document.*

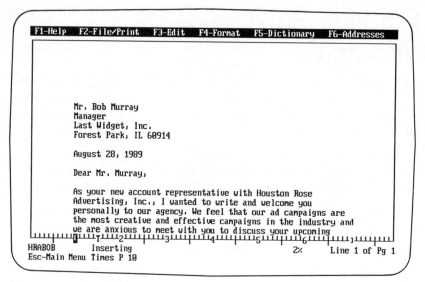

F1-Help   F2-File/Print   F3-Edit   F4-Format   F5-Dictionary   F6-Addresses

```
Mr. Bob Murray
Manager
Last Widget, Inc.
Forest Park, IL 60914

August 28, 1989

Dear Mr. Murray,

As your new account representative with Houston Rose
Advertising, Inc., I wanted to write and welcome you
personally to our agency. We feel that our ad campaigns are
the most creative and effective campaigns in the industry and
we are anxious to meet with you to discuss your upcoming
```

HRABOB   Inserting   2%   Line 1 of Pg 1
Esc-Main Menu Times P 10

Fig. 10.13. The document with the address pasted in.

Professional Write uses its own default copy format to select the address book information and place it in the document. You can tailor the information you place into the document, as the next section explains.

Specifying the Copy Format

Although Professional Write comes with a built-in copy format, you can rearrange or change the fields as necessary to get the effect you want.

Start by displaying the copy format Professional Write uses as the default. Do this by pressing F6 to open the Addresses menu and selecting the **Specify copy format** option. Figure 10.14 shows the screen that is then displayed.

You can modify this format in any way. You can enter new field identifiers by typing over the existing identifiers, or you can press Ctrl-E to remove the existing information.

If you want to include punctuation (for example, between City and State), you can enter it on the copy form and it is placed automatically in the document. Figure 10.15 shows the new copy format.

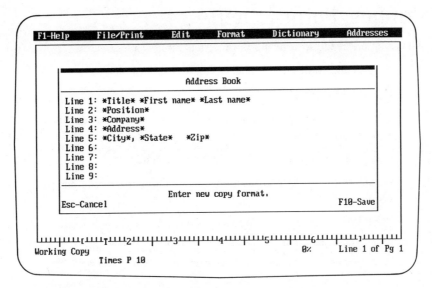

Fig. 10.14. *The default copy format.*

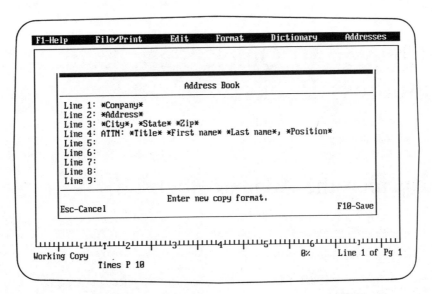

Fig. 10.15. *The new copy format.*

Printing Form Letters

When you are ready to print the form letters, follow these steps:

1. Display the form letter model on the Create/Edit screen.

2. Open the File/Print menu by pressing F2.

3. Choose the **Print working copy** option. (You can press Ctrl-O, if you prefer.)

4. Check the options on the Print Options screen.

5. At the **Data file to merge** option, enter the name of the address file that stores the records you plan to merge.

6. Press Enter. Professional Write then displays the search form.

7. Enter search instructions, if necessary, and press F10. Professional Write locates the records you specified and starts printing.

> You also can use files from dBASE, Professional File, or PFS: FILE as the data for your form letters. To find out more about merging these data types with Professional Write documents, consult your program's documentation.

Chapter 10 Quick Start: Using Address Books

This section reviews the procedures you have learned about using address books and printing form letters.

Opening the Address Book File

The first step in creating an address book is to create the address book file. To do this, follow these steps:

1. Start Professional Write.

2. When the Main menu is displayed on-screen, select the **Create/Edit** option.

3. From the Create/Edit screen, press F6 to open the Addresses menu.

4. Choose the **Select address book** option. Professional Write displays a screen, telling you that ADDRESS.SPC is the address book being used.

5. Backspace over the existing file name and press F7. Professional Write prompts you to enter a name (and path, if necessary) for the new address book file.

6. Press Enter. The program provides a screen on which you can enter a description of the file.

7. Type a description of the file.

8. Press Enter. The first blank record of your new address book is displayed.

Entering Address Book Information

To enter information into the address book, follow these steps:

1. From the working copy, open the Addresses menu by pressing F6.

2. If you want to use the current file, select the **Add an address** option. (If you need to open another file first, use the **Select address book** option first.)

3. Position the cursor in the field to which you want to add information.

4. Type the information for the field.

5. Press Enter or Tab to go to the next field.

6. Continue entering information in the fields as necessary.

7. When you finish entering all necessary information in the address book record, press F10 to add the record to the address book file and to display a blank record.

Deleting Records

To delete records in the address book, follow these steps:

1. Use the search form to locate the record(s) you want to delete.

2. Press the F9 key. Professional Write warns you that you are about to delete the record.

3. Press Enter. The record is deleted, and the next record found according to the search instruction is displayed.

Creating a Form Letter Model

To create the form letter model, follow these steps:

1. Compose the document in the usual way, as you would any other letter in Professional Write.

2. When you are ready to add the field identifiers, move the cursor to the proper position and type an asterisk, the field name (exactly as it is spelled in the address book but without the colon), and another asterisk.

3. Press Enter to get to the next line, and proceed to enter field identifiers as necessary.

4. When you finish creating the form letter model, open the File/ Print menu and select the **Save working copy** option.

Pasting Address Book Information into the Document

To copy address book information into the working copy, follow these steps:

1. Open the document into which you want to paste the information.

2. Open the address book by choosing **Select address book** from the Addresses menu (if the address book isn't already active).

3. When the first record of the address book is displayed, select **Find an address**. The search form is then displayed.

4. Type the search instructions and press F10 to begin the search.

5. When Professional Write displays the correct address, press F8 to paste the information into the document. Professional Write then removes the address book from the screen and displays the document with the address in place.

Printing Form Letters

To print the form letters, follow these steps:

1. Display the form letter model in the Create/Edit screen.

2. Open the File/Print menu by pressing F2.

3. Choose the **Print working copy** option. (You can press Ctrl-O, instead, if you prefer.)

4. Check the options on the Print Options screen to make sure that they are set the way you want them.

5. At the **Data file to merge** option, enter the name of the address file that stores the records you plan to merge.

6. Press Enter. Professional Write then displays the search form.

7. Enter search instructions, if necessary, and press F10. Professional Write locates the records you specified and starts printing.

Chapter Summary

This chapter introduced you to a terrific timesaving feature of Professional Write. By using the program's address book feature, you always have immediate, on-line access to hundreds (or thousands) of names, addresses, and other information pertinent to your business needs. In the next chapter, you learn to automate some of your Professional Write tasks by creating macros that do the work for you.

11

Using Macros

T his chapter introduces you to a feature that can save you a considerable amount of time and keystrokes: macros.

You may be familiar with the term *macro* if you have used other programs, such as 1-2-3, WordStar, or dBASE IV. Basically, a macro is similar to a mini-program that you assign to one key; you can then run the whole set of program lines by pressing the key to which the macro is assigned. From another perspective, you can think of a macro as a kind of beefed-up speed key—a speed key to which you can assign any operation that you want done.

For example, suppose that at the end of every sales letter, you include the following text:

Thank you very much for your time and consideration. If you have any questions, please don't hesitate to call.

Sincerely,

Casey Carlson
Account Representative

Using a Professional Write macro, you can automate the program so that the text is entered for you. If you were entering this text manually, you would require several minutes for data entry. When you assign this text to a macro, however, Professional Write can enter the entire section in a few seconds.

You can create macros to do a wide variety of things, including:

❑ Opening a file

❑ Adding a section of text you use frequently

❑ Setting new margins

❑ Changing a marked block to a particular font

❑ Running the spelling checker

❑ Opening an address book

❑ Adding a header or footer

With Professional Write, you can create macros that execute automatically, or macros that begin executing, then pause and wait for your input, and then finish executing. The latter macros are called *interactive* macros.

Understanding the Macros Menus

When you create and work with menus, you deal primarily with two menus: the Macros menu (see fig. 11.1) and the Recording Options menu (see fig. 11.2). Tables 11.1 and 11.2 give you some insight into the options available on these menus.

Table 11.1
Options on the Macros Menu

Option	Description
List macros	Displays a list of all macros that have been created
Record a macro	Begins the recording process
Erase a macro	Enables you to remove a macro from disk

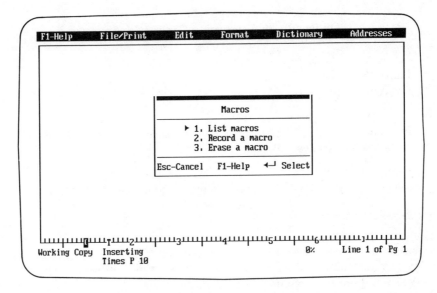

Fig. 11.1. *The Macros menu.*

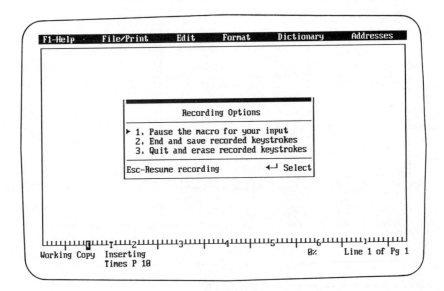

Fig. 11.2. *The Recording Options menu.*

Table 11.2
Options on the Recording Options Menu

Option	Description
Pause the macro for your input	Enables you to create an interactive macro that pauses at a predefined place and waits for your input
End and save recorded keystrokes	Stops recording and saves the keystrokes as a macro
Quit and erase recorded keystrokes	For those ''oops-I-didn't-mean-to-do-that'' moments; removes recorded keystrokes and turns off recording.

There is one other screen you should be familiar with, even though it is not a menu: the Save Recorded Keystrokes screen (see fig. 11.3). This screen is displayed, as you might expect, after you choose **End and save recorded keystrokes** from the Recording Options menu.

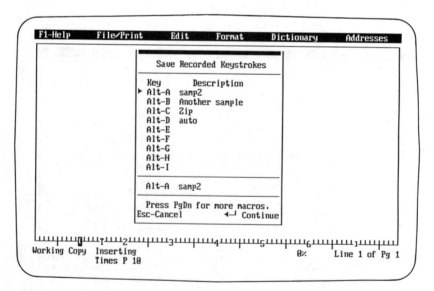

Fig. 11.3. *The Save Recorded Keystrokes screen.*

The next section explains how you can create a simple macro to help with your word processing tasks.

Creating a Macro

For best results, begin to create the macro where you want the macro to begin in your document. Because you basically create the macro by recording the keystrokes, you need to start at the place where you will be using the macro.

For example, suppose that you want the macro to open a file you use often. The macro must be able to do the following tasks:

❑ Select **Create/Edit**

❑ Select **Get a file**

❑ Enter the file name.

❑ Press Enter.

Because you want this macro to begin at the Main Menu, you need to go to the Main Menu before you begin to record the macro. Similarly, if your macro will be inserting a paragraph of text into a document, you should open a document before you begin to create the macro.

Creating a Basic Macro

Creating a basic macro involves the following steps:

❑ Go to the place where you want to start the macro.

❑ Turn on the recording feature.

❑ Go through all the operations you want the macro to record.

❑ Turn off the recording feature.

❑ Save the keystrokes.

This section explains all the steps necessary for creating your own macros. The section that follows this one explains how to create and use interactive macros.

To create a macro that enters a closing for a letter, follow these steps:

1. Open a new document. (If a document is currently in the working copy, select **Erase working copy** from the File/Print menu to erase the file from the screen.)

2. Press Alt-0 (zero) to display the Macros menu. (If you prefer, you can open the File/Print menu and select the **Use macros** option.)

3. From the Macros menu, choose the **Record a macro** option. A screen is shown, alerting you that you are about to begin recording the macro. Press Enter. Professional Write returns you to the document, and the word Recording is displayed in the status line at the bottom of the screen (see fig. 11.4).

4. Type *If you have any questions, please call.* and press Enter twice.

5. Now type *Sincerely,* and press Enter three times.

6. Press Alt-0 to turn off recording. The Recording Options menu appears.

7. Select **End and save recorded keystrokes** and press Enter. The Save Recorded Keystrokes screen is displayed, showing you a list of available macro names.

8. Position the cursor on the macro key you want to use and press Enter to select the key. (You will execute the macro by pressing these keys.)

9. Enter a macro description to remind you of the function of the macro (see fig. 11.5).

10 Press Enter. Professional Write displays the working copy again.

Now that the macro has been saved, you can play it back and insert the closing in your document whenever you need it. Before you learn to play back macros, however, you should know something about interactive macros.

Creating an Interactive Macro

An *interactive macro* performs a task up to a certain point and then waits for input from the user before continuing. Suppose, for example, that you want to create a macro to add the report heading for a weekly report you create. The heading itself stays the same from week to week, but the

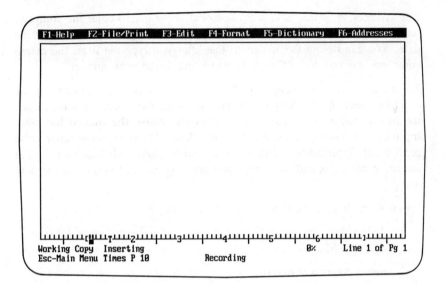

Fig. 11.4. *Professional Write displays* Recording *in the status line at the bottom of the screen.*

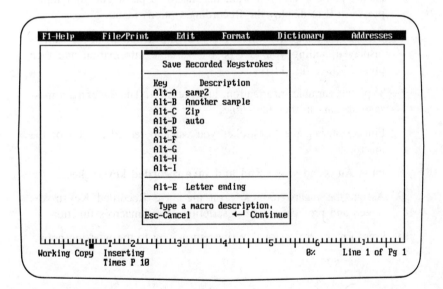

Fig. 11.5. *Entering a macro description.*

date changes. You can have a Professional Write macro enter the company name and the report heading and then pause, waiting for you to enter the date. You can design the macro so that after you type the date, the macro completes the task by adding your name and department number.

To create a pausing macro, simply record the macro as explained in the preceding section. At the point where you want the macro to pause, open the Macro menu (press Alt-0) and select the **Pause the macro for your input** option. Then type the input (which changes from report to report) and press Enter. Professional Write saves the macro, and each time you use the macro, it pauses operation at the appropriate point until you enter the new date.

To create an interactive macro, follow these steps:

1. At the place where you want the recording to begin, press Alt-0 to open the Macros menu.

2. Select **Record a macro**.

3. Type the text (or make the menu selections) that comprise the first part of the macro.

4. At the point where you want the macro to pause for your input, press Alt-0 to display the Recording Options menu.

5. Select the **Pause the macro for your input** option. A message is displayed, telling you to type the variable information and then press F9 (see fig. 11.6).

6. Type the variable information, and press F9. The Recording message appears in the status line.

7. Finish entering the keystrokes you want to record as part of the macro.

8. Press Alt-0 and select **End and save recorded keystrokes**.

9. Assign the macro to a key on the Save Recorded Keystrokes screen and provide a brief description of the macro's function.

10. Press Enter. Professional Write returns you to the working copy.

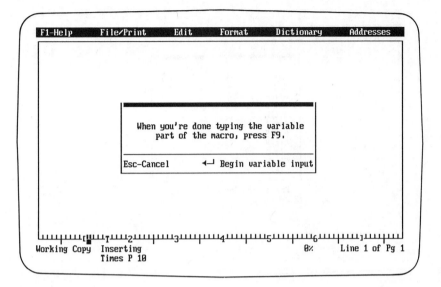

Fig. 11.6. *Professional Write prompts you to enter the variable information.*

Running Macros

To play a macro, you press the key combination you assigned to it (such as Alt-A, Alt-B, and so on). If the macro does not run properly, create the macro again, paying careful attention to the keystrokes you enter.

Listing Macros

Because macros are "invisible," you may occasionally need a reminder about the various macros you have created and the functions of each of those macros. To display a list of macros you have created, follow these steps:

1. Press Alt-0 to display the Macros menu.

2. Choose the **List macros** option. The Macro Definitions screen is displayed (see fig. 11.7).

3. When you are ready to go back to the Macros menu, press Esc.

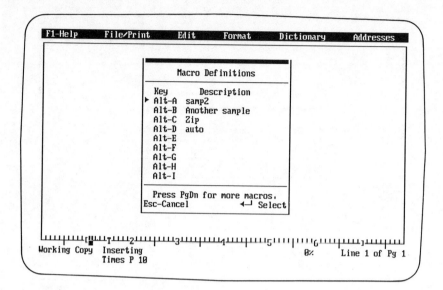

Fig. 11.7. *The Macro Definitions screen.*

Editing Macros

Professional Write provides no way to edit a macro, short of re-creating it. When you re-create a macro, you simply select **Record a macro** from the Macros menu and enter the macro's key combination. Professional Write warns you that this macro exists, and asks whether you want to overwrite it (see fig. 11.8).

Erasing Macros

The procedure for erasing macros is simple. When you want to delete a macro that has become obsolete, follow these steps:

1. Press Alt-0 to display the Macros menu.

2. Choose the **Erase a macro** option.

3. From the list of macros that is displayed, use the ↓ key to move the highlight to the macro you want to erase and press Enter.

4. Professional Write warns you that you are going to erase the macro; press Enter to continue.

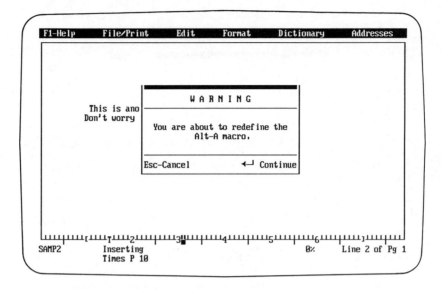

Fig. 11.8. Professional Write warns you against overwriting a macro.

Now that you have learned everything there is to know about creating basic and interactive macros, you are ready to try a few yourself. You can use the macros listed in the following section as they are or tailor them to fit your needs.

Sample Macros

This section gives you a cross-section of macro types that you can create for your word processing tasks.

Adding a *GRAPH* Command Line

To create a macro that inserts a *GRAPH* command line and pauses while you enter the name of the graph you want to use, follow these steps:

1. Open a document.

2. Press Alt-0.

3. Select the **Record new macro** option.

4. At the left margin of the document, type *GRAPH_. (*Note:* Be sure to leave a space in place of the underscore character.)

5. Press Alt-0 to display the Recording Options menu.

6. Choose **Pause the macro for your input**; then type the name of the graph and press F9.

7. Type * and press Enter; then press Alt-0.

8. Select **End and save recorded keystrokes** to save the macro.

9. Enter Ctrl-G as the name for the *GRAPH* macro, and type a short description.

10. Press Enter.

Adding a New Page Line

The following steps create a macro that inserts a *NEW PAGE* marker:

1. Open a document.

2. Press Alt-0.

3. Select the **Record new macro** option.

4. Position the cursor where you want the new page to begin.

5. Type *NEW PAGE* and press Enter.

6. Press Alt-0.

7. Choose **End and save recorded keystrokes** to save the macro.

8. Enter Ctrl-N as the name for the *NEW PAGE* macro, and type a short description.

9. Press Enter.

Adding Footers Automatically

Use the following steps to create a macro that adds a footer to your document file:

1. Open a document.

2. Press Alt-0.

3. Select the **Record new macro** option.

4. Press F4 to open the Format menu.

5. Choose **Set footer**.

6. Type *BrightStar Toys, Quarterly Report* in the **Footer 1:** line (or a footer that is appropriate for your needs).

7. Modify any other settings on the Footer screen, as necessary.

8. Press Enter.

9. Press Alt-0.

10. Select **End and save recorded keystrokes**.

11. Enter Ctrl-F as the name for the footer macro, and type a short description.

12. Press Enter.

Chapter 11 Quick Start: Creating Macros

This section reviews the basic procedures you have learned in this chapter.

Creating a Basic Macro

To create a macro that enters a letter closing, follow these steps:

1. Open a new document.

2. Press Alt-0 (zero) to display the Macros menu.

3. From the Macros menu, choose the **Record a macro** option.

4. Type *If you have any questions, please call.* and press Enter twice.

5. Now type *Sincerely,* and press Enter three times.

6. Press Alt-0 to turn off recording. The Recording Options menu appears.

7. Select **End and save recorded keystrokes** and press Enter. The Save Recorded Keystrokes screen is displayed, showing you a list of available macro names.

8. Position the cursor on the macro key you want to use and press Enter to select the key. (You will execute the macro by pressing these keys.)

9. Enter a macro description to remind you of the function of the macro.

10. Press Enter. Professional Write displays the working copy again.

Creating an Interactive Macro

To create an interactive macro, follow these steps:

1. At the place you want the recording to begin, press Alt-0 to open the Macros menu.

2. Select **Record a macro**.

3. Type the text (or make the menu selections) that comprise the first part of the macro.

4. At the point where you want the macro to pause for your input, press Alt-0 to display the Recording Options menu.

5. Select the **Pause the macro for your input** option. A message is displayed, telling you to type the variable information and then press F9.

6. Type the variable information, and press F9. The Recording message appears in the status line.

7. Finish entering the keystrokes you want to record as part of the macro.

8. Press Alt-0 and select **End and save recorded keystrokes**.

9. Assign the macro to a key on the Save Recorded Keystrokes screen and provide a brief description of the macro's function.

10. Press Enter. Professional Write returns you to the working copy.

Listing Macros

To display a list of macros you have created, follow these steps:

1. Press Alt-0 to display the Macros menu.

2. Choose the **List macros** option. The Macro Definitions screen is displayed.

3. When you are ready to go back to the Macros menu, press Esc.

Erasing Macros

When you want to delete a macro, follow these steps:

1. Press Alt-0 to display the Macros menu.

2. Choose the **Erase a macro** option.

3. From the list of macros that is displayed, highlight the macro you want to erase and press Enter.

4. Professional Write warns you that you are going to erase the macro; press Enter to continue.

Chapter Summary

This chapter concluded the book by teaching you how you can use macros to streamline some of your repetitive word processing tasks. By using macros to enter text, change formats, and perform other routine operations, you can further reduce the time you spend processing words. In the process, you might make your life a little easier.

Features New in Professional Write 2.1

T his appendix highlights the new features and changes in Professional Write 2.1.

The Preview Feature

Probably the most significant enhancement available in Professional Write 2.1 is the preview feature. Preview, which is covered in detail in Chapter 8, enables you to view the document on-screen the way it will appear in print, complete with font sizes and styles, graph placement, and headers and footers. You have several options for the way you view the document in preview mode, and you can make font changes from within preview.

Font Information

As you know, Professional Write supports a range of fonts. Previously, the program supported both portrait and landscape orientation, but you had no way of knowing which orientation or size had been chosen for a particular block of text. With Version 2.1, the status line at the bottom of the screen shows the font's name, size, and orientation. (Chapter 7 includes information on installing and working with fonts.)

305

Formatting Changes

A few changes enhance the way you set and work with the margins of your document (see Chapter 5):

❏ Now you can change margins either by positioning the cursor on the ruler line and pressing [(for left margin) or] (for right margin), or you can press F8 and type a numeric value for the margins.

❏ Additionally, you can change existing margins without first highlighting the area as a block. When you select **Set left/right margins** from the Format menu, Professional Write asks whether you want to insert new margins or change the margin for the current block. If you select **Change margins of current block**, Professional Write highlights the entire block and asks you whether you want to continue.

Enhanced Printer Support

The list of printers supported by Professional Write has been expanded. More than 150 printers now can be used with the Professional Write program. In addition to the numerous dot-matrix printers that are compatible with the program (some of which have limited font capability), Professional Write supports PostScript printers, as well as cartridge fonts and soft fonts for the Hewlett-Packard family of laser printers. (See Chapter 8 for more information.)

File Compatibility Changes

The last major enhancement in Professional Write 2.1 concerns the transfer of files among programs. For example, now Professional Write can accept graphics that you produce with PFS: First Graphics. This file compatibility is also useful for people who have some experience with WordPerfect 5.0, PFS: First Choice 3.0, Microsoft Word 4.0, and OfficeWriter 6. Now Professional Write can read directly the files produced in these programs. (Chapter 4 provides information on importing text into Professional Write. Appendix D explains using Professional Write text in PFS: First Publisher documents.)

B

Professional Write
Speed Keys

T hroughout this book, you have seen references to speed key combinations. Speed keys enable you to bypass the menu selection sequences and carry out operations quickly.

The speed keys in this reference section are presented according to function. For an alphabetical listing of all available speed keys, see your program documentation.

Working with Files

When You Want To	Use This Speed Key
Open a file	Ctrl-G
Save a file	Ctrl-S

Moving within the Document

When You Want To	Use This Speed Key
Jump to another page	Ctrl-J
Jump to start of block	Ctrl-Q
Jump to end of block	Ctrl-Z

Editing the Document

When You Want To	Use This Speed Key
Check spelling of a word	Ctrl-A
Check spelling of document	Ctrl-V
Delete a word	Ctrl-W
Delete a line	Ctrl-L

Working with Blocks

When You Want To	Use This Speed Key
Mark a block	Ctrl-T
Mark a rectangle	Ctrl-R
Copy a block	Ctrl-C
Paste a block	Ctrl-P
Erase a block	Del

Enhancing the Document

When You Want To	Use This Speed Key
Boldface a word	Ctrl-B
Underline a word	Ctrl-U
Center a line	Ctrl-X
Start drawing feature	Ctrl-Y

Formatting the Document

When You Want To	Use This Speed Key
Change margins	Ctrl-[
Indent	Ctrl-N
Change tabs	Ctrl-K
Double space	Ctrl-D

Using Special Features

When You Want To	Use This Speed Key
Use a macro	Alt-0 (zero)
Find and replace	Ctrl-F
Use the calculator	Ctrl-M
Preview the working copy	Ctrl-PrtSc
Print the working copy	Ctrl-O

Editing and Cursor-Movement Keys

▶ T his appendix lists for quick reference the keys you use for moving the cursor and editing.

Editing Keys

When you are editing a document, a few keys make your life easier. These keys are shown in the following list:

Key	Function
Backspace	Erases character to the left of the cursor position
Ins	Toggles the insert mode on/off
Del	Deletes character at cursor position (unless a block is highlighted, and then Del deletes the entire block)
Ctrl-A	Checks the spelling of the word at the cursor position

311

Key	Function
Ctrl-V	Checks the spelling of the document, beginning at the cursor position
Ctrl-W	Deletes the word at the cursor position
Ctrl-L	Deletes the line at the cursor position

Cursor-Movement Keys

The following list shows the keys you use to move the cursor around within the document:

Key	Moves cursor
↑	Up one line
↓	Down one line
→	Right one character
Ctrl-→	Right one word
←	Left one character
Ctrl-←	Left one word
Home	Beginning of current line
Ctrl-Home	Beginning of document
End	End of current line
Ctrl-End	End of document
PgUp	Up one screen
Ctrl-PgUp	To preceding page
PgDn	Down one screen
Ctrl-PgDn	To following page
Tab	To next tab on ruler
Shift-Tab	To previous tab on ruler
Ctrl-J	To another page

You can use the arrow keys even before you have text in the document. Other cursor-movement keys, like Home or End, for example, do not work until you have entered text.

D

Using Professional Write Documents with PFS: First Publisher

As you may know, in addition to Professional Write, Software Publishing Corporation produces a variety of business software products. One of these products, PFS: First Publisher, can be used to give your Professional Write documents a "designer" look.

What Is First Publisher?

First Publisher is a desktop publishing program that enables you to turn routine memos, letters, reports, and newsletters into professional-looking, graphically designed documents. Do you want to create a sophisticated logo for your company? Are you responsible for producing a multipage annual report? Would your business benefit from the advantage of publishing a client newsletter? First Publisher provides you with all the software tools you need to create, design, lay out, illustrate, and print documents that will impress your audience.

313

How Do You Use Professional Write with First Publisher?

It's a simple matter to turn your Professional Write documents into a desktop-published piece by using First Publisher. Because First Publisher directly supports files that are created in Professional Write, you can import text directly into First Publisher without losing any formats or text styles. If you have specified fonts in your Professional Write document, those fonts are kept in First Publisher, if the font file used by First Publisher (MASTER.FNT) contains the necessary instructions to work with that font. (For more information on setting up fonts to work with First Publisher, see *Using PFS: First Publisher,* published by Que Corporation.)

Basically, the steps involved in using a Professional Write file in a First Publisher document are as follows:

1. Create the file in Professional Write (see fig. D.1).

2. Save the file.

3. Exit Professional Write.

4. Start First Publisher.

5. When First Publisher's work area is displayed, select **Get text** from the Text menu. *Note:* If you are adding this text to an existing document, first position the cursor at the point you want the text to be placed.

6. Highlight the name of the file you want to import. (You need to enter the path to the Professional Write data file after the **Path:** setting, if the file is in a directory other than the one you are working with.)

7. Select the Get button by clicking it (if you have a mouse) or by pressing F1.

8. First Publisher recognizes automatically that you have specified a Professional Write file. The program may request that you enter the path to the Professional Write program files.

9. If you have used fonts that are not available in First Publisher, the program will ask you to enter the path to the directory that stores the files from the Fonts Disk. If the fonts still are not found, First Publisher will ask you whether you want to have the program automatically substitute other characters or fonts for the fonts not found. When you press F1, First Publisher imports the document and displays it in the work area.

```
F1-Help    F2-File/Print    F3-Edit    F4-Format    F5-Dictionary    F6-Addresses


                          Houston Rose Advertising
                             History Unfolds...


                    From the Wild West to the Enchanted East


            In 1888, not too many people were looking for an advertising
            agency. Lotions, potions, and sundries tended to sell
            themselves; medicine men pushed the fermented whiskey tonics
            in the suspicious-looking brown glass bottles. No one needed
            a company to represent their product--there just wasn't
            enough competition. If you had a product, you got attention.
            Only the rare wallflower was overlooked on the general store
            shelves.

            On a dusty, dry day in July, 1888, Hugo Higgenmeyer had an
            idea for a new product. Unlike most others in his time,


 HRAHUGO           Inserting                              7%     Line 2 of Pg 1
 Esc-Main Menu Times P 10
```

Fig. D.1. *The document created in Professional Write.*

You then can perform any number of operations on the file. Starting with the example in figure D.1, for instance, you may want to use First Publisher to do any of the following things:

- ❏ Create a better heading for the report
- ❏ Change the font used
- ❏ Make the report into three columns
- ❏ Add a graphic element and reposition the text around the graphic
- ❏ Draw rules or boxes, or both, to highlight information

> If you are planning to import your Professional Write document into First Publisher, first remove all lines that you have entered with the draw feature. Because First Publisher doesn't recognize the line as such, question marks (?) will be substituted in place of the individual line characters.

Sample Documents

This section provides you with examples of how you can take the design of your Professional Write documents one step further by enhancing them with First Publisher.

Business Stationery

A business creates its own identity by the type of business cards, letterhead, and envelopes it uses. Because many of your clients may get their first impression of you through the mail, it is imperative to look good in print. First Publisher can take an ordinary letter, as shown in figure D.2, and give it a special identity (see fig. D.3).

The letter looks pretty good, and, if it is printed on a laser printer, the quality will help make a good impression. If you spruce up the original letter by adding the graphic design shown in figure D.3, however, the letter becomes an entirely different document. After you finish with the letter, you can save the design work as a template so that you can use the letterhead design again.

Annual Reports

Similar to business stationery, reports benefit from a professional, polished look. Do you want to include a cover page that incorporates graphics? Do you want to use special, ornate lettering in the heading? Would the report look best in a multicolumn format? First Publisher gives you many options for organizing and laying out your text in the most appealing way possible. Figure D.4 shows a report created in Professional Write; figure D.5 shows the report after it has been finished with First Publisher.

Company Newsletters

The last sample shown in this appendix is the company newsletter. In Professional Write, because your design and layout capabilities are limited, a company newsletter can be nothing more than pages of text with headers, footers, and graphs. With First Publisher, you can create multicolumn documents with a variety of art elements and special design features. Figure D.6 shows a ''newsletter'' done in Professional Write; figure D.7 shows the same newsletter after it has been finished with First Publisher.

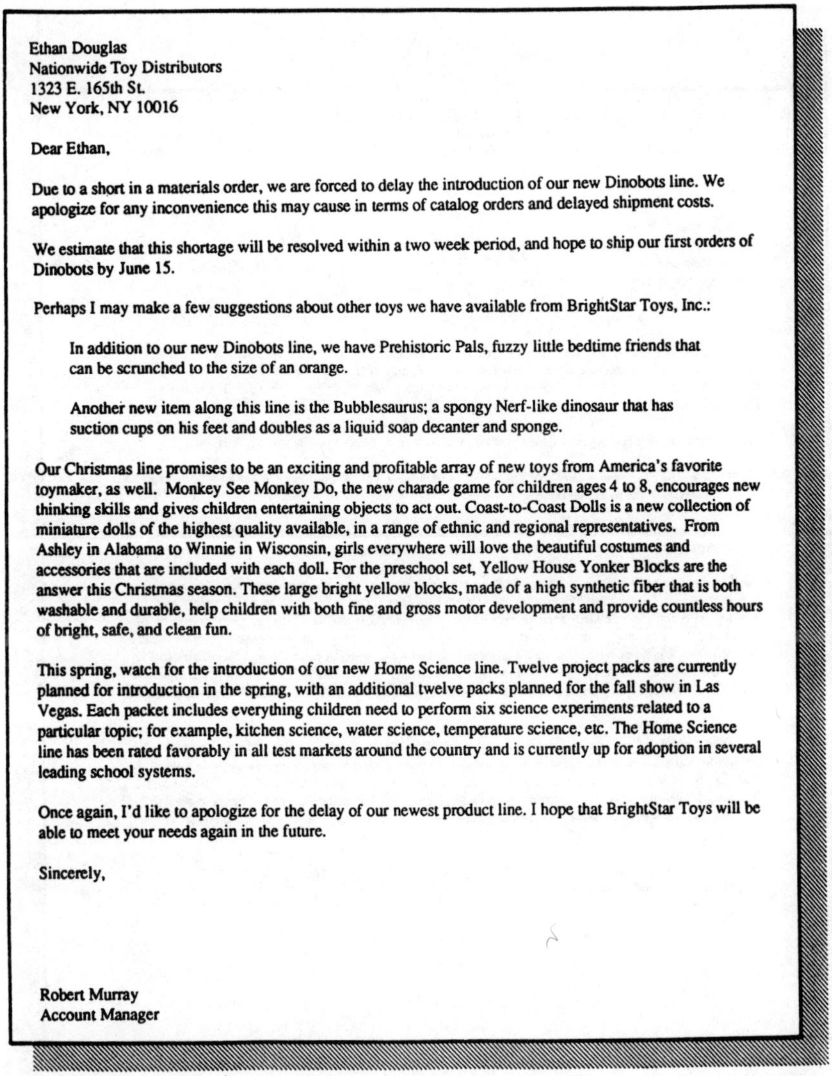

Ethan Douglas
Nationwide Toy Distributors
1323 E. 165th St.
New York, NY 10016

Dear Ethan,

Due to a short in a materials order, we are forced to delay the introduction of our new Dinobots line. We apologize for any inconvenience this may cause in terms of catalog orders and delayed shipment costs.

We estimate that this shortage will be resolved within a two week period, and hope to ship our first orders of Dinobots by June 15.

Perhaps I may make a few suggestions about other toys we have available from BrightStar Toys, Inc.:

> In addition to our new Dinobots line, we have Prehistoric Pals, fuzzy little bedtime friends that can be scrunched to the size of an orange.

> Another new item along this line is the Bubblesaurus; a spongy Nerf-like dinosaur that has suction cups on his feet and doubles as a liquid soap decanter and sponge.

Our Christmas line promises to be an exciting and profitable array of new toys from America's favorite toymaker, as well. Monkey See Monkey Do, the new charade game for children ages 4 to 8, encourages new thinking skills and gives children entertaining objects to act out. Coast-to-Coast Dolls is a new collection of miniature dolls of the highest quality available, in a range of ethnic and regional representatives. From Ashley in Alabama to Winnie in Wisconsin, girls everywhere will love the beautiful costumes and accessories that are included with each doll. For the preschool set, Yellow House Yonker Blocks are the answer this Christmas season. These large bright yellow blocks, made of a high synthetic fiber that is both washable and durable, help children with both fine and gross motor development and provide countless hours of bright, safe, and clean fun.

This spring, watch for the introduction of our new Home Science line. Twelve project packs are currently planned for introduction in the spring, with an additional twelve packs planned for the fall show in Las Vegas. Each packet includes everything children need to perform six science experiments related to a particular topic; for example, kitchen science, water science, temperature science, etc. The Home Science line has been rated favorably in all test markets around the country and is currently up for adoption in several leading school systems.

Once again, I'd like to apologize for the delay of our newest product line. I hope that BrightStar Toys will be able to meet your needs again in the future.

Sincerely,

Robert Murray
Account Manager

Fig. D.2. *A letter composed in Professional Write.*

 BrightStar Toys, Inc.
1980 Westchester Ln., Suite 202
New York, NY 10014

Ethan Douglas
Nationwide Toy Distributors
1323 E. 165th St.
New York, NY 10016

Dear Ethan,

Due to a short in a materials order, we are forced to delay the introduction of our new Dinobots line. We apologize for any inconvenience this may cause in terms of catalog orders and delayed shipment costs. We estimate that this shortage will be resolved within a two week period, and hope to ship our first orders of Dinobots by June 15.

Perhaps I may make a few suggestions about other toys we have available from BrightStar Toys, Inc.:

In addition to our new Dinobots line, we have Prehistoric Pals, fuzzy little bedtime friends that can be scrunched to the size of an orange.

Another new item along this line is the Bubblesaurus; a spongy Nerf-like dinosaur that has suction cups on his feet and doubles as a liquid soap decanter and sponge.

Our Christmas line promises to be an exciting and profitable array of new toys from America's favorite toymaker, as well. Monkey See Monkey Do, the new charade game for children ages 4 to 8, encourages new thinking skills and gives children entertaining objects to act out. Coast-to-Coast Dolls is a new collection of miniature dolls of the highest quality available, in a range of ethnic and regional representatives. From Ashley in Alabama to Winnie in Wisconsin, girls everywhere will love the beautiful costumes and accessories that are included with each doll. For the preschool set, Yellow House Yonker Blocks are the answer this Christmas season. These large bright yellow blocks, made of a high synthetic fiber that is both washable and durable, help children with both fine and gross motor development and provide countless hours of bright, safe, and clean fun.

This spring, watch for the introduction of our new Home Science line. Twelve project packs are currently planned for introduction in the spring, with an additional twelve packs planned for the fall show in Las Vegas. Each packet includes everything children need to perform six science experiments related to a particular topic; for example, kitchen science, water science, temperature science, etc. The Home Science line has been rated favorably in all test markets around the country and is currently up for adoption in several leading school systems.

Once again, I'd like to apologize for the delay of our newest product line. I hope that BrightStar Toys will be able to meet your needs again in the future.

Sincerely,

Fig. D.3. *The letter created with a letterhead banner in First Publisher.*

BrightStar Toys, Inc.
1989 Annual Report

1989 has been a record breaking year for BrightStar Toys, Inc. This report will detail the overall changes that have occurred in our company in the last 12 months; namely, the changes in staff, in housing, and in operations. Perhaps it would be quicker to list the areas that haven't changed!

Beginning on page two of this report, you will see material written by each of the departmental managers, summarizing the activities that have taken place in their departments during the last calendar year. The last three pages of the report are dedicated to future plans for 1990. Inserted inside the back cover of the report, you will find an Employee Response Card. Carrying on our tradition of the last 15 years, we ask you to fill out this card, listing your best and worst moments of the last year, and making any suggestions you might have for improvements in BrightStar's future. Thanks very much for your support during the last year.

New Hires and New Promotions

As you know, BrightStar has added some very important people to our staff in the last year. In this section, you will be introduced to each of these people and find out a little more about their roles at BrightStar.

In Operations, **Mary Lou Beasley** was hired as a balance and distribution clerk. Coming from a ten-year employment with AT&T, Mary Lou brings BrightStar a solid understanding of employee needs and will assist Mark Homeston with payroll on a regular basis.

In Marketing, **Roger Reynolds** joins us from the prestigous Ridge, Watson, and Wheeler advertising firm in Boston, MA. Roger will be our Junior Marketing Manager and will be responsible for the Dinobots line, the CarGo line, and the Powerpuff Dolls.

Lindy Walker has also joined the Marketing department in order to use her copywriting skills to help us create some innovative new campaigns for this season's hottest toys. Welcome aboard, Lindy!

Janice Hopkins, Associate Production Director, has come to BrightStar from a fast-paced computer assembly company. She brings with her a fundamental understanding of both electronics and computer hardware and will greatly benefit the production lines of all our toys.

The Publications staff would like to announce the promotion of **Summer Davidson** to Desktop Publishing Director. In her new role, Summer will instruct and direct her staff to produce all materials previously typeset on our new desktop publishing systems. (Next year, you can expect to see the Annual Report done on desktop, as well!)

Other promotions/hires include the following:

* **Roger Plotnik**, promoted to 3rd Shift Supervisor
* **Ann Raymond**, promoted to Copywriter

Fig. D.4. A report created in Professional Write.

 # BrightStar Toys, Inc.

1989 Annual Report

1989 has been a record breaking year for BrightStar Toys, Inc. This report will detail the overall changes that have occurred in our company in the last 12 months; namely, the changes in staff, in housing, and in operations. Perhaps it would be quicker to list the areas that haven't changed!

Beginning on page two of this report, you will see material written by each of the departmental managers, summarizing the activities that have taken place in their departments during the last calendar year. The last three pages of the report are dedicated to future plans for 1990. Inserted inside the back cover of the report, you will find an Employee Response Card. Carrying on our tradition of the last 15 years, we ask you to fill out this card, listing your best and worst moments of the last year, and making any suggestions you might have for improvements in BrightStar's future. Thanks very much for your support during the last year.

About the Editor

Jim Watkins has been with BrightStar's PR department for 12 years. He's just recently inherited the Annual Report.

New Hires and New Promotions

As you know, BrightStar has added some very important people to our staff in the last year. In this section, you will be introduced to each of these people and find out a little more about their roles at BrightStar.

In Operations, Mary Lou Beasley was hired as a balance and distribution clerk. Coming from a ten-year employment with AT&T, Mary Lou brings BrightStar a solid understanding of employee needs and will assist Mark Homeston with payroll on a regular basis.

In Marketing, Roger Reynolds joins us from the prestigous Ridge, Watson, and Wheeler advertising firm in Boston, MA. Roger will be our Junior Marketing Manager and will be responsible for the Dinobots line,

Fig. D.5. The report after First Publisher enhancements are added.

Houston Rose Advertising
History Unfolds...

Houston Rose Advertising, Inc.

From the Wild West to the Enchanted East

In 1888, not too many people were looking for an advertising agency. Lotions, potions, and sundries tended to sell themselves; medicine men pushed the fermented whiskey tonics in the suspicious-looking brown glass bottles. No one needed a company to represent their product--there just wasn't enough competition. If you had a product, you got attention. Only the rare wallflower was overlooked on the general store shelves.

On a dusty, dry day in July, 1888, Hugo Higgenmeyer had an idea for a new product. Unlike most others in his time, Hugo's product, a kind of a bath salt that was made from crushed rose petals, did have competition. How would he call attention to his product so people would stop using their old standards? He and best friend Jeremiah Houston found the answer; they would advertise. Jeremiah drew and painted signs with pictures of people bathing with Rosey's Bath Salts. The important thing, Hugo stressed, was that the people in the signs had to look as though they were completely happy and relaxed.

Rosey's Bath Salts sold well enough to allow Hugo to quit his carpentry and Houston to leave his farm. Moving into a boarding house in the city, the pair began to create a whole line of concoctions that eventually became the largest line of toiletry items to hit the west for the next 20 years.

Hugo and Houston both found wives and married during their years as co-presidents of Houston Rose Toiletries. Houston had no children, but Hugo and his wife Marjorie had one son, William. William was born in 1908 in St. Louis, Missouri.

In 1949, William Higgenmyer made a decision to carry on the tradition of Houston Rose Toiletries--yet to capitalize on his father's first major business talent--advertising--and sell the retail portion of the business.

Lotions, potions, and sundries tended to sell themselves; medicine men pushed the fermented whiskey tonics in the suspicious-looking brown glass bottles. No one needed a company to represent their product--there just wasn't enough competition. If you had a product, you got attention. Only the rare wallflower was overlooked on the general store shelves.

On a dusty, dry day in July, 1888, Hugo Higgenmeyer had an idea for a new product. Unlike most others in his time, Hugo's product, a kind of a bath salt that was made from crushed rose petals, did have competition. How would he call attention to his product so people would stop using their old standards? He and best friend Jeremiah Houston found the answer: they would advertise. Jeremiah drew and painted signs with pictures of people bathing with Rosey's Bath Salts. The important thing, Hugo stressed, was that the people in the signs had to look as though they were completely happy and relaxed.

Rosey's Bath Salts sold well enough to allow Hugo to quit his carpentry and Houston to leave his farm. Moving into a boarding house in the city, the pair began to create a whole line of concoctions that eventually became the largest line of toiletry items to hit the west for the next 20 years.

Hugo and Houston both found wives and married during their years as co-presidents of Houston Rose Toiletries. Houston had no children, but Hugo and his wife Marjorie had one son, William. William was born in 1908 in St. Louis, Missouri.

In 1949, William Higgenmyer made a decision to carry on the tradition of Houston Rose Toiletries--yet to capitalize on his father's first major business talent--advertising--and sell the retail portion of the business.

Company History Compiled and Published
by reVisions Plus, Inc., 1989

Fig. D.6. *The Professional Write newsletter.*

Houston Rose Advertising, Inc.

Vol. 2   History Unfolds...   October, 1989

From the Wild West to the Enchanted East

In 1888, not too many people were looking for an advertising agency. Lotions, potions, and sundries tended to sell themselves; medicine men pushed the fermented whiskey tonics in the suspicious-looking brown glass bottles. No one needed a company to represent their product--there just wasn't enough competition. If you had a product, you got attention. Only the rare wallflower was overlooked on the general store shelves.

On a dusty, dry day in July, 1888, Hugo Higgenmeyer had an idea for a new product. Unlike most others in his time, Hugo's product, a kind of a bath salt that was made from crushed rose petals, did have competition. How would he call attention to his product so people would stop using their old standards? He and best friend Jeremiah Houston found the answer: they would advertise. Jeremiah drew and painted signs with pictures of people bathing with Rosey's Bath Salts. The important thing, Hugo stressed, was that the people in the

signs had to look as though they were completely happy and relaxed.

Rosey's Bath Salts sold well enough to allow Hugo to quit his carpentry and Houston to leave his farm. Moving into a boarding house in the city, the pair began to create a whole line of concoctions that eventually became the largest line of toiletry items to hit the west for the next 20 years.

Hugo and Houston both found wives and married during their years as co-presidents of Houston Rose Toiletries. Houston had no children, but Hugo and his wife Marjorie had one son, William. William was born in 1908 in St. Louis, Missouri.

In 1949, William Higgenmeyer made a decision to carry on the tradition of Houston Rose Toiletries--yet to capitalize on his father's first major business talent--advertising--and sell the retail portion of the business.

Current News...

1989 has been a record breaking year for BrightStar Toys, Inc. This report will detail the overall changes that have occurred in our company in the last 12 months; namely, the changes in staff, in housing, and in operations. Perhaps it would be quicker to list the areas that haven't

changed!
Beginning on page two of this report, you will see material written by each of the departmental managers, summarizing the activities that have taken place in their departments during the last calendar year. The last three pages of the report are dedicated to future plans for 1990. Inserted inside the back cover of the report, you will find an Employee

Response Card. Carrying on our tradition of the last 15 years, we ask you to fill out this card, listing your best and worst moments of the last year, and making any suggestions you might have for improvements in BrightStar's future. Thanks very much for your support during

1

Fig. D.7. The newsletter finished with First Publisher.

Glossary

ASCII. An acronym for the American Standard Code for Information Interchange. ASCII is the "common denominator" way of saving and exchanging data from various programs.

Baud rate. The rate at which data is transferred by modem; also called the *communication speed*.

Clipboard. The Professional Write clipboard is an unseen area to which you can copy or move text.

Context-sensitive. Professional Write has a context-sensitive help system, which means that the program is sensitive to the placement of the cursor and displays help on any task you specify with the cursor.

Cursor. The small flashing underline that marks the place where characters appear on-screen when you type.

Cursor control keypad. The keys on the right side of the computer keyboard that allow you to move the cursor. Sometimes this keypad is separate, and sometimes it functions as a toggle with the numeric keypad as well.

Data file. A file in which data is stored.

Data-entry form. Can be used to refer to the Address Book form on which you enter names and addresses.

Database management. The term used to refer to the process of gathering, storing, and using data on a particular subject.

Delimited ASCII. A type of ASCII file in which individual data items are separated by characters such as the comma or quotation marks.

Field. A field in an address book that stores an individual data item, such as Name, Address, City, or State.

Fixed-length ASCII. A type of ASCII file in which the data items are stored in a columnar format.

Footers. Information lines that are printed along the bottom margin of a document.

Function keys. The keys marked F1 through F10, usually on the left or across the top of the keyboard.

Headers. Information lines included across the top of a document or report.

High resolution. Resolution refers to the quality of the screen display or printed output. The higher the resolution, the better the quality.

Insert cursor. When the insert cursor is active, the cursor appears as a flashing rectangle. Any characters typed are inserted at the cursor position.

Justified. Justified text aligns at both the left and right margins. Space is added between words so that the right margin aligns.

Left-justified. Left-justified text aligns along the left margin only.

Low resolution. This phrase refers to the quality of the screen display or printed output. The lower the resolution, the poorer the quality.

Macro. A macro is a series of recorded keystrokes that you can activate by pressing one key combination.

Mail merge. You can merge print form letters, labels, and envelopes by merging text in a document with data from the address book.

Menu bar. The bar across the top of the Professional Write. It lists the available menus.

Message line. The line at the bottom of the screen reminding you of important keys and giving instructions about different forms.

Nonjustified. Nonjustified text has an uneven (ragged) right margin.

Numeric keypad. The numeric keypad is a set of keys used for entering numbers. It consists of a group of keys located to the right of the keys used for typing the alphabet. On some computer keyboards, the numeric keypad also functions as a cursor control keypad.

Order of precedence. The order of mathematical operations in which a program computes the answer to an equation.

Overwrite mode. Also called *replace mode*, this mode is active when the replace cursor is being used. The replace cursor is a small flashing underline when the program is in overwrite mode.

Pausing macro. A macro that stops and waits for user input.

Pixels. The small dots of light that make up all characters and graphics on a computer screen.

Print head. The mechanism on the printer that controls the placement of the pins on paper.

QWERTY keyboard. The standard alphabetic keyboard found on ordinary computers and typewriters.

RAM. Random-access memory, which is the amount of memory made available for programs in your computer.

Record. Each entry in an address book that includes one person's (or company's) name, address, and other information items.

Replace cursor. When the replace cursor is active, characters that you type overwrite existing text.

Right-justified. Text that is aligned along the right margin, but not the left.

Ruler. You change margins, set indents, and control tabs by changing the settings on the ruler line at the bottom of the screen.

Search form. The form displayed when you select **Find an address** from the Addresses menu, enabling you to enter search instructions and find a particular form.

Search instructions. Instructions that tell Professional Write what data to search for in the database.

Selected text. Text that has been highlighted.

Speed keys. Key combinations that enable you to bypass certain menu selections. Available speed keys are shown in the menus to the right of the option.

Status line. The status line gives you important information about the size of the file; the name of the file; the font size, style, and orientation; and the line or column number of the cursor.

Text block. A highlighted section of text.

Working Copy. The area in which you create and work on the document. It is located below the status line.

Index

N

More Computer Knowledge from Que

1-2-3 Release 3 QuickStart

Developed by Que Corporation

More than 100 two-page illustrations help you learn the fundamental operations of 1-2-3 Release 3. This fast-paced visual approach guides you step-by-step through 1-2-3 worksheets, reports, graphs, databases, and macros.

$19.95 USA
Order #973
0-88022-438-X
433 pp.

Using PFS: First Publisher

by Katherine Murray

From word processing basics to advanced layout features, this text is power-packed with program and design tips! Includes a Quick Start lesson, step-by-step explanations of the program's capabilities, and coverage of DeskMate.

$22.95 USA
Order #937
0-88022-401-0
388 pp.

Using PFS: First Choice

by Katherine Murray

An excellent introduction to Versions 2 and 3 of this popular integrated program. A series of Quick Start tutorials leads readers step-by-step from First Choice fundamentals through coverage of each module. Shows how to use First Choice as an integrated system, as well as how to interface with other programs.

$22.95 USA
Order #984
0-88022-401-0
516 pp.

Using Harvard Graphics

by Steve Sagman and Jane Graver Sandlar

An excellent introduction to presentation graphics! This well-written text presents both program basics and presentation fundamentals to create bar, pie, line, and other types of informative graphs. Includes hundreds of samples!

$24.95 USA
Order #941
0-88022-407-X
550 pp.

1-2-3 Release 2.2 QuickStart

Developed by Que Corporation

Que's award-winning graphics approach makes it easy for you to get up and running with 1-2-3 Release 2.2! More than 200 pages of illustrations explain the program's worksheets, reports, graphs, databases, and macros. Also covers Release 2.01.

$19.95 USA
Order #1041
0-88022-502-5
450 pp.

Using 1-2-3 Release 3

Developed by Que Corporation

Only the spreadsheet experts at Que can bring you this comprehensive guide to the commands, functions, and operations of new 1-2-3 Release 3. Includes a comprehensive Command Reference, a useful Troubleshooting section, and easy-to-follow instructions for Release 3 worksheets, graphics, databases, and macros.

$24.95 USA
Order #971
0-88022-440-1
862 pp.

Using 1-2-3 Release 2.2, Special Edition

Developed by Que Corporation

Learn professional spreadsheet techniques from the world's leading publisher of 1-2-3 books! This comprehensive text leads you from worksheet basics to advanced 1-2-3 operations. Includes Allways coverage, a Troubleshooting section, a Command Reference, and a tear-out 1-2-3 Menu Map. The most complete resource available for Release 2.01 and Release 2.2!

$24.95 USA
Order #1040
0-88022-501-7
850 pp.

Upgrading to 1-2-3 Release 3

Developed by Que Corporation

This versatile text helps you evaluate your upgrading needs, then gets you up and running with the new features of 1-2-3 Release 3. Covers hardware and operating system requirements, plus helpful techniques and troubleshooting tips.

$14.95 USA
Order #1018
0-88022-491-6
388 pp.

Upgrading and Repairing PCs
by Scott Mueller

The ultimate resource for personal computer upgrade, repair, maintenance, and troubleshooting! This comprehensive text covers all types of IBM computers and compatibles—from the original PC to the new PS/2 models. Defines your system components and provides solutions to common PC problems.

$27.95 USA
Order #882
0-88022-395-2
750 pp.

MS-DOS User's Guide, 3rd Edition
by Chris DeVoney

Updated for Version 4.0! Includes expanded EDLIN coverage and an introduction to the DOS shell. Also contains several extended tutorials, basic command syntax, and in-depth DOS data. This is a must for everyone who uses DOS!

$22.95 USA
Order #838
0-88022-349-9
756 pp.

Managing Your Hard Disk, 2nd Edition
by Don Berliner

Learn the most efficient techniques for organizing the programs and data on your hard disk! This hard-working text includes management tips, essential DOS commands, an explanation of new application and utility software, and an introduction to PS/2 hardware.

$22.95 USA
Order #837
0-88022-348-0
600 pp.

Networking Personal Computers, 3rd Edition
by Michael Durr and Mark Gibbs

The most in-depth coverage of local area networks! Learn LAN standards, LAN hardware, LAN installation, and practical solutions to common LAN problems. The text also covers networking IBM-compatible PCs with Macintosh machines.

$22.95 USA
Order #955
0-88022-417-7
400 pp.

Free Catalog!

Mail us this registration form today, and we'll send you a free catalog featuring Que's complete line of best-selling books.

Name of Book _____

Name _____

Title _____

Phone ( ) _____

Company _____

Address _____

City _____

State _____ ZIP _____

Please check the appropriate answers:

1. Where did you buy your Que book?
   ☐ Bookstore (name: _____)
   ☐ Computer store (name: _____)
   ☐ Catalog (name: _____)
   ☐ Direct from Que
   ☐ Other: _____

2. How many computer books do you buy a year?
   ☐ 1 or less
   ☐ 2-5
   ☐ 6-10
   ☐ More than 10

3. How many Que books do you own?
   ☐ 1
   ☐ 2-5
   ☐ 6-10
   ☐ More than 10

4. How long have you been using this software?
   ☐ Less than 6 months
   ☐ 6 months to 1 year
   ☐ 1-3 years
   ☐ More than 3 years

5. What influenced your purchase of this Que book?
   ☐ Personal recommendation
   ☐ Advertisement
   ☐ In-store display
   ☐ Price
   ☐ Que catalog
   ☐ Que mailing
   ☐ Que's reputation
   ☐ Other: _____

6. How would you rate the overall content of the book?
   ☐ Very good
   ☐ Good
   ☐ Satisfactory
   ☐ Poor

7. What do you like *best* about this Que book?
   _____
   _____

8. What do you like *least* about this Que book?
   _____
   _____

9. Did you buy this book with your personal funds?
   ☐ Yes   ☐ No

10. Please feel free to list any other comments you may have about this Que book.
    _____
    _____
    _____

que

Order Your Que Books Today!

Name _____

Title _____

Company _____

City _____

State _____ ZIP _____

Phone No. ( ) _____

Method of Payment:

Check ☐ (Please enclose in envelope.)

Charge My: VISA ☐   MasterCard ☐

American Express ☐

Charge # _____

Expiration Date _____

Order No.	Title	Qty.	Price	Total

You can **FAX** your order to **1-317-573-2583**. Or call **1-800-428-5331, ext. ORDR** to order direct.
Please add $2.50 per title for shipping and handling.

Subtotal _____

Shipping & Handling _____

Total _____

que

BUSINESS REPLY MAIL

First Class Permit No. 9918   Indianapolis, IN

Postage will be paid by addressee

11711 N. College
Carmel, IN 46032

BUSINESS REPLY MAIL

First Class Permit No. 9918   Indianapolis, IN

Postage will be paid by addressee

11711 N. College
Carmel, IN 46032